Disclosure Behavior of European Firms around the Adoption of IFRS

AF702338

Michael H. R. Erkens

Disclosure Behavior of European Firms around the Adoption of IFRS

With a foreword by Prof. Dr. Axel F. A. Adam-Müller

Springer Gabler

Dr. Michael H. R. Erkens
Rotterdam, The Netherlands

Dissertation Trier University, Fachbereich IV – BWL, Germany, 2012

ISBN 978-3-658-13440-2 ISBN 978-3-658-13441-9 (eBook)
DOI 10.1007/978-3-658-13441-9

Library of Congress Control Number: 2016935390

Springer Gabler
© Springer Fachmedien Wiesbaden 2016
This work is subject to copyright. All rights are reserved by the Publisher, whether the whole or part of the material is concerned, specifically the rights of translation, reprinting, reuse of illustrations, recitation, broadcasting, reproduction on microfilms or in any other physical way, and transmission or information storage and retrieval, electronic adaptation, computer software, or by similar or dissimilar methodology now known or hereafter developed.
The use of general descriptive names, registered names, trademarks, service marks, etc. in this publication does not imply, even in the absence of a specific statement, that such names are exempt from the relevant protective laws and regulations and therefore free for general use.
The publisher, the authors and the editors are safe to assume that the advice and information in this book are believed to be true and accurate at the date of publication. Neither the publisher nor the authors or the editors give a warranty, express or implied, with respect to the material contained herein or for any errors or omissions that may have been made.

This Springer Gabler imprint is published by Springer Nature
The registered company is Springer Fachmedien Wiesbaden GmbH

Foreword

The provision of relevant, meaningful and understandable accounting information is an essential part of any firm's interaction with capital markets. In this monograph, Michael Erkens analyzes two dimensions of how European firms communicate with capital markets and what exactly they communicate.

The first dimension relates to language as one of the key components of information provision. Michael Erkens documents the various positive effects of making annual reports in English available to investors. These effects solely depend on the language in which the information is being published, not on what specific information is being provided.

The second dimension of capital market communication takes the reporting language as given and focusses on a particular type of information to be disclosed. Using the natural experiment of the adoption of IFRS 7, Michael Erkens provides evidence for a significant extent of non-disclosure and, hence, non-compliance with this accounting standard. He also provides insights into a variety of determinants of this behavior. His results support the view that any attempt to harmonize accounting standards across Europe should be accompanied by, inter alia, appropriate measures of enforcement. Not the least in this respect, Michael Erkens' research points to various directions for future research.

This monograph is a revised version of Michael Erkens' doctoral dissertation that was submitted to the Department of Business Administration at Trier University on 5 June 2012 and defended on 26 July 2012 with *summa cum laude*.

During the research process, Michael Erkens got financial support from the EU's Marie Curie INTACCT network that allowed him to spend several months at HEC Paris where the ideas for the first part of the dissertation were developed. A significant proportion of the research on the second part was carried out while the author visited the University of Chicago's Booth School of Business, again for several months. Project-specific financial support for the second part was provided by the German Research Foundation through grant AD 176/3-1 which is gratefully acknowledged.

Prof. Dr. Axel F.A. Adam-Müller

Acknowledgements

The implementation of this thesis could not have been possible without the significant contribution and kind support of a number of people. First of all, I would like to express my thanks and appreciation to my supervisor, Professor Axel Adam-Müller. He provided me with great personal support, encouragement, and guidance during the implementation of this thesis and made various stays abroad possible. I would also like to thank the members of my committee, Professor Matthias Wolz and Professor Lutz Richter.

I am also very grateful to Professor Hervé Stolowy and Professor Thomas Jeanjean for their personal support, encouragement, guidance, helpful comments, and constructive creative criticism of my ideas.

I would also like to thank my colleagues, David Kreppel and Tobias van der Neut, as well as Caroline Hilgers, Dr. Ursel Mueller and Roswitha Nierhoff. Thank you for creating a great and fun work environment.

I gratefully acknowledge financial support from the INTACCT network, which was funded under the European's Commission 6th Framework Marie Curie (Contract No. MRTN-CT-2006-035850) and the project-specific support of the German Research Foundation (DFG, AD 176/3-1). Large parts of this research were carried out while I was visiting HEC Paris (2009, 2010) and the University of Chicago's Booth School of Business (2011, 2012). Thank you very much to all faculty members and PhD students for your support and valuable discussions.

My special thanks and appreciation go to Dr. Ying Gan, Wolfgang and Gabi Erkens, and Dr. Ralf Erkens, who supported me wherever and whenever it was possible.

Dr. Michael H.R. Erkens

Abstract

This dissertation was submitted in partial fullfillment of the requirements for the degree of *doctor rerum politicarum (Dr. rer. pol.)* at the Department IV at Trier University, Germany (Fachbereich IV – BWL, Universität Trier).

The thesis consists of two self-contained disclosure studies focusing on European firms around the adoption of International Financial Reporting Standards (IFRS) in 2005. The first disclosure study investigates the economic consequences of increasing financial report visibility, measured by the use of English as a reporting language for firms from non-English-speaking countries. We sample 113 firms that started publishing their annual report in English (in addition to their local language) during 2004-2007 while not cross listing, not joining a major stock index and not engaging in major M&A activity. Taking into account the endogeneity of the reporting language, with a difference-in-differences setting and propensity score matching, and controlling for confounding factors, we find that adoption of English in the annual report is associated with lower information asymmetry, greater analyst following and more foreign investors. This suggests that language *per se* is an attribute of the firm's visibility and an important determinant of firms' disclosure choices.

The second study examines corporate risk management disclosures for nearly 400 firms across 20 European countries. Our analysis reveals that firms' average compliance with mandatory disclosure rules is 66% only. This is surprisingly low given that all firms prepare their financial statements in accordance with IFRS. The average voluntary disclosure index is 40%. We offer various explanations for why firms do not fully comply with mandatory disclosure rules. Both mandatory and voluntary disclosures vary significantly across countries. We document that firms' reporting practices are shaped by managers' reporting incentives, market demands, as well as country specific institutional and cultural factors. We explore the role of enforcement and find that strong legal enforcement is particularly important if markets' demand for accounting information is high. Finally, we exploit cultural differences across countries and provide evidence for direct and indirect influences of cultural variables on mandatory and voluntary disclosures. Overall, the level of observed disclosure falls short of the standard setters' intentions. Our results emphasize the notion that the mere application of IFRS is not sufficient to guarantee consistent financial reporting.

Contents

List of Tables

List of Figures

Chapter 1

Introduction

The analysis of disclosure, its determinants and economic consequences is a major issue in both accounting and finance research. Researchers try to answer three major questions: (1) what attitude do firms take towards accounting disclosure, either general or specific?; (2) why do some firms disclose less (or more) information than other firms?; and (3) what are the economic consequences associated with (non-)disclosure? The first kind of research question is commonly referred to as "disclosure level evaluation", the second kind of question is known as "disclosure determinant analysis", whereas the third kind of research question is known as "disclosure consequences analysis". Each of the two chapters of this thesis, which are presented as self-contained papers, addresses and investigates one of the research questions outlined above. Chapter 2 focuses on the last question and analyzes the economic consequences associated with a very specific disclosure choice: the publication of an annual report in English by European firms from non-English speaking countries. Chapter 3 addresses the former two research questions. It presents an empirical investigation of corporate risk management disclosures of firms from 20 European countries. Chapter 3 therefore not only focuses on the actual level of disclosure, but also analyzes the determinants of the observed disclosure patterns. This introductory chapter presents the research areas to be addressed in each chapter and summarizes their main results and contributions.

In Chapter 2 we analyze the economic consequences associated with the publication of an English annual report for firms from non-English speaking countries. We show that the disclosure of financial reports in English comes with lower information asymmetry, greater analyst following, and more foreign investors. Therefore, we sample 113 European firms that started publishing their annual report in English in addition to their local language annual report during 2004 and 2007. We control for cross-listing, joining a major stock index, major M&A activity, the adoption of International Financial Reporting Standards (IFRS), and the amount of information disclosed. We also take into account the endogeneity of the reporting language by employing a difference-in-differences (DID) setting in conjunction with a propensity score matching (PSM). Our results are robust to different econometric techniques.

A large body of literature documents important benefits of voluntary disclosure for a firm's liquidity and its cost of capital. This work often implies that these benefits can be obtained by simply increasing the quantity and quality of disclosure. However, this assumption is challenged by the visibility literature, which suggests that large groups of securities are often overlooked by investors due to their low visibility. One reason for that are various new regulations which came into existence over the past decade (such as the Dodd-Franck Act in the U.S., or the adoption of IFRS in Europe). These new regulations forced firms to disclose more and more information to external users. As a consequence of these regulations, it became difficult for firms to use disclosure levels for differentiation purposes, to draw interest, and to increase their visibility. Even the implementation of a new investor relation strategy involves much more than simply increasing the amount of information to be disclosed. According to Bushee and Miller (2012), firms have to foster increases in media and analyst coverage, as well as addressing institutional investors directly besides simply increasing disclosure levels. Prior work also documents that certain firm characteristics, such as size, liquidity and exchange listing, tend to attract institutional investors and security analysts, solving the visibility problem (see, for example, Baker et al. 2002). The combination of both streams of literature suggests that some firms – notably smaller firms on minor exchanges – face significant challenges in improving visibility and attracting investors, since most strategies (cross-listing, implementing a new investor relation strategy) involve significant costs and are therefore confined to relatively large firms. Bushee and Miller (2012), for example, estimate the indirect costs associated with an adoption of a new investor relation strategy to about 25% of the CEO's time, and 50% of the CFO's time.

An alternative and relatively straightforward strategy to become more visible is to adopt English as an external reporting language and to disclose all narrative and financial information in an additional language. This disclosure strategy ultimately reduces information asymmetries since previously inaccessible information becomes now available to external users who are not familiar with the firm's local language. Swedish firm Getupdated Internet Marketing AB (formerly Eastpoint AB), for instance, stated in its 2007 annual report (its first to be released in English): "Because language is the only barrier on the Internet, a presence in the major language groups is a prerequisite for profitable international growth" (p. 8). Developing a foreign market for the company's products increases firm visibility as more foreign customers will become aware of the company. As a consequence, we expect that foreign investors and analysts also will be attracted to the company, resulting in changes of the overall information environment.

Predicting the role of increasing a firm's international exposure through the release of an English annual report is, however, far from being obvious. On the one hand, one may argue that "going international" and reporting in English is simply not an issue. Firstly, financial institutions are sophisticated investors. They recruit analysts on a worldwide basis. Even if most financial analysts are fluent in English and U.K. or U.S. based, not all of them are native speakers. They are able to understand different languages. Secondly, financial data exists for all listed firms in databases. It is therefore not necessary to go back to the local language annual report to get access to financial data. On the other hand, one may think that "going international" is an issue. Firstly, past research documented that non-financial information matters for analysts and investors both in the U.S. and world-wide (e.g., Chang and Most 1985; Vergoossen 1993). The disclosure of narrative information – which can only be found in the firm's annual report – has become a much more important source of information over the past years. Secondly, there are indirect and direct costs of a translation. If there were no benefits from issuing an English annual report, why do some firms decide to issue an English report albeit costly? Thirdly, Merton's (1987) investor based recognition hypothesis states that investors will only in firms they are familiar with. One important familiarity attribute is *language* (Chui et al. 2010). Under this view, we hypothesize that firms issuing an annual report in English will (1) experience a decrease in information asymmetry, (2) an increase in their analyst following, and (3) attract new and more foreign investors.

To test these hypotheses, we created a sample of firms that have adopted English for their financial reporting. From the "Global Reports database" we identified all firms from non-English speaking European countries which issued an English annual report for the first time between 2004 and 2007. We then excluded all firms listed on the NEXT segment (Euronext) or Prime segment that require firms to publish in English. We also dropped firms engaging in a merger-acquisition activity, firms joining major stock market indices, and firms cross-listing at foreign exchanges. Our final sample consists of 113 firms from 15 countries with 12 different languages spoken. In studying the economic consequences of an English annual report adoption, we use proxies for information asymmetry, analyst following and ownership structure. To proxy for information asymmetry we use companies' bid-ask spreads and zero return days. We measure analyst following as the number of analysts issuing at least one EPS forecast during the year. Our measure of the internationality of ownership counts the number of foreign owners in relation to the number of total owners for each firm-year observation.

To demonstrate the language relevancy, our research design needs to address two major problems: (1) a commitment to greater visibility has effects both in terms of "news" (an annual report in English adoption signals information about the firm's future prospects) and "information asymmetry" (adoption is a way to disseminate information to investors), and these effects have to be separated; and (2) there may be a self-selection bias. Our research design attempts to address each of these concerns. Firstly, we use a difference-in-differences setting, an empirical estimation technique commonly used in the economics literature (see Cheng and Xu 2006; Altamuro and Beatty 2010). This setting is able to test the economic consequences of using English. We compute our proxies before and after the adoption of English, for treatment firms and for a control group of firms (determined with a propensity score matching procedure – see below). If the adoption of English has economic consequences, we expect to see differences in the economic consequences between the treatment and control groups after the adoption. The use of a control group and the computation of time differences (before and after the change) provide natural controls for any confounding factors, such as the adoption of IFRS in 2005. Secondly, we address a potential self-selection problem by implementing a propensity score matching procedure according to which we select our control firms. This methodology is becoming increasingly popular in the accounting literature (see DeHaan et al. 2012; Iskandar-Datta and Jia 2013; Lawrence et al. 2011). Propensity score matching essentially estimates each firm's propensity to make a binary choice as a function of observables, and matches firms with similar propensities. It involves two stages: In the first stage, we estimate the probability of publishing an annual report in English with a Logit model. This enables us to identify control firms that (1) have the same predicted propensity to use English as the treatment firms (adopters), and (2) continue to use the local language only for external reporting. In the second stage, we estimate the difference-in-differences estimation for treatment firms (adopters) and control firms (firms that continue to use only the local language but show the same propensity as our sample firms to issue an English annual report).

In a series of univariate and multivariate tests, we find that firms publishing an annual report in English experience a decrease in information asymmetry, and an increase in analyst following and foreign ownership relative to control firms. Our results are similar in robustness checks using an approach suggested by Heckman (1979) in which we control for unobservable factors associated with the decision to adopt English. We also provide an analysis over time and plot the effects of all economic consequences around the adoption year. This analysis suggests that the consequences stem from changes in ownership.

We contribute to the literature in three ways. Firstly, we are the only study analyzing the consequences of using English as a disclosure strategy in the accounting literature. Secondly, we contribute to the growing field of research on non-numerical information by showing the importance for market participants of the language used in annual reports. Thirdly, we add to the international accounting literature by showing that language is a means of improving accessibility to financial statement besides the actual accounting standards applied.

Chapter 3 addresses the so-called "disclosure level evaluation", as well as the "disclosure determinant analysis" research question. We evaluate the impact of accounting for derivatives and risk management on the scope of corporate risk management and financial instruments disclosure. First of all, we are the first to provide evidence that firms do not fully comply with mandatory disclosure rules and to give detailed information on how much firms mandatorily and voluntarily disclose on their risk management activities (disclosure level evaluation). Afterwards, we analyze the determinants of the observed disclosure patterns. Besides analyzing firm-level characteristics, we focus on institutional and cultural differences across countries to explain disclosure levels (determinant analysis).

Corporate risk management relies on operational and financial instruments. So far, the understanding of how, to what extent and to what effect these instruments are being used is rather limited. Several empirical studies across different countries and periods of time have provided inconclusive answers. Lack of sufficiently detailed and reliable data is the most likely reason for this inconclusiveness. Existing studies have either used questionnaire data, suffering from non-response biases and strategically biased answering (Bodnar et al. 2012; Bodnar et al. 1996, 1998; Bodnar et al. 1995), or very limited data drawn from audited financial statements such as notional or fair values of financial derivatives, ignoring other risk management instruments (for example, Judge 2006; Magee 2009). This study is a large empirical study based on an entirely new data set. The adoption of IAS 32, IAS 39 and IFRS 7 requires firms to publish significantly more detailed information on risk management in general and the use of financial instruments in particular. This new data allows for a detailed, in-depth analysis of the determinants for risk management and financial instruments disclosure.

Prior disclosure studies are part of the accounting literature. These studies try to empirically identify those firm characteristics that have explanatory power for what and how much is being disclosed by a firm. The first study on disclosure of corporate finance information is by Raffournier (1995) who uses an unweighted disclosure index consisting of 30 disclosure items and regresses this index on company size, leverage, profitability, internationality, auditor size and other independent variables. His main finding is that size and internationality seem to be the only characteristics that determine the level of financial disclosure. Ahmed and Takeda (1995) perform a related study on disclosure by banks. They are the first to analyze information on financial derivatives. Lopes and Rodrigues (2007) focus on the determinants of disclosure for financial instruments by corporations and find that the degree of disclosure is positively related to firm size, type of auditor (BIG 4 vs. non-BIG 4), listing status and to business sector. Iatridis (2008) provides comparable results for another set of firms. Excellent survey articles on disclosure and determinant studies are provided by Healy and Palepu (2001) and Core (2001), see also Chavent et al. (2006).

The objective of the project is twofold: First, by using a change in the accounting rules regarding corporate risk management disclosure, we aim to better understand how and to what extent companies manage their risks. Second, we want to gain insights if – and how – companies inform investors about the risks they are exposed to and their approach to manage these risks. We therefore exploit a change in the disclosure requirements for publicly listed firms. As effective of 2005, the new International Accounting Standards 32 and 39 and the new International Financial Reporting Standard 7 (effective as of 2007) require firms to publish significantly more information about their risk management in general and the use of financial instruments in particular. Prior to this change, such information was relatively scarce to the effect that empirical studies on corporate risk management had to rely on very limited data sets. This was a major impediment for the validity of these studies. By analyzing the newly availaible data, we are able to provide new and better insights into companies' risk management and their disclosure strategies.

Apart from any data availability concerns, there is, however, an intense debate on whether a unique set of accounting standards such as IFRS truly increases transparency and enhances comparability of financial reports across industries and countries. The common understanding is that a single set of accounting standards *per se* is not sufficient for transparent and internationally comparable financial reporting and disclosure (Ball et al. 2000; Ball et al. 2003; Holthausen 2003). Apart from managerial incentives and markets' demand for information, a country's institutional environment, its strength of enforcement, as well as its cultural values are expected to affect corporate financial reporting. In this study, we provide an in-depth analysis of the determinants of firms' disclosure behavior. We offer various explanations for why firms may not fully comply with mandatory disclosure rules. We also analyze the determinants of firms' voluntary disclosure patterns.

Our working sample consists of 385 firms from 20 European countries. We constructed three disclosure indices: a total disclosure index, a mandatory index, and a voluntary disclosure index. Each index is based on the requirements and/or recommendations of IAS 32, IAS 39, and IFRS 7. We do not penalize firms for the non-disclosure of irrelevant items. Our findings reveal a huge variation in corporate risk management disclosure. The average of the total disclosure index is at 51.38%, of the mandatory index it is at 66.29%, and the average of the voluntary disclosure index lies at 39.48%. The finding that firms on average comply to only 66% with mandatory disclosure rules causes for serious concern, given that all firms are subjected to the same set of accounting standards.

Our study consists of three main sets of analyses. The first set focuses on the general determinants of disclosure. We classify the determinants of disclosure into four groups: *managers' incentives, business structure, accounting standards,* and *countries' institutions.* We find that each group exhibits a significant impact on the mandatory and voluntary disclosure index. Our results are corroborated even if we (1) extract country-fixed effects, (2) collapse our data set at the country level, and (3) control for a possible endogeneity problem of enforcement via a two stage least squares (2SLS) regression.

The second set exploits the role of enforcement for corporate disclosure behavior. we expect and find that the perception of the strength of enforcement at the firm level is an important determinant of firms' disclosure practices. Assuming that outsiders' demand for information shape a firm's perception of enforcement, we find that the impact of enforcement is indeed much stronger the larger the information demands from outsiders.

The third set examines the role of culture for corporate disclosure practices. At a descriptive level, we perform a k-means cluster analysis of 20 different cultural values yielding five cultural clusters. We find that both the mandatory and voluntary disclosure indices vary significantly across these clusters. Via a multilevel regression analysis we further explore this finding. We find that cultural clusters (and cultural values) have an impact on firms' disclosure practices.

We contribute to the literature in various ways. First, we provide evidence that the adoption of IFRS is not sufficient for a transparent and comparable reporting and disclosure behavior. Prior studies have found comparable results (Ball et al. 2000; Ball et al. 2003; Ball 2006; Holthausen 2003, 2009). They use, however, indirect measures of reporting and disclosure quality rather than a more straightforward measure of disclosure quantity. We are the first to analyze the impact of disclosure incentives on recent disclosure indices using a large international data set of firms that have to follow the same set of accounting standards. Second, we contribute to the literature on the role of differences between local GAAP and IFRS and find that these differences have a significant impact on firms' disclosure practices (Bae et al. 2008b; Ding et al. 2007). Third, we contribute to the growing literature on the impact of enforcement and institutions on disclosure practices and disclosure quantity/quality (Armstrong et al. 2010b; Christensen et al. 2011; Hail and Leuz 2006; Leuz 2010). Prior studies have focused on the impact of enforcement on various financial market outcomes (e.g. stock liquidity or information asymmetries), or on accounting quality (e.g. timely loss recognition or earnings quality). To our best knowledge, no study directly examines the influence of enforcement on (1) firms' compliance with mandatory accounting rules, and (2) firms' voluntary disclosure choices. Finally, we also contribute to the growing literature on the role of culture in accounting. Existing evidence documents that cultural values have a significant impact on managers, analysts and stakeholders. This is the first study that provides a comprehensive overview of the impact of cultural values on firms' disclosure practices.

The rest of the thesis is organized as follows: Chapter 2 analyzes the economic consequences associated with the publication of an English annual report for European firms from non-English speaking countries. Chapter 3 investigates disclosure levels of nearly 400 firms from 20 European countries with regard to risk management and financial instruments disclosure according to IAS 32, IAS 39, and IFRS 7. Chapter 3 also analyzes the determinants of the observed disclosure levels and focuses on the role of enforcement and cultural values. Chapter 4 presents the main conclusions of the thesis.

Chapter 2

The Economic Consequences of Increasing the International Visibility of Financial Reports

2.1 Introduction

Attracting investors' attention is a challenge for listed firms. Prior research finds that certain characteristics (size, liquidity, cross-listing) are associated with firm visibility (see, e.g., Baker et al. 2002; Bushee and Miller 2012). Firms lacking these characteristics are often neglected by investors and intermediaries. Prior research (Bushee and Miller 2012) also suggests that voluntary disclosure can improve analyst and investor following, and ultimately reduce the cost of capital. However, since such research generally focuses on highly-visible firms, it is not clear whether simply increasing disclosure is sufficient to overcome visibility and familiarity barriers. In addition, over the past decades several new disclosure and financial regulations have forced companies to disclose more information to external users, making it more difficult for firms to use disclosure levels for differentiation purposes, to attract interest and increase their visibility.

To become more visible, some firms adopt an investor relations strategy involving more than simply changing disclosure practices (Bushee and Miller 2012). Other firms try to enhance their visibility by cross-listing in countries where the firm is not incorporated, such as the US or the UK (Baker et al. 2002). Both these strategies, however, involve significant costs and are confined to relatively large firms.

An alternative and relatively straightforward strategy is to adopt English as an external reporting language. Besides press releases and more informal communication channels, the most commonly used communication interface between a firm and its third parties is still the annual report. Smaller firms' annual reports are generally published in the language of the country where the company is incorporated. If the country of origin is a non-English speaking country, the information disclosed in the local-language annual report is, to put it baldly, inaccessible to external users who cannot understand the reporting language. At firm level, one way round this problem is to publish a second annual report in English, which is the "lingua franca of international business" (Charles 2007). Swedish firm Getupdated Internet Marketing AB (formerly Eastpoint AB), for instance, stated in its 2007 annual report (its first to be released in English): "Because language is the only barrier on the Internet, a presence in the major language groups is a prerequisite for profitable international growth" (p. 8). Nextevolution AG, a German firm, explained in its first annual report in English in 2006 that "[it] decided to adjust [its] investor relations work to the international capital market standards. Therefore, [it is] reporting about the development of [the] company […], both in German and English" (p. 17). Hence, developing a foreign market for the company's products increases firm visibility as more foreign customers will become aware of the company. As a consequence, we expect that foreign investors and analysts also will be attracted to the company, resulting in changes of the overall information environment.

The goal of this study is to analyze the economic consequences of using English as an external reporting language for firms from non-English speaking countries. To rule out the possibility of our findings being driven by one specific effect, we study a range of economic consequences. Specifically, we test the relationship between publishing an Annual Report in English (ARE)[1] and information asymmetry, plus analyst and investor behavior.

It is not obvious whether releasing an annual report in English and thereby increasing the international visibility of the company has any effect on the firm's information environment. Opponents may argue that reporting in English is simply a non-issue. Financial institutions are sophisticated investors, able to understand any language used in the world. Moreover, financial data exist for all listed firms in financial databases, so information should be

[1] For the sake of simplicity, in the rest of this study we use the expression "annual report in English" or ARE to mean the English-language version of the annual report.

available to all interested users, whatever their language. From this standpoint, the use of English should not have any economic consequences. We label this possibility "Language irrelevance". Alternatively, perhaps the reporting language does matter, for two reasons at least. First, there are costs associated with issuing an ARE. As well as the direct costs of translation (probably negligible at firm level), indirect costs arise because the firm's annual reports will become readily available to a large class of sophisticated (mostly US and UK based) investors, who are likely to challenge managers' views and decisions. It is unlikely that rational managers would incur these costs without expected benefits. A second reason draws on Merton (1987, 489), who suggests that investors will only invest in firms they are familiar with (and we believe that one very important familiarity attribute is *language*). In line with this familiarity argument, Chui et al. (2010), for example, show that the foreigners' familiarity with a given country's equity market is positively related to momentum profits. Following this view, we expect that firms issuing an ARE will (i) experience decreasing information asymmetry, (ii) increase their analyst following, and (iii) attract more foreign investors. We label this possibility "language relevance".

We use a sample of firms that decided to publish an ARE in addition to their local-language annual report. We call these firms "ARE adopters" (or treatment firms) in the rest of this study, as they have adopted a new reporting policy. The sample is drawn from the Global Reports database, which states the language used by firms in their annual reports.

To discriminate between the "language irrelevance" and "language relevance" possibilities, our research design needs to avoid two pitfalls. The first pitfall is that the adoption of English in the annual report may result from "other events" that influence the economic consequences investigated. For instance, if a French firm merges with a US firm, the combined enterprise will likely use English in its annual report and therefore benefit from lower information asymmetry and more analyst following. Moreover, if a German firm acquires a US firm, the same is likely to happen. We expect a similar behavior for firms that cross-listed, became part of a major stock index or were engaged in merger and acquisition activity. To avoid such ex-ante confounding effects, our research strategy is twofold. First, we exclude from our treatment sample all firms that cross-listed during or after the period of investigation, firms that joined a major stock index or a stock index that requires external reporting in English and firms engaging in merger and acquisition activities in the two years prior to adoption of English (as a target or an initiator), Second, we adopt a difference-in-differences setting where control firms are not randomly chosen. We first model the decision to use English for firms from non-English speaking countries, and then select control firms that have the closest propensity to use English in their annual report to the treatment firms but do not actually do so. The selection process for control firms helps to control the observable differences between control and treatment firms.

The second pitfall is that our treatment firms are likely to experience changes in their disclosure policies after the adoption of an ARE. More specifically, firms which issue an ARE may increase their disclosure levels or adopt financial reporting standards as part of their strategy to become "international". To mitigate the impact of this post-adoption effect, we include in our difference-in-differences regressions a number of control variables to take into account these effects.

Our first univariate test consists of observing our proxies for information asymmetry, analyst following and the presence of international investors before and after the change. We focus on information asymmetries between the firm and (i) investors, and (ii) information intermediaries. While information asymmetries arise due to asymmetric information between insiders and outsiders of the firm, they are are also affected by the general information environment and infrastructure laid out by the company, even in the presence of information. To proxy for information asymmetries we use companies' bid-ask spreads and zero returns.We observe that information asymmetry decreases by almost 29.3% when measured by the bid-ask spread and by 39.6% when measured by the zero-return days, while analyst following increases (on average, ARE adopters increase the number of analysts from 0.5 to 1.7, i.e., by more than one analyst) and the proportion of foreign ownership surges by 17 points (which represents an additional 2.5 foreign owners on average). These magnitudes are much lower for control firms. In other words, ARE adopters experience a decrease in information asymmetry and an increase in analyst following and foreign ownership relative to control firms. In a series of multivariate tests, we introduce control variables for the quantity of information disclosed, accounting standards, size, leverage and other control variables. Findings are similar. We carry out a number of additional analyses to check the robustness of our findings. First, we use an approach suggested by Heckman (1979) in which we control for unobservable factors associated with the decision to adopt an ARE. Second, we investigate whether the economic consequences of adopting an ARE vary with country size. We find that firms incorporated in "large countries" benefit more from adopting an ARE than firms domiciled in "small countries". The visibility effects resulting from the ARE seem to complement rather than substitute the visibility brought by a country. Finally, we provide an analysis of the economic effects over time that reinforces our findings. We plot the effects of adoption of an ARE. We find that most of the decrease in information asymmetry follows changes in ownership, and that changes in analyst following trail changes in information asymmetry. This suggests that the economic consequences of ARE adoption stem from changes in ownership.

Our study makes three contributions to the literature. First, the consequences of using a widespread language (English) in the accounting literature have never been studied before. However, language (or cultural and familiarity aspects, which are related) has been put forward as a possible explanation for a home investment bias (e.g., Dvorak 2005), the superiority of country-specialized analysts over industry specialists (Sonney 2009), more accurate forecasts by local analysts compared to foreign analysts (e.g., Bae et al. 2008a), different investment styles between domestic and foreign investors in conjunction with investor sophistication (e.g., Grinblatt and Keloharju 2000, 44, 66), a higher trading volume for local equity than foreign equity (see, e.g., Grinblatt and Keloharju 2001, 1054; Hau 2001a, 768), greater proximity between the company and its local investor base (e.g., Rauch 1999; Grinblatt and Keloharju 2001, 1054), lower information asymmetry (e.g., Hau 2001a, 768), and broader international ownership (e.g., Kalev et al. 2008, 2377). In contrast to this study, none of these articles *directly* tests the consequences of using a specific language.

Second, our study contributes to the growing field of research on non-numerical information. Baginski et al. (2004) investigate why managers augment voluntary earnings forecasts with explanations for forecasted performance. Tetlock et al. (2008) quantify the language used in financial news stories in an effort to predict firms' accounting earnings and stock returns and Li (2010a) applies a linguistic analysis to some sections of annual reports. Hales et al. (2011) mention that "although we often think of financial reporting in terms of numbers, language is, in fact, the medium through which companies communicate much of the information on their past and projected future performance" (p. 224). Our study contributes to this field by showing the importance for market participants of the language (English or local) used in annual reports.

Third, we also add to the international accounting literature. There has been some debate over the desirability of common financial reporting standards: although the adoption of International Accounting Standards (IAS) and International Financial Reporting Standards (IFRS) is found to be associated with a lower cost of capital and transaction costs, a higher market value (Leuz and Verrecchia 2000) and reduced home bias (Covrig et al. 2007), these effects seem to be confined to early adopters and are economically relatively modest in magnitude. We argue that before we even reach the question of accounting standards, the first barrier to understanding and comparing financial statements and increasing transparency is the language barrier. Using English for external reporting and disclosure purposes is therefore the only way to address anyone outside the firm easily and directly, and reduce the costs of information acquisition. We show that the language used in the annual report is a means of improving accessibility to financial statements for users of information.

The rest of the chapter is organized as follows. In the following section, we provide some background on annual report language and develop our hypotheses. Section 2.3 describes the methodology, variables and sample, and section 2.4 presents our empirical evidence. Section

2.5 provides additional analyses to confirm the validity of our study. Section 2.6 concludes the chapter.

2.2 Motivation and Hypothesis Development

2.2.1 Importance of Language for Financial Statements Users

Past literature concentrates on accounting as a language, not on the language used in annual reports *per se*. In this study, we investigate whether the language used in the annual report has economic consequences, making the implicit assumption that the annual report is useful to investors.

Annual reports are comprehensive documents consisting of a variety of components, such as a presentation of the firm (history, products, operating and financial review), a letter from the Chairman, a management discussion and analysis section and a full set of financial statements. The literature on accounting information generally holds the view that accounting and financial statement data are not the only source of information for capital markets (e.g., Gonedes 1976). The annual report is part of a network including complementary instruments such as preliminary announcements and analyst presentations. Insider trading, for example, sends information to capital markets (Seyhun 1998): analysts and ratings agencies receive information before its publication in financial statements, and they convey this information to the capital markets through their own publications. However, surveys and other research evidence have shown that the annual report is a vital, though not sufficient, source of information for analysts both in the US and elsewhere (e.g., Chang and Most 1985; Vergoossen 1993). Chang et al. (1983) showed that the annual report was used as a basis for investment decisions. Barker (1998) concludes that the research literature has paid insufficient attention to the role of accounting information in direct communication between companies and fund managers. The importance of narratives and one-to-one contact also underlines the importance of language as an ingredient of the informational efficiency of markets. For instance, Nickerson and de Groot (2005) state that "European corporations will be increasingly reliant on the non-financial texts within the annual reports, as a means to distinguish themselves from competitors" (p. 328).

Hales et al. (2011) underline the importance of annual reports, as the qualitative information contained in financial reporting and diclosure is not completely subsumed by the "hard" numbers produced by the financial accounting system. This is why we argue that an ARE enhances the information environment of a firm, and hence reduces information asymmetry in the market, even when the actual accounting figures are already accessible through financial databases such as Datastream©, Global©, Infinancials© or Worldscope©.

Information asymmetry originates not only from unawareness of a firm's figures, but also through a lack of knowledge of corporate strategies, goals and management estimations. These ingredients of the information environment of a firm can typically be found in the firms' annual report.

2.2.2 Hypothesis Development

Information asymmetry exists because some investors possess private information about a firm that is unavailable to other investors. Economic theory and empirical evidence suggests that greater disclosure reduces information asymmetry (Diamond and Verrecchia 1991). This is because voluntary disclosure "levels the playing field" among investors and because public and private information are seen as substitutes. The associated disclosure literature implicitly assumes that all disclosure is read and utilized by market participants, but this assumption is contradicted by a large body of literature on firm visibility and its impact on price (e.g., Chan et al. 2005). This literature follows Merton's (1987) suggestion that investors will only invest in firms they are familiar with.

In this study, we argue that issuing an ARE is a way for firms to increase their visibility to investors and financial analysts. Several factors underlie this positive association. First, English is a *lingua franca*: in terms of native speakers[2], it is the world's second most common language (after Mandarin and on an equal footing with Spanish). Second, English is the language of business: stock exchanges located in English-speaking countries represent 65% of the world stock market capitalization[3], and 93% of financial analysts who are members of the CFA institute are located in English-speaking countries.[4]

The visibility of a firm and the existence of information asymmetry can be captured by two often-used and cited proxies for informational advantage: "market proximity" and "familiarity". Market proximity and familiarity can concern geographical, economic, industrial, and cultural characteristics and among other effects, reduce information asymmetry in the market. Our proxies for information asymmetry are bid-ask spreads and zero-return trading days. Cultural and geographical proximity themselves are mainly influenced and connected by the existence of a common language. Rauch (1999, 10, 25, 30) points out that a common language and colonial ties are of particular importance for product design, and shows that both have effects on matching international buyers and sellers for more differentiated products. In addition, his analysis confirms that search costs – which can in our case be interpreted as translation costs – are a great barrier to trade for those products. Various

[2] Source: http://www2.ignatius.edu/faculty/turner/languages.htm.
[3] Source http://www.world-exchanges.org/statistics.
[4] See www.cfa.institute.com.

studies have explicitly linked the existence of a common language to trading behavior, portfolio allocation decisions, and information asymmetry. Tesar and Werner (1995), for example, focus on "language, institutional and regulatory differences and the cost of obtaining information about foreign markets" (p. 479). They suggest that "geographic proximity seems to be an important ingredient in the international portfolio allocation decision" (p. 485). In their study on gross cross-border equity flows between 14 countries, Portes and Rey (2005) find that a language dummy is a significant factor in certain specifications for asset trade. Sarkissian and Schill (2004, 795) report as their main result that there is more cross-listing activity across countries that share a similar language or colonial ties, since there is lower information asymmetry. Hau (2001b), in his study on transaction data from the Xetra trading system at the German Security exchange, finds that traders outside Germany in non-German-speaking locations face an information disadvantage, and trade less and with lower profitability. He remarks that "the information barrier may be either linguistic or geographic in nature" (p. 1962).

Lundholm (1988) argues that public information may also complement private information. In this case, disclosure leads all investors to have more information; however, disclosure leads some investors to be better informed than others. This complementarity effect arises when some investors are better able to process the information disclosed or when the disclosure leads some investors to acquire private information (Kim and Verrecchia 1994). We posit that the issuance of an annual report in English in addition to the local language likely reduces the complementarity effect of disclosures and, therefore, information asymmetries related to the stock. That is, the decision to issue an annual report in English likely lowers the information processing costs for investors that do not speak the local language and, therefore, reduces the information asymmetries between the foreign and domestic investors.

In addition, if information processing costs associated with language barriers act as an impediment to financial analysis, some investors may choose to refrain from considering the company as an investment alternative. Merton (1987) suggests that "if, for each firm, investors must pay a significant 'set-up' (or 'receiver') cost before they can process detailed information released from time to time about the firm, then this fixed cost will cause any one investor to follow only a subset of traded securities." Issuing an annual report in English may, therefore, increase the number of investors analyzing the company and, therefore, increase the market efficiency and decrease information asymmetries related to the stock.

Finally, institutional theory (Meyer and Rowan 1977) suggests that formal mechanisms can allow organizations to be perceived as more legitimate. Based on legitimacy theory (Fiss and Zajac 2004; Westphal and Zajac 1994), we argue that investors could perceive annual reports issued in English to be more credible than those issued only in the local language. More credible disclosures are likely to lead to less private information search and lower information asymmetries related to the company stock.

We recognize that there are arguments for increased information asymmetry with the release of English annual reports. Specifically, if companies issuing an annual report in English attract more foreign investors and if foreign shareholders by nature suffer from greater information asymmetry than local shareholders, then information asymmetry may increase. However, we argue that the reduced information asymmetries from decreased language barriers offset the increased information asymmetries from more investors with greater geographic and cultural distances. We, therefore, predict an overall reduction in information asymmetry from issuing English annual reports. This leads to our first hypothesis:"

> **Hypothesis 1**: *Firms adopting English in their annual report experience a reduction in information asymmetry.*

As a second hypothesis, we focus on analysts' response to ARE adoption, which can be a strategy to channel information through intermediaries such as financial analysts (Beaver 1981) in order to increase firm visibility and attract investors. A huge body of literature exists on analyst following and the accuracy of analyst forecasts (see, for instance, Baker et al. 2002; Ali et al. 2007; Arya and Mittendorf 2007; Lehavy et al. 2011).[5] Most of these studies indicate that analysts prefer to follow large firms listed on major exchanges with lower performance volatility (O'Brien and Bhushan 1990; Lang and Lundholm 1996).

Some of the most recent studies on analyst following even mention the possible effect of domestic analysts' informational advantages compared to foreign analysts, due to language knowledge and cultural proximity. Bae et al. (2008b) assume that the decision to follow firms is based on the costs and benefits of following foreign firms. On the cost side they expect that "costs presumably include primarily the direct costs of acquiring information about a new firm". In their empirical tests they include a dummy variable indicating the existence of a common language between analysts and the firm followed by those analysts. The results confirm their expectation: foreign analyst following is greater when the firm's country and the analyst's country share a common language or colonial history. Bae et al. (2008a, 599) refine this finding further not by looking at the existence of a "common language", but by focusing on the "English language" specifically. They assume that foreign analysts are likely to be fluent in English, and therefore expect those analysts "to be at a disadvantage with regard to firms in countries where English is not the main language". Ramnath et al. (2008) take a

[5] For a review, see Ramnath et al. (2008).

similar position and propose that future research might consider the effects of cultural differences across countries on analysts' decision processes and forecasts. Our study differs from past literature by focusing on the firm's point of view rather than the analyst's point of view. Our second hypothesis addresses all these issues and is expressed as follows:

> **Hypothesis 2**: *Firms adopting English in their annual report increase their analyst following.*

Finally, we examine whether foreign ownership depends on the reporting language. There is a large body of empirical literature examining the firm characteristics associated with institutional investor ownership (see, for instance, Bushee 2001; Dahlquist and Robertsson 2001). These articles consistently find that institutions prefer larger firms that are listed on stock indexes and major exchanges. The possible interaction between language or cultural proximity and foreign ownership is less often mentioned in prior studies than the potential links between liquidity and language proximity. Grinblatt and Keloharju (2001, 1055) show that investors are more likely to trade in stocks of firms that share (or at least communicate in) the same language as the investor, and have a similar cultural background because of greater information flows between market participants with the same language or historical ties. They point out that "if a company perceives that a large proportion of its shareowners prefer a particular language, the company may choose to communicate in that language". They also find that Finland-domiciled companies that publish their annual reports both in Finnish and Swedish are able to tap an abnormally large Swedish-speaking investor base, both in Finland and Sweden. They expect that "firms in other countries should be able to do the same to increase their investment appeal. For example, US companies, which generally publish their annual reports only in English, might be able to expand their investor base by publishing their annual reports also in, say, Spanish and Japanese" (Grinblatt and Keloharju 2001, 1071). Pagano et al. (2002) find that a common language fosters "clustering" of institutions in countries that are geographically or culturally close to their country of incorporation. They believe this is mainly due to informational reasons. Kalev et al. (2008, 2377) compare the investor behavior of foreign and local investors on the Helsinki Stock Exchange. They expect and confirm "that information about single-listed stocks is more apparent to local investors who do not face language, distance or culture barriers". Hence, foreign ownership is smaller for firms that do not communicate in English, since the informational disadvantage for foreign investors is greater than with companies that publish their accounts in English as well as their local language. Graham et al. (2009) provide evidence that investor competence is an important determinant in investment decisions, especially for international investment. Holding competence constant, disclosing an ARE enables firms to target more competent investors, as it lowers the "language barrier".

Taken together, based on prior empirical evidence we hypothesize that a firm's international visibility is positively affected by adopting an ARE. Our third hypothesis is therefore:

> **Hypothesis 3**: *Firms adopting English in their annual report attract more foreign investors.*

2.3 Methodology, Variable Description and Sample

As outlined in the previous section, economic theory suggests that commitment to increasing visibility should enhance the firm's information environment. The difficulty lies in demonstrating this relationship empirically. There are three major problems: First, a commitment to greater visibility has effects both in terms of "news" (ARE adoption signals information about the firm's future prospects) and "information asymmetry" (adoption is a way to disseminate information to investors), and these effects must be separated; second, there may be self-selection bias; and third, the proxies used to measure economic consequences may also influence findings. Our research design attempts to address each of these concerns.

2.3.1 Methodology

The Difference-In-Differences (DID) Methodology

To assess the impact of international reporting strategies on our proxies, we can study the effect across firms by explicitly controlling for other determinants of the information environment, or we can examine changes in the proxies around the adoption of an ARE strategy ("pre-post adoption study"). Each option has advantages and disadvantages (Leuz and Verrecchia 2000). The cross-sectional design is less prone to confusing the "news" and "information asymmetry" effects of a commitment to increasing visibility. The change in economic consequences that occurs when the firm adopts English in the annual report indicates both a change in expectations about the firm's future performance and a change in the information environment. The former occurs around the switch and its direction depends on the news or information content of the disclosure. The latter is permanent and captures the reduction in information asymmetry and increase in liquidity: its direction is therefore independent of the news content. By estimating a cross-sectional relationship between our proxies and the firm's reporting strategy well after firms have changed disclosure regime, we should be able to separate the two effects and focus on the "information asymmetry" effect. A "pre-post adoption study" design observes the behavior of our proxies around the reporting change and hence mitigates the possibility that some other unobserved variable (rather than the disclosure policy) is responsible for the cross-sectional differences in the proxies.

To test our hypotheses and address the research design issues outlined above, we use a difference-in-differences (DID) setting, an empirical estimation technique commonly used in economics and in the accounting literature (see Cheng and Xu 2006; Wang et al. 2009; Altamuro and Beatty 2010). Let us take a hypothetical example in which a firm decides to adopt English for external reporting purposes and publishes an ARE for 2006 (in the early months of 2007). Let us also assume that in the year the change becomes effective and known to interested parties (year 2007, called year 1 in our statistical treatments), an outcome variable (e.g., analyst following) increased by 50% compared to the year before the change became effective (year 2006, called year 0 in our treatments). To estimate the impact of the change on analyst following, we could simply conduct a "before and after" analysis and conclude that adoption of an ARE is associated with a 50% increase in analyst following. The problem is that there could be an unrelated trend towards more analyst following over time, and it is impossible to know whether the firm's decision to publish an ARE or the time trend caused this increase in analyst following.

One way to identify the impact of ARE adoption is to run a DID regression. If there is another comparable firm that did not change its external reporting language, this could be used as a control to compare the year-on-year changes between ARE adopters and non-adopters. More precisely, we will estimate the following equation:

$$\begin{aligned} &Economic\ consequence = \beta_0 + \beta_1 Treatment + \beta_2 Time + \beta_3 Treatment \times Time \\ &+ \beta_s Control\ variables + \varepsilon \end{aligned} \tag{E2.1}$$

Where

- *Economic consequence* is the economic consequence analyzed (analyst following for instance – we also use information asymmetry and foreign ownership);

- *Treatment* is a dummy coded 1 if the firm adopted English at some point in time, 0 otherwise;

- *Time* is a time dummy coded 1 from the year the change becomes effective (i.e., one year after the period concerned by the annual report, 2007 for the 2006 annual report, in our example) and 0 until the year the change becomes effective;

- *Treatment* × *Time* is the interaction of the *Treatment* dummy and the *Time* dummy;

- *Control variables* vary across the dependent variables. These variables are included to control for factors, other than time and language, associated with the economic consequence analyzed. They are presented below.

This setting can test the economic consequences of using English. We compute our proxies before and after the adoption of English, for treatment firms and for a control group (determined with a propensity score matching procedure – see below). If the adoption of English has economic consequences, we expect to see differences in the economic consequences between the treatment and control groups after the adoption. The use of a control group and the computation of time differences (before and after the change) provide natural controls for any confounding factors, such as the adoption of IFRS in 2005. The following table indicates the predicted value of an economic consequence for each of the possible scenarios.

Predicted *Economic consequence*	Time = 0	Time = 1
Treatment = 0	β_0	$\beta_0+\beta_2$
Treatment = 1	$\beta_0+\beta_1$	$\beta_0+\beta_1+\beta_2+\beta_3$

In the regression, β_0 represents the average for control companies before the initiation of an ARE, β_1 represents the difference between the two groups before the initiation, β_2 represents the time trend in the control group, and β_3 represents the difference in the change over time between the treatment and control groups. Assuming that both groups have the same analyst following trend over time, we have now controlled for a possible time trend effect. We can thus identify the true impact of ARE adoption on analyst following (β_3).

Under our DID procedure, a significant β_3 can be interpreted in at least four different ways. A first interpretation is that issuing an ARE is indeed associated with economic consequences. A second possible explanation is that an ARE contains more information than a local-language annual report. Under this interpretation, a significant β_3 would not mean that using English has economic consequences, but that *increased disclosure in the English version* of the annual report has economic consequences. However, past research suggests that firms do not "take advantage" of the English version to report additional information and increase transparency. Campbell et al. (2005), for instance, carry out a content analysis of voluntary disclosure in an international comparison context. They examine the validity of volumetric comparison by recording word and sentence counts, using both original German documents and their English translations published by German companies themselves. They find that the English rendering of German environmental narrative is generally faithful to the German, suggesting that companies do not deliberately discriminate by reporting jurisdiction. In other words, we can study the use of English *per se* because there is no difference in content between the local-language annual report and the ARE.

A third explanation for a significant β_3 is that firms that adopted an ARE committed to disclose more information in their annual report after the adoption. Following this reasoning, β_3 does not capture the economic consequences of adopting an ARE, but the economic consequences of *increased disclosure* (either in the local language or its English equivalent). To control for this disclosure effect, we include a variable that captures the extent of disclosure beyond the country average for both control and treatment firms. It is intended to reflect any information effect associated with the adoption of an ARE.

A last possible reason for a significant β_3 is self-selection if factors associated with the issuance of an ARE are also associated with outcome variables. We will see below in Table 2.1, Panel B that English adopters are smaller than other listed firms and have more growth opportunities. Since these factors are potentially correlated with the economic consequences analyzed, we implement a propensity score matching (PSM) procedure initially proposed by Rosenbaum and Rubin (1983).

Despite the possibility to control for time trends and common company characterisitics by choosing an appropriate set of control firms, the DiD estimator nevertheless can result in downward-biased standard errors due to a potential auto-correlation of the outcome variable (Bertrand et al. 2004). What is important for DiD to work is that the difference between treatment and control group is relatively stable over time in absence of the treatment. This can be examined by comparing the outcome variable before the treatment between treatment and control group. One should also correct the standard errors for clustering on the time variable. We indirectly address the former concern in a robustness analysis when analyzing the effects of adopting English over time (see Figure 2.1 and section 2.5.3). As can be seen from Figure 2.1, the differences between treatment and control group with regard to bid-ask spreads, analyst following, and foreign ownership are fairly stable up to three years prior to the treatment. Only the difference with regard to zero-return days reveals a potential time trend. With regard to the second concern, all standard errors are clusterd by time and firm.

The Propensity Score Matching (PSM) Procedure

The standard "proper" DID approach relies on a natural experiment, i.e., some change is expected to affect treatment for one group more than another, but the two groups should not otherwise differ. For this to work properly, the natural experiment should be exogenous (i.e., the change must not be a reaction to behavior) and unlikely to encourage people to "play the system" and change their behavior in unpredictable ways. In other words, the choice of a matching sample is a critical step in our methodology.

The key problem in estimating the cross-sectional regression is that firms *choose* their reporting strategy, and their decision will take the costs and benefits of reporting in English into consideration. To mitigate the self-selection problem, we use a non-random control sample of firms which have the same propensity to adopt English, but did not do so. This methodology, known as "propensity score matching", is becoming increasingly popular in the accounting literature (see Armstrong et al. 2010c; Lawrence et al. 2011) and involves two stages.

In the first stage, we estimate the probability of publishing an ARE with a Logit model. This enables us to identify control firms that (i) have the same predicted propensity to use English as the treatment firms (adopters), or (ii) continue to use the local language only for external reporting. In the second stage, we estimate Equation 2.1 (E2.1) for treatment firms (adopters) and control firms (firms that continue to use only the local language but show the same propensity as our sample firms to issue an ARE). Propensity score matching essentially estimates each firm's propensity to make a binary choice as a function of observables, and matches firms with similar propensities. As Rosenbaum and Rubin (1983) showed, if the propensities were known for each firm year, they would incorporate all the information about possible self-selection issues, and propensity score matching could achieve optimal efficiency and consistency. In practice, the propensity must be estimated and selection is not only on observables, so the estimator may be both biased and inefficient.

At the general level, we hypothesize that the decision to issue an ARE is driven by external financing needs, as suggested by Jeanjean et al. (2010). In other words, the issuance of an ARE should be related to the desire to attract new investors. More precisely, we expect the following variables to influence the likelihood of using an ARE: firm size, profitability, growth opportunities, leverage, international sales, ownership structure and issuance of debt or equity. The rationale for including these variables in our propensity score procedure is discussed below.

Bonaccorsi (1992) develops a theoretical analysis of the obstacles preventing small firms' internationalization: limited resources, lack of scale economies and perceived high risk for international operations. Consistent with this framework, we expect the benefits of an ARE to increase with a firm's *Size*.

All other things being equal, a highly profitable firm generates a large free cash flow. This lowers the need for external financing. If the annual report is used to increase the visibility of the firm, then the need for an ARE should decrease with ROA and ARE adoption should show a negative association with *Return on assets*. Prior research has divided firm value into two components (Myers 1977): the assets-in-place, which are valued independently of the firm's future investment opportunities, and the growth options, which are valued on the basis of the firm's future investment decisions. As it depends on future discretionary expenditures by managers, the value of growth options is subject to far more uncertainty than the value of assets-in-place. Myers (1977) notes that firms with abundant growth opportunities are more likely to be in need of external financing to fund current and future profitable projects. Reporting in English as well as the local language could facilitate fund-raising by enlarging the base of potential investors. This is why ARE adoption should be positively related to *Growth opportunities*.

Myers and Majluf (1984) show that firms may refuse to issue stock, sometimes choosing to pass up valuable investment opportunities because of information asymmetries between the company and investors. Their findings are based on the assumptions that (i) managers know more about the firm's value than potential investors and (ii) managers act in the interest of existing shareholders, but also that (iii) investors interpret the firm's actions rationally. They also show that companies are less likely to seek external equity financing as their leverage increases. Since the issuance of an annual report in English is positively associated with companies' equity financing needs (Jeanjean et al. 2010), and based on the pecking order theory (Myers and Majluf 1984), we expect the issuance of an annual report in English to be negatively related to the company's *Leverage*.

Raffournier (1995, 266) states that companies are induced to comply with the usual practices of countries in which they operate and that more international operations require more broadly accepted practices ("The more international the operations of a firm, the larger is the inducement"). Raffournier confirms his hypothesis based on as sample of Swiss companies by using international sales as an indicator for the degree of internationalization of a firm. We expect this relationship to hold in an international setting and, therefore, expect the issuance of an annual report in English to be positively related to *Foreign sales*.

Past research (Dahlquist and Robertsson 2001) showed that institutional shareholders prefer to invest in firms with a widespread ownership. If the adoption of English is related to the desire to attract new shareholders, then we should observe that issuance of an ARE is negatively associated with the proportion of *Closely held shares*.

Finally, we expect the likelihood of issuing an ARE to be positively associated with the issuance of debt or equity in the future. We therefore anticipate a positive and significant coefficient on *Future debt increase* and *Future equity increase*.

In addition to these eight variables, we also include industry and year dummies to control for fixed factors correlated with industry or year. We estimate the following Logit for each country:

$$Log\left[\frac{\Pr(ARE=1)}{1-\Pr(ARE=1)}\right]=\alpha_0+\alpha_1 Size+\alpha_2 Return\ on\ assets+\alpha_3 Growth\ opportunities$$
$$+\alpha_4 Leverage+\alpha_5 Foreign\ sales+\alpha_6 Closely\ held\ shares+\alpha_7 Future\ equity\ increase$$
$$+\alpha_8 Future\ debt\ increase+\sum_k \alpha_{9,k} Industry+\sum_t \alpha_{10,t} Year$$

(E2.2)

To estimate Equation 2, we use the global reporting universe described later in this section. Table 2.1, Panel A, reveals that the sample size is 11,338 firm-year observations, 49.5% classified as publishing an ARE and 50.5% as publishing only in their local language.

As noted by Li and Prabhala (2006), propensity-score matching estimators are consistent estimators for treatment effects (the adoption of English in the annual report in our case) if the assignment to treatment is not endogenous, i.e., if unobserved variables that affect the assignment process are not related to the outcomes. In other words, a PSM procedure controls for self-selection on observable but not unobservable factors. We think that including control variables in our second stage equation and studying several outcomes (information asymmetry, analyst following, foreign ownership) provide controls for these unobservable factors. Moreover, we believe that our sampling procedure (i.e.: the exclusion of firms that cross list, join a major stock index or engage in M&A activity) mitigates the possible effect of self-selection since ARE adopters are excluded if these events occur either concomitantly or after the adoption of English. Consistent with past research, we also provide additional tests in which we control for unobservable factors in our analysis.

2.3.2 Variable Description

Variable descriptions are presented in the Appendix to Chapter 2.

Dependent Variables

In studying the economic consequences of ARE adoption, we use proxies for information asymmetry, analyst following and ownership structure. To proxy for information asymmetry we use companies' bid-ask spreads and zero returns. Although previous literature has found various other proxies for information asymmetries, such as share price volatility (Leuz and Verrecchia 2000), analyst following and forecast accuracy (Lang et al. 2003), price impact of trades and probability of informed trading (Chan et al. 2008), availability of SEC filings and third-party credit ratings (Sufi 2007), we follow Welker (1995), Healy et al. (1999) and Leuz and Verrecchia (2000). According to Leuz and Verrecchia (2000), among the different proxies for information asymmetry, the bid-ask spread is the best option to address the adverse selection problem that arises on share trading (p. 99). Less information asymmetry implies less adverse selection, which, in turn, implies smaller bid-ask spreads. This measure is also used in other studies as a proxy for information asymmetry (e.g., Lev 1988; Armstrong et al. 2011).

As the bid-ask spread is not the only existing proxy for information asymmetry, we add a second proxy for adverse selection and information asymmetry. The most important premise for this proxy is having data for all sample firms available that is consistent across markets. Since detailed transaction data are of relatively poor quality in some countries, we use a measure that is based on observed zero daily returns. We therefore use the proportion of zero-return days as a second proxy. If the benefits associated with trading do not outweigh the costs, then market participants will elect not to trade. Hence, illiquidity will be visible in infrequent trading, reflected in days without price movements, and therefore in observed zero returns (Lesmond et al. 1999). Moreover, this measure requires only a time series of daily equity returns. Finally, the use of the proportion of zero-return days as a measure for information asymmetry is consistent with Daske et al. (2008) and Ashbaugh-Skaife et al. (2006), who find that a zero-return metric is a summary measure of the extent to which firm-specific information is reflected in share price. We follow Bekaert et al. (2007) and define the zero-return metric as the number of zero-return trading days over the firm's fiscal year divided by the total number of trading days in the fiscal year. Higher values for this proxy correspond to greater information asymmetry. Using the zero-return metric is convenient in our setting because the information necessary to compute it is readily available consistently across markets.

Our next proxy relates to analyst following. Since analysts serve as information intermediaries, their presence should tend to increase transparency. We measure analyst following as the number of analysts issuing at least one EPS forecast during the year.[6] Our fourth measure of economic consequences relates to the internationality of ownership. Data on ownership are provided by Thomson Ownership. This database indicates the country of residence (the "country" column) as well as the number of shares owned by each shareholder. We compute three measures of the internationality of ownership. For each measure, we count the number of "Foreign owners" (FO) for each firm-year observation.[7] FO are defined as (1)

[6] It would have been interesting to identify financial analysts, their location and first language in order to directly test whether firms are able to attract more UK or US-based analysts, and/ or analysts with English as their first language by issuing an ARE. This is not possible, as IBES has eliminated the possibility of matching analysts with their employers.

[7] We did not use the alternative method of computing the total shareholdings of non-local owners, because we found inconsistencies in the continuity of this data as provided by Thomson Ownership.

owners from a country whose language is different from the one used in the firm's country of incorporation; (2) owners from any country that is not the firm's country of incorporation; (3) owners from an English-speaking country. Consider for instance a German firm, with four shareholders: one German, one Austrian, one Italian, and one British. Our three metrics set FO respectively at 2 (as Austria's language is German), 3, and 1.

Control Variables

For each dependent variable, we add control variables in Equation 2.1 (E2.1). In all regression models, we include industry-, country-, and year-fixed effects. Our specifications therefore control for differences in countries' ARE adoption rates as well as time trends.

For all regressions, we also control for the quantity of information disclosed. There is a possibility that the adoption of English is accompanied by more disclosure; this additional disclosure is likely to be associated with our outcome variables (information asymmetry, analyst following and foreign ownership). To control for this disclosure effect, we include a variable named *Quantity of information,* computed as the number of pages in the local-language annual report, scaled by the average number of pages in all sampled (local-language) annual reports in the country. This variable captures the extent of disclosure beyond the country average and is intended to reflect any information effect associated with adoption of English.

We follow prior literature to control for firm characteristics that are related to our variables of interest. In the spread regression, we control for *Size*, *Return variability*, *Share turnover* and *International standards* (Chordia et al. (2000), Leuz and Verrecchia (2000) Daske et al. (2008), Daske et al. (2013)). In the zero-return regression, we control for *International standards, Size, Return variability*, occurrence of a *Loss, Growth opportunities* and *Analyst following* (Chordia et al. (2000), Leuz and Verrecchia (2000), Daske et al. (2008), Daske et al. (2013)). In the analyst following regression, we control for *Size*, *Return on assets* and *Growth opportunities (Bae et al. 2008b).* We expect to find greater analyst following for bigger firms, and for firms with higher profitability and growth opportunities. In the foreign ownership regression, we control for *International standards*, *Size*, *Financial leverage*, *Return on assets*, and *Growth opportunities* (Dahlquist and Robertsson 2001).

2.3.3 Sample

To test our hypotheses, we created a sample of firms that have adopted English for their financial reporting (i.e., publish both a local-language annual report and an ARE). The primary data source is the "Global Reports database" (GR database). The GR database is part of Infinancials (http://www.infinancials.com) which covers more than 70,000 listed active companies around the world and aggregates data from WVB, Factset, Thomson Reuters, and Morningstar. The GR database provides access to annual and interim reports for more than 40,000 global companies from 126 countries. From this database, we selected all firms from non-English speaking European countries which issued an annual report (in any language) from 2004 to 2007. We restricted our sample to European firms because of the harmonization of European regulations, which gives us a homogenous set of countries where cross-border movements of goods, services and people are facilitated (see Bekaert et al. 2010).[8] We dropped all pre-2004 observations because the European Union decided to mandate the adoption of IFRS for all listed firms in 2005, and the transition process required all 2004 financial statements to be restated under IFRS. This makes it possible to control for the potential influence of accounting standards on the attributes measured, as both treatment and control firms are impacted by IFRS adoption due to its mandatory nature. The following table 2.1 presents our sample selection and descriptive statitsics.

Table 2. 1 Sample Selection and Descriptive Statistics

Panel A: Sample selection

	Number of firm-year observations	%
Total number of annual reports stated in Global Reports (Infinancials) with available financial data over the period 2004-2007	11,338*	
Split between:		
- Number of firm-year observations with an annual report in English (A)	5,607	49.5
- Number of firm-year observations without an annual report in English (B)	5,731	50.5

	Number of "adopters"
Adopters identified among firm-year observations with an annual report in English (A)	208
Exclusion of cross-listed firms	-24
Sub-total	184
Exclusion of companies listed in the NEXT segment	-6
Sub-total	178
Exclusion of firms with merger & acquisitions activity	-36
Sub-total	142
Elimination of companies with missing data	-29
Final sample	113

Observations to compute propensity scores (PS) in section IV are taken from sub-samples A and B. For each "Treatment group" firm in section 2.4, we choose one "Control group" firm that must: (i) be located in the same country, (ii) have a similar propensity to use English to the treatment firm the year preceding the change to English, (iii) not issue an ARE either before or after the change observed for our treatment firm.
See the Appendix to Chapter 2 for a description of variables.

[8] Although Switzerland does not belong to the European Union (EU), it is included in our sample because it is part of the EFTA (European Free Trade Association) and is highly integrated with the EU.

Panel B: Descriptive statistics of financial data

	N (Firms)	Mean	Median	N (Firms)	Mean	Median	N (Firms)	Mean	Median	p-value (t-test)	p-value (MW U-test)	p-value (t-test)	p-value (MW U-test)
	(Universe)			(Treatment)			(Control)			(Treatment vs Universe)		(Treatment vs Control)	
Size (Sales)	3,543	4.549	4.732	113	4.002	4.385	107	4.406	4.458	0.002	0.000	0.005	0.009
Return on assets	3,543	0.017	0.036	113	0.002	0.030	107	0.014	0.029	0.305	0.866	0.453	0.066
Growth opportunities	3,543	1.672	1.306	113	2.154	1.452	107	1.503	1.189	0.000	0.000	0.000	0.000
Leverage	3,543	0.516	0.541	113	0.507	0.522	107	0.508	0.519	0.469	0.450	0.542	0.419
Foreign sales	3,543	0.225	0.000	113	0.119	0.000	107	0.181	0.000	0.000	0.000	0.002	0.015
Closely held shares	3,543	0.363	0.362	113	0.337	0.289	107	0.314	0.247	0.275	0.176	0.512	0.377
Future equity increase	3,543	0.435	0.000	113	0.584	1.000	107	0.495	0.000	0.006	0.006	0.222	0.222
Future debt increase	3,543	0.738	1.000	113	0.814	1.000	107	0.757	1.000	0.977	0.977	0.666	0.666

See the Appendix to Chapter 2 for a description of variables.

As shown in Table 2.1, Panel A, from this initial database of 3,543 firms (11,338 firm-year observations over the period 2004-2007), we analyzed the external language(s) used for each firm-year observation (Local language/English/Both). Out of the 11,338 observations, 49.5% publish an ARE at least once, whereas 50.5% publish only local-language annual reports.

From the GR database, we were able to identify firms which issued a local-language annual report and an ARE between 2004 and 2007. We hand-collected and checked the languages of annual reports before and after the change date as identified from this database (208 changes in all).[9] Even if the choice of language is independent of the decision to adopt different accounting policies[10], we believe that companies listed in the US or UK will be tempted to publish an ARE to facilitate understanding of their financial statements by US or UK investors, and consequently we excluded cross-listed firms from our sample. We also excluded firms listed on the NEXT segment (Euronext) or Prime segment that require firms to publish an ARE in English. This resulted in elimination of 30 firms during the period 2004-2009[11] so as to avoid simultaneity in the consequences of adopting an ARE and the benefits of cross-listing.[12] We also dropped 36 firms engaging in merger-acquisition activity during 2004-2009 (as initiator or target) according to the SDC Platinum Database, because such firms engaged could experience changes in ownership or analyst following that are unrelated to the issuance of an ARE. We also checked that no firms joined a major stock market index, as this event would enhance the visibility of the firm. We finally dropped 29 companies with missing data on some of our independent variables. Our final working sample consists of 113 firms.

In Table 2.1, Panel B, we provide descriptive statistics on financial data for the universe (11,338 firm-year observations for 3,543 firms), the treatment sample (113 firms) and the control sample (107 firms).[13] Note that there are fewer control firms than treatment firms, as the same firm can be a control firm for more than one treatment firm (but not for the same adoption year). On average, mean (median) firm size, measured as the log of sales, is 4.002 (4.385) for treatment firms, which appears to be smaller than for the entire universe: 4.549 (4.732). This difference is significant in both the mean and the median. The mean (median)

[9] Annual reports were collected from the www.infinancials.com website, or if unavailable, from the firms' websites.

[10] For example, foreign companies listed in the US must prepare a 20-F form, which of course is in English. However, the annual report of these companies (which is a separate document from the 20-F form) may still be published in their local language. In addition, evidence on whether the 20-F form is the source of the information is mixed, because the information release date is generally unclear (see Lang et al. 2003).

[11] We include in our initial dataset all firms that first issued an ARE in the period 2004-2007. Consequently, we exclude all firms that cross-listed up to two years after the last adoption of an ARE.

[12] To test the robustness of our results with regard to this hypothesis, we run the basic model including companies listed in the US or UK. Findings are robust to the inclusion of cross-listed firms in our sample.

[13] For the composition and selection of our control sample, see below.

return on assets (ROA) is 0.2% (3.0%) for the treatment group. These figures are statistically indistinguishable from the mean (1.7%) and median ROA (3.6%) for all listed firms. The growth opportunities of the treatment firms equal an average (median) 2.154 (1.452), compared to 1.672 (1.306) for all listed firms. Firms that adopted an ARE appear to have more growth opportunities than the whole universe (p-value of the t-test = 0.000, p-value of the Mann-Whitney U test = 0.000). One unexpected finding concerns leverage: its mean (median) value is 50.7% (52.2%) for the ARE adopters, which is comparable to the 51.6% (54.1%) for all listed firms. Surprisingly, firms from our treatment group exhibit a lower proportion of foreign sales (mean of 11.9%) than the entire universe (22.5%). However, intra-industry variation in the proportion of ARE could explain this finding. Firms with an ARE do not differ from the entire universe in terms of ownership structure: on average, their closely held shares represent 33.7% of the total number of shares, versus 36.3% for the whole universe. Firms that adopt an ARE seem to lever funds either through equity or debt offerings more frequently than other firms. On average, 58.4% (81.4%) of ARE adopters issued equity (debt) during the period versus 43.5% (73.8%) for all firms. The proportion of future equity increases differs statistically and economically across sub-samples, whereas the proportion of future debt increases is statistically indistinguishable.

To summarize, ARE adopters are smaller, have more growth opportunities, lower international sales and more funding needs than the average listed firm in their respective countries. Meanwhile, the group of all ARE adopters is smaller, has more growth opportunities and lower international sales than the group of all control firms. However, at the firm-to-firm level we control for these differences by the propensity-score matching procedure.

Table 2.2 provides descriptive statistics for our treatment sample. Panel A reports the country of origin and Panel B the industry classification of our sample.

Table 2. 2 Descriptive Statistics of the Treatment Sample

Panel A: Distribution of adopters by country and languages spoken

Country name	N	%	Main language spoken
Austria	3	2.7	German
Belgium	1	0.9	Dutch
Denmark	10	8.8	Danish
Finland	3	2.7	Finnish
France	5	4.4	French
Germany	28	24.8	German
Greece	10	8.8	Greek
Italy	11	9.7	Italian
Netherlands	4	3.5	Dutch
Norway	12	10.6	Norwegian
Poland	1	0.9	Polish
Portugal	4	3.5	Portuguese
Spain	2	1.8	Spanish
Sweden	13	11.5	Swedish
Switzerland	6	5.3	German
Total	113	100.0	

*Multi-lingual countries: For Belgium and Switzerland, we chose the language spoken by the majority of the population: Dutch (Flemish) for Belgium

Panel B: Distribution of adopters by industry

Industry	N	%
Mining-Construction	5	4.4
Manufacturing	31	27.4
Transportation	8	7.1
Trade	11	9.7
Finance-Insurance	27	23.9
Services	31	27.4
Total	113	100

See the Appendix to Chapter 2 for a description of variables.

Panel A reveals that the sample firms come from 15 different countries. Eight countries (Germany, Sweden, Norway, Italy, Denmark, Greece, Switzerland and France) account for nearly 84% of the observations. Those eight countries have relatively well-developed capital markets, a useful factor in computation of information asymmetry measures; yet across and within these markets, firms are likely to differ substantially in terms of transparency and liquidity. Firms also differ in terms of dominant local language, with 12 different languages used in the sample countries. Panel B of Table 2.2 reveals that three sectors (Manufacturing, Service and Finance) account for more than 78% of the observations.

2.4 Empirical Findings

We expect the adoption of English in the annual report to have consequences for visibility. However, it could be argued that most adoptions occurred around 2005 and that the effects shown reflect an IFRS effect rather than a visibility effect resulting from ARE publication. It is also probable that the likelihood of ARE adoption is correlated with factors associated with visibility. To control for alternative explanations, we benchmark our findings against a control group comprising firms selected for their likelihood of publishing an ARE in a multivariate analysis. We describe selection of the control firms before presenting a change analysis of the economic consequences before and after ARE adoption. In a third paragraph, we use a Difference-in-Differences (DID) setting.

2.4.1 First Stage of the Propensity Score Matching Procedure

We first report the results of the first stage of the propensity score matching. The selection equation (E2.2) was estimated country by country to determine the likelihood of ARE adoption for each firm-year observation. As we cannot report the regression results for each country, Table 2.3 reports the estimated coefficients for the whole sample, to demonstrate the economic intuition of our model. Findings are quite similar across countries.

Table 2. 3 Results of the Logit Regression in Preparation of the Propensity Matching

	Predicted signs	Coefficients	z	p
Size (sales)	+	0.494	26.393	0.000
Return on assets	-	-0.599	-3.740	0.000
Growth opportunities	+	0.244	11.215	0.000
Leverage	-	-1.245	-11.131	0.000
Foreign sales	+	0.017	18.160	0.000
Closely held shares	-	-0.006	-7.435	0.000
Future equity increase	+	0.434	9.006	0.000
Future debt increase	+	0.194	3.600	0.000
Industry effects		Included		
Year effects		Included		
Country effects		Included		
Constant		-2.198	-8.919	0.000
Number of observations		11,338		
Chi square		2261.572		
p(chi2)		0.000		
Nagelkerke R-square		0.382		
Pct classified in sample		73.602		

A logit regression is run for each country. The dependent variable is coded 1 if the firm issues an annual report in English, 0 otherwise. As we cannot display the tables for all the countries, this table presents the results for a logit regression run on all firms with available data (N = 11,338). See the Appendix to Chapter 2 for a description of variables.

Overall, the model is significant (Chi^2 = 2261.572, p = 0.000) and correctly classifies 73.6% of the observations when run on the universe. At country level, the percentage of correctly classified firms per country ranges from 68.8%[14] for Italy to 90.9% for the Netherlands. On average, when Equation 2.2 is estimated country by country, 77.4% of the observations are correctly classified. These percentages are significantly higher than in a naïve model (no ARE adopters) that would have correctly classified 50.5% of observations (see Table 2.1, Panel A).

All coefficients are significant, with the predicted signs. The coefficient on *Size* is positive (coeff = 0.494, z = 26.393), suggesting that large firms tend to issue an ARE more frequently. This finding is consistent with intuition. As expected, the coefficient on *Return* is negative (coeff = -0.599, z = -3.740), suggesting that profitable firms tend to issue an ARE less frequently. Firms with high *growth opportunities* tend to issue an ARE more frequently (0.244, z = 11.215), whereas the opposite is true for more highly-leveraged firms (coef = -1.245, z = -11.131). These findings are consistent with the idea that firms use English to increase their visibility and thus raise funds. Consistent with our expectation, the more international the sales, the more likely the issuance of an ARE as indicated by the positive and significant coefficient on *Foreign sales* (coef = 0.017, z = 18.160). The firm's ownership structure is associated with the likelihood of issuing an ARE: the coefficient on *Closely held shares* is negative (-0.006) and significant (z = -7.435), consistent with the idea that closely held firms are not prone to issue an ARE. Finally, firms that will issue debt or equity in the future have a greater tendency to issue an ARE, as the coefficients on *Future equity increase* and *Future debt increase* are positive (0.434 and 0.194 resp.) and significant (resp. z = 9.006, z = 3.600). Overall, our findings suggest that firms issue an ARE when they need to raise money, or in response to demands from external parties (such as investors or customers). Findings are similar if we run Equation 2.2 country by country.

The treatment group consists of all firms that decided to issue an ARE for the first time between 2004 and 2007. For each treatment group firm, we select one control group firm that meets all three of the following conditions: First, it must be located in the same country; second, it must have a similar propensity to use English as the treatment firm the year preceding the adoption of English; and third, it must not adopt an ARE either before or after the change observed for our treatment firm. The mean (median) difference in the propensity scores between treatment and control firms is 0.0058 (0.0009). As propensity scores are expressed in percentages, this emphasizes that our matching procedure works reasonably well. In section 2.5 we use an alternative test to address this issue by including in all specifications of our basic model firm characteristics that turned out to be important for distinguishing

[14] The country with the second-lowest proportion of correctly classified firms is Germany, with a rate of 72.7%.

treatment and control firms. We also rerun our tests, excluding all treatment firms for which the difference in propensity scores was higher than 0.005. Findings are similar in magnitude and significance.

2.4.2 Univariate Findings

As a first pass on the economic consequences of issuing an ARE, we tabulate a simple before/after test in Table 2.4 for our four variables of interest for treatment and control firms. For each variable, we tabulate the mean value for up to three years before the change (subject to data availability) and up to three years after the change (subject to data availability). We then test the statistical and economic significance of the change.

Table 2. 4 Univariate Findings

	N (Total)	Mean (before) (a)	Mean (after) (b)	Difference (b-a)	T-test	p-value
Bid ask spread – Treatment (i)	546	0.034	0.024	-0.010	-3.505	0.000
Bid ask spread - Control (ii)	560	0.030	0.038	0.008	2.694	0.007
Difference (i-ii)	.	0.004	-0.014	-0.018	.	.
T-Test	.	1.388	-4.903	-3.667	.	.
p-value	.	0.166	0.000	0.000	.	.
Zero return – Treatment (i)	614	0.390	0.235	-0.154	-6.121	0.000
Zero return - Control (ii)	629	0.363	0.321	-0.043	-1.742	0.082
Difference (i-ii)	.	0.026	-0.085	-0.112	.	.
T-Test	.	1.044	-3.563	-3.992	.	.
p-value	.	0.297	0.000	0.000	.	.
Analyst following – Treatment (i)	772	0.413	1.003	0.590	10.557	0.000
Analyst following - Control (ii)	772	0.481	0.633	0.152	2.603	0.009
Difference (i-ii)	.	-0.069	0.370	0.439	.	.
T-Test	.	-1.413	5.522	5.093	.	.
p-value	.	0.158	0.000	0.000	.	.
Foreign ownership – Treatment (i)	772	0.104	0.273	0.170	10.844	0.000
Foreign ownership - Control (ii)	772	0.105	0.200	0.095	5.645	0.000
Difference (i-ii)	.	-0.001	0.073	0.074	.	.
T-Test	.	-0.084	3.597	2.661	.	.
p-value	.	0.933	0.000	0.008	.	.

This table presents a before / after test for the four variables of interest for treatment firms. For each variable, we tabulate the mean value for up to three years before the change (subject to data availability) and up to three years after the change (subject to data availability). We then test the statistical and economic significance of the change. See the Appendix to Chapter 2 for a description of variables.

On average, the mean bid-ask spread drops from 3.4% to 2.4% for our treatment firms. This represents a 29.3% reduction in the bid-ask spread after ARE adoption. This change is economically (and statistically) significant (p-value of t-test = 0.000). The mean bid-ask spread for the control sample increases from 3% to 3.8%. This finding strongly supports our hypothesis that ARE adoption enhances a firms' information environment – particularly in times of economic downturns such as the financial crisis which started in 2007. While the mean difference of the bid-ask spread between treatment and control firms was not significant in the pre-adoption period (t = 1.388, p = 0.166), it becomes highly significant after the adoption (t = -4.903, p = 0.000). As a consequence, the difference-in-differences is significant (t = -3.667, p-value of t-test = 0.000). Similar patterns are observed for zero-return days, analyst following and foreign ownership. The number of zero-return days decreases from 39% of the trading days to 23.5% after the change for treatment firms. The difference in the zero-return measure between treatment and control firms after controlling for time trend effects is -0.112 (p-value = 0.000).

The log of analyst following increases from 0.413 per firm to 1.003 after the release of an ARE. This represents an increase in analyst following from 0.51 analyst per firm on average to 1.72. Compared to control firms and taking possible time trend effects into account, the difference between both groups is 0.439 (p-value = 0.000), that is an increase by one analyst on average. The proportion of foreign owners of treatment firms more than doubles (from 10.4% to 27.3%). The difference between treatment and control firms before and after the change is 7.4% and significant (p-value = 0.008).

These changes are all the more significant since our sample excludes firms that (i) cross-list, (ii) have been included in a major stock market index or a stock index that requires external reporting in English, (iii) engage in M&A activity during the period. We tabulate in section 2.5 an analysis of the economic consequences over time, which confirms that they follow ARE adoption.

2.4.3 Difference-In-Differences Regressions

We now present our findings controlling for confounding factors. We estimate Equation E2.1 using a double clustering on firm and time dimension (Petersen 2009).[15] Table 2.5 presents the results. It consists of four panels: Panel A and Panel B (findings for H1 Information asymmetry), Panel C (findings for H2 Analyst following) and Panel D (findings for H3 Foreign ownership).

[15] Observations are pooled three years before (after) ARE adoption, and we compute the mean economic consequence before (after) ARE adoption.

Table 2. 5 Difference-In-Differences Analysis with a Propensity Score Matching

	Panel A		Panel B		Panel C		Panel D	
	Ln(Bid-Ask Spread)		Zero Daily Return		Analyst Following		Foreign Ownership	
	coef.	p-value	coef.	p-value	coef.	p-value	coef.	p-value
Treatment	0.147	0.049	0.028	0.158	0.013	0.852	0.009	0.637
Time	0.056	0.340	-0.019	0.409	0.045	0.072	0.039	0.055
Treatment * Time	-0.182	0.001	-0.065	0.000	0.297	0.000	0.030	0.030
Quantity of information	-0.105	0.099	-0.013	0.339	0.160	0.019	0.012	0.405
IFRS	0.064	0.351	-0.008	0.793	0.150	0.026	0.036	0.195
Log of market value	-0.398	0.000	-0.013	0.209				
Share turnover	-0.240	0.000						
Return variability	-0.014	0.382	-0.003	0.709				
Growth opportunities			0.004	0.593			0.037	0.001
Loss			-0.017	0.240				
Number of analysts			-0.060	0.000				
Size (Sales)					0.106	0.000	0.044	0.000
Lag return on assets					0.006	0.003		
Leverage							-0.009	0.851
Return on assets							-0.001	0.190
Country effects	Included		Included		Included		Included	
Industry effects	Included		Included		Included		Included	
Year effects	Included		Included		Included		Included	
Number of observations	1,061		1,173		1,200		1,305	
F	94.209		133.340		29.095		20.520	
Prob>F	0.000		0.000		0.000		0.000	
R-square	0.678		0.650		0.340		0.304	

The difference-in-differences analysis is based on all companies issuing an English version of their annual report and selected control companies with data available over the period. Control firms are comparable with treatment firms on the basis of a propensity score matching (same country, same year). The table reports regression results for the dependent variables, independent variables and control variables. We use four dependent variables in the analyses. Each panel displays the results of the analyses we run. Panel A: *Bid-ask spread* is the yearly median value of the absolute value of the daily bid-ask spread scaled by the mid point between the bid and ask price. *Panel B: Zero daily return*: number of zero-return trading days over the firm's fiscal year divided by the total trading days of the fiscal year. Panel C: *Analyst following* equals ln(1+ # of analysts). Panel D: *Foreign ownership* is the number of "foreign" investors over the total number of investors, as identified in the Thomson Ownership database. We define a "foreign" investor as an investor located in a different country that uses a different language from the country of the company in which she invests. Note that all standard errors are clustered following White (1980). The R^2s are consistent with prior research (Leuz and Verrecchia (2000); Bae et al. (2008a); Daske et al. (2008)). See the Appendix to Chapter 2 for a description of variables.

The main coefficient of interest is coefficient β_3 which translates the value of the effect of ARE adoption after controlling for time effects and factors that affect all comparable firms.

Panel A tabulates findings for the bid-ask spread, our first proxy for information asymmetry. Coefficient β_1 is positive (0.147) and significant (p = 0.049), which means that there is a difference between the treatment and control sample before the adoption of English.

Coefficient β_2 is positive (0.056) and non-significant (p = 0.340), showing that there is no difference for the control sample before and after the adoption. The β_3 coefficient is negative (-0.182) and significant (p = 0.001). This means that, after controlling for time effects and factors that affect all firms, ARE adoption is associated with lower information asymmetry. In other words, by publishing an ARE, firms can reduce their bid-ask spread by more than 18.2% compared to the control group. This figure is much lower than the 29% decrease reported in Table 2.3 but remains economically significant. Control variables are usually significant and consistent with prior literature. *Quantity of information* is negative (-0.105) and barely significant (p = 0.099). Consistent with intuition, firms with a better overall information environment exhibit smaller bid-ask spreads and hence less information asymmetry. *International standards* is positive (0.064) and non-significant (p = 0.351), consistent with Daske et al. (2008) who find a modest average effect of IFRS adoption on their proxies for information asymmetry. Coefficients on *Firm size* (Log of market value) and *Share turnover* are negative and significant. Consistent with intuition, large firms and firms with frequently traded shares exhibit less information asymmetry. Finally, the coefficient on return variability is non-significant (p = 0.382).

Findings for the zero-return measure are presented in panel B. They are qualitatively similar to the results for the bid-ask spread: Coefficient β_1 is positive (0.028) and non-significant (p = 0.158), which means that there is no difference between the treatment and control sample before ARE adoption. Coefficient β_2 is negative (-0.019) and non-significant (p = 0.409), showing that there is no difference for the control sample before and after ARE adoption. The β_3 coefficient is negative (-0.065) and significant (p = 0.000). This suggests that, after controlling for time and other factors that affect all firms, the initiation of issuing English annual reports is associated with a 6.5 point reduction in the number of zero-return days. Given that the mean percentage of zero-return days before the adoption of English is 39% for treatment firms (see Table 2.3), this represents a decrease of more than 16% (6.5/39).

Findings for analyst following are presented in Panel C. Coefficient β_1 (0.013) is positive and non-significant (p = 0.852), which means that the treatment group and the control sample are indistinguishable before the adoption. Coefficient β_2 is positive (0.045) and significant (p = 0.072), which shows that there is a common time-trend for the control and treatment groups. More importantly, the β_3 coefficient is positive and significant (0.297, p = 0.000). Hence, the adoption of English translates into a 29.7% increase in the number of analysts who follow the firm. Compared to Table 2.3, this effect is much lower, underlying the need to control for other factors. *Quantity of information* is positive (0.160) and significant (p = 0.019), showing that the general amount of disclosed information is an important determinant of analyst following. All other control variables are consistent with prior literature.

Panel D tabulates findings for foreign ownership. Coefficient β_1 (0.009) is not significant (p = 0.637), which shows that there is no difference between the treatment and control sample before the adoption. Coefficient β_2 is positive (0.039) and significant (p = 0.055), which again shows that there is a common time-trend effect for the control and treatment groups. More importantly, the β_3 coefficient is positive and significant (0.030, p = 0.030). After controlling for time effects and other factors, this means that the adoption of English translates into a 3.0 point increase in the number of foreign owners. Control variables are usually significant and consistent with prior literature (see Dahlquist and Robertsson 2001) with the notable exception of *International standards,* which appears to be non-significant (p = 0.195), whereas Covrig et al. (2007) showed that the voluntary adoption of IAS/IFRS is associated with a lower home investment bias. Note, however, that our sample includes mandatory IAS/IFRS adopters, and past literature has shown that the benefits of the transition to IFRS may be restricted to early adopters (see Christensen et al. 2008).

As already outlined above, we have three different definitions of foreign ownership (FO). FO is defined as (1) owners from a country whose language is different from the one used in the firm's country of incorporation (FO1); (2) owners from any country that is not the firm's country of incorporation, even if the foreign owner shares the same language (FO2); (3) owners from an English-speaking country (FO3). The definition FO3 is not suitable, as we would miss on average about 70 percent of owners who do not come from an English speaking country. In our main analysis, we focus only on definition FO1. We, however, remodel the univariate tests with the second definition. Results obtained from these tests are relatively consistent. However, with regard to the main regression model, our findings are not significant when we use this alternative definition. We explain this difference in results as follows. By definition, FO1 is more restrictive than FO2, which leads to a higher proportion of foreign owners. We compute the variable FO-diff as the difference between FO2 and FO1. Given that FO1 represents shareholders from a different country and that do not speak the same language (e.g., an Italian shareholder of an Austrian firm) and that FO2 include foreign shareholders from a different country even if they speak the same language (e.g., an Italian shareholder of an Austrian firm or a German shareholder for an Austrian firm), FO-diff captures the proportion of foreign shareholders who speak the same language as the firm (e.g., a German shareholder of an Austrian firm). Table 2.6 below displays univariate statistics concerning the variable FO-diff.

Table 2. 6 Univariate Test Statistics for Differences in Ownership Measures

	N (Total)	Mean (before) (a)	Mean (after) (b)	Difference (b-a)	T-test	p-value
FO - Diff - Treatment(i)	551	0.054	0.064	0.010	0.697	0.486
FO - Diff - Control (ii)	529	0.010	0.019	0.008	1.676	0.094
Difference (i-ii)	.	0.044	0.045	0.001	.	.
T-Test	.	4.132	4.206	0.219	.	.
p-value	.	0.000	0.000	0.827	.	.

These results suggest that English adopters (treatment companies) have a higher percentage of non-national shareholders with a shared language (e.g., Austrian firms attracting German owners) than control companies. This difference is significant before and after the initiation of issuing an annual report in English. We also note that this percentage of "non-national shareholders with a shared language" does not increase significantly after the initiation of an annual report in English.

In other words, English adopters (treatment companies) internationalize their ownership before adopting English by attracting non-national shareholders with a shared language. The "next step" is to use English in the annual report to attract new investors.

Overall this suggests a process by which companies expand their investor base. They first look for new shareholders with a pool of investors with a cultural proximity – proxied by language; before attracting new investors by using English. This is indeed consistent with Grinblatt and Keloharju (2001) who document that investors are more likely to hold, buy, and sell the stocks of firms that communicate in the investor's native tongue.

Taken as a whole, all four panels are consistent with the hypotheses that ARE adoption is associated with lower information asymmetry, greater analyst following and higher foreign ownership. Our findings are also consistent with the idea that firms try to make up for a lack of visibility by using English for their external reporting purposes.

2.5 Additional Analyses

In this section, we test the robustness of our findings. First, we report our findings when alternative specifications are applied to deal with the self-selection issue. Second, we replicate our main analysis for groups of countries: we expect that the reduction in information asymmetry associated with ARE adoption will be more prevalent for firms from countries whose language is relatively uncommon. Third, we analyze at what points in time the economic consequences of ARE publication occur.

2.5.1 Alternative Specifications to take Self-Selection into Account

To overcome the self-selection issue, we apply a propensity score matching procedure using a control sample that is "identical", except for the ARE decision, to the treatment sample. However, the selection process is based on the fitted values of our selection model (E2.2), that is, the observable differences between control and treatment firms. In other words, we use smaller sets of information to evaluate managers' decisions than the information sets used by managers and investors. Failing to take into account a relevant factor to select control firms may lead to inappropriate inferences about treatment effects, especially if unobserved variables that affect the assignment process are also related to the outcomes.

As recalled by Tucker (2010), there are two potential sources of selection bias. "Selection bias due to observables" arises from sample differences that researchers can observe but fail to control for, and "selection bias due to unobservables" arises from the unobservable and thus uncontrolled sample differences that affect managers' decisions and their consequences. To overcome the first potential self-selection issue, we apply a propensity score matching procedure to select control companies with a similar propensity to issue an annual report in English as the treatment companies. However, we recognize that the selection process is based on the fitted values of our selection model (Equation 1) for observable differences between control and treatment companies. While we attempt to account for the potential factors influencing the issuance of an English annual report, it is impossible to control for all factors. Failing to account for relevant factors to select control companies may lead to inappropriate inferences, especially if unobserved variables that affect the selection process are also related to the outcomes.

To mitigate this concern and address the second selection bias due to unobservables, we apply the Heckman (1979) two-stage approach. The first stage is to estimate the decision model for the initiation of an English annual report. We model this decision via Equation 1. Again, our model is run on a country-by-country basis. The percentage of correctly-classified companies ranges from nearly 70 percent to more than 90 percent. The mean over all countries is nearly 80 percent. This highlights that our model is correctly specified and identifies most of the factors that result in the (non-) issuance of an English annual report. As noted in Li and Prabhala (2006), the validity of the Heckman (1979) methodology relies on the "restriction exclusion", or the existence of at least one variable that explains the decision to adopt English but not the outcome variables. For each outcome, at least one independent variable of the first stage is not a control variable in the second stage.

The second stage is to add a bias correction variable in the form of the Inverse Mills ratio (obtained from Equation E2.1) to the main regression in Equation E2.2 We continue to run our analysis with the matched control sample to control for time trends, factors associated with the outcome variables, and omitted factors which are constant over time. We report the regression results with the Inverse Mills ratio included in the regression in Table 2.7.

Table 2. 7 Difference-In-Differences Analysis Including Controls for Self Selection

	Ln(Bid-Ask Spread)		Zero Daily Return		Analyst Following		Foreign Ownership	
	coef.	p-value	coef.	p-value	coef.	p-value	coef.	p-value
Treatment	0.150	0.045	0.027	0.184	0.006	0.936	0.010	0.590
Time	0.056	0.305	-0.020	0.390	0.050	0.082	0.037	0.056
Treatment * Time	-0.181	0.002	-0.065	0.000	0.301	0.000	0.029	0.032
Inverse Mills ratio	-0.262	0.432	0.128	0.205	-0.600	0.057	0.146	0.170
Quantity of information	-0.108	0.095	-0.012	0.358	0.162	0.014	0.011	0.428
IFRS	0.060	0.374	-0.007	0.834	0.146	0.028	0.038	0.159
Log of market value	-0.405	0.000	-0.008	0.414				
Share turnover	-0.242	0.000						
Return variability	-0.014	0.375	-0.003	0.679				
Growth opportunities			0.003	0.627			0.040	0.000
Loss			-0.017	0.251				
Number of analysts			-0.060	0.000				
Size (Sales)					0.085	0.002	0.050	0.000
Lag return on assets					0.006	0.002		
Leverage							-0.022	0.664
Return on assets							-0.001	0.167
Country effects	Included		Included		Included		Included	
Industry effects	Included		Included		Included		Included	
Year effects	Included		Included		Included		Included	
Number of observations	1,061		1,173		1,200		1,305	
F	94.779		131.562		29.227		19.592	
Prob>F	0.000		0.000		0.000		0.000	
R-square	0.679		0.651		0.344		0.307	
Adjusted R-square	0.667		0.639		0.323		0.285	

We test the economic consequences of an ARE by running our DID regressions, taking self-selection of matched firms into account by adding to our models the inverse Mills ratio (IMR) computed from the fitted value obtained in Equation 2.2. See the Appendix to Chapter 2 for a description of variables.

Overall, the signs, magnitude and significance levels of our variable of interest (β_3) are very consistent with those reported in Table 2.5. The IMR proves to be significant for the analyst following model (at the 10% level), and non-significant in the other three models. However, as noted in Li and Prabhala (2006), the validity of these inferences relies on the "restriction exclusions", that is, the existence of at least one variable that explains the decision to adopt English but not our outcome variables. For each outcome, at least one independent variable of the first stage is not a control variable in the second stage.

To test the robustness of our results with regard to possible omitted variables, we also included in all specifications of our basic model firm characteristics that turned out to be important for distinguishing treatment and control firms. As shown in Table 2.1, Panel B these are the proportion of foreign sales to total sales, growth opportunities, return on assets, and future equity increases. Untabulated results show that the signs, magnitude and significance levels of our variable of interest (β_3) are very consistent.

2.5.2 Impact of Countries

In this section, we show that the effect of ARE adoption differs across countries. The rationale is as follows. We hypothesize that English helps to increase the firm's visibility, because more investors are able to understand the annual report. Consequently, the magnitude of the effect should differ between a relatively widespread and well-known language (say Spanish) and a relatively rare language (say Danish). We test this prediction by running our DID regressions for two sub-samples. The first sub-sample (labeled "big countries") comprises all observations from countries whose languages are commonly spoken. The second sub-sample is made up of observations from "small countries" (in terms of the number of speakers of their language). The first group includes all countries where French, German or Spanish are the official language. The second group includes countries whose official languages are Danish, Dutch, Finnish, Greek, Italian, Norwegian, Polish, Portuguese, or Swedish.[16]

[16] This distribution is based on the number of speakers (see Lewis (2009)).

Table 2. 8 Difference-In-Differences Analysis by Group of Countries

	Panel A				Panel B				Panel C				Panel D			
	Ln(Bid-Ask Spread) - Big countries		Ln(Bid-Ask Spread)- Small countries		Zero Daily Return - Big countries		Zero Daily Return - Small countries		Analyst Following - Big countries		Analyst Following - Small countries		Foreign Ownership - Big countries		Foreign Ownership - Small countries	
	coef.	p-value	coef.	p-value	coef.	p-value	coef.	p-value	coef.	p-value	coef.	p-value	coef.	p-value	coef.	p-value
Treatment	0.259	0.041	0.041	0.609	0.035	0.253	0.030	0.251	-0.032	0.803	0.077	0.382	-0.005	0.883	0.025	0.215
Time	0.156	0.005	-0.043	0.436	0.021	0.360	-0.026	0.369	-0.042	0.228	0.101	0.048	0.003	0.822	0.057	0.050
Treatment * Time	-0.146	0.102	-0.219	0.024	-0.098	0.003	-0.042	0.079	0.375	0.007	0.236	0.000	0.044	0.068	0.031	0.117
Quantity of information	-0.022	0.777	-0.217	0.003	-0.006	0.812	-0.015	0.333	0.143	0.080	0.136	0.157	-0.022	0.442	0.037	0.004
IFRS	-0.026	0.776	0.011	0.931	-0.040	0.277	0.057	0.281	0.133	0.143	0.264	0.017	0.045	0.264	0.043	0.262
Log of market value	-0.452	0.000	-0.358	0.000	-0.011	0.465	-0.025	0.021								
Share turnover	-0.233	0.000	-0.254	0.000												
Return variability	0.030	0.317	-0.035	0.086	-0.002	0.917	-0.003	0.671								
Growth opportunities					0.013	0.377	0.001	0.910					0.052	0.000	0.024	0.058
Loss					-0.013	0.596	-0.018	0.278								
Number of analysts					-0.090	0.000	-0.029	0.050								
Size (Sales)									0.082	0.028	0.140	0.000	0.048	0.000	0.039	0.000
Lag return on assets									0.004	0.139	0.007	0.001				
Leverage													-0.069	0.424	0.063	0.262
Return on assets													-0.001	0.258	-0.001	0.233
Industry effects	Incl.		Incl.		Incl.		Incl.		Incl.		Incl.		Incl.		Incl.	
Country effects	Incl.		Incl.		Incl.		Incl.		Incl.		Incl.		Incl.		Incl.	
Year effects	Incl.		Incl.		Incl.		Incl.		Incl.		Incl.		Incl.		Incl.	
Constant																
Number of observations	459		602		467		706		473		727		509		796	
F	51.098		46.663		17.458		227.257		24.872		17.644		19.261		21.432	
Prob>F	0.000		0.000		0.000		0.000		0.000		0.000		0.000		0.000	

Table 2.8 shows that publishing an ARE has economic consequences mainly in "small countries". We focus our comments on the interaction term between *Treatment* and *Time*, our variable of interest (β_3). On the bid-ask spread, we find a negative (-.146) but non-significant coefficient (p = 0.102) for "big countries", whereas it is negative and significant for small countries (-0.219, p = 0.024). This suggests that the decrease in information asymmetry is concentrated in firms that originally use a language unlikely to be understood by many speakers.

For the zero daily return, the overall picture is dissimilar: the number of zero-return days is reduced by 9.8% in big countries versus 4.2% in small countries. Note however, that the coefficient on *Size* is negative and significant (-0.025, p = 0.021) for smaller countries, showing that the number of zero-return days is smaller for larger firms. This is not the case in big countries, where the coefficient is non-significant (p = 0.465). This suggests that the effect of firm size to some extent outstrips the effect of publishing an ARE in smaller countries. An alternative explanation might be that the bid-ask spread and zero-return days capture different dimensions of information asymmetry.

The same pattern arises for analyst following: although coefficients are positive for both "big" and "small" countries, they appear much higher in big countries (0.375) than in small countries (0.236). This difference is both economically and statistically significant (p = 0.007 for "big" countries and 0.000 for "small" countries). Note however, that the time trend is different in big and small countries. The coefficient on *Time* is positive and significant in small countries, suggesting that the number of analysts following a firm increased by 10.1% after ARE adoption (around 2005). This is not the case in big countries, where the coefficient on *Time* (-0.042) is negative and non-significant (p = 0.228). This reveals that there was a general trend towards greater analyst focus on smaller countries over time, probably because of the adoption of IFRS (positive and significant coefficient for small countries (0.264, p = 0.017). This suggests that a modest increase in small countries after controlling for time-trend effects has more economic significance than the increase in big countries. Concerning foreign ownership, β_3 is positive for both the small and big countries sub-samples and marginally significant for big countries. Again, the coefficient for small countries is smaller than the coefficient for big countries. As with analyst following, a time-trend effect in small countries attenuates the magnitude of the coefficient and reduces its significance.

Taken together, the evidence for a "small vs. big language effect" on the four variables of interest is mixed. On the one hand, for some dependent variables the effect of language is more pronounced in countries with a relatively rare spoken language – especially taking into account time-trend and size effects. On the other hand, it seems that institutional factors –

which have stronger links with bigger countries – do also play a significant role in determining the effect of the variable β_3 on the four dependent variables. In these cases, the effect is more pronounced in bigger countries.

2.5.3 Temporal Analyses of Consequences

In our main analyses we show that ARE adoption is associated with a decrease in bid-ask spreads, a decrease in zero-return trading days, and an increase in analyst following and foreign ownership. However, it remains unclear at what point in time and to what extent these consequences appear, and how far each one causes the others. Therefore, we tabulate a simple "year test" in Table 2.9 for our four variables of interest for treatment and control firms. For each variable, we tabulate the mean value for three years before the change and three years after the change. We then test the statistical and economic significance of the change.

Table 2. 9 Analysis over Time

	3 years before	2 years before	1 years before	Adoption year	1 years after	2 years after	3 years after
Bid-ask spread - Treatment	0.054	0.046	0.030	0.018	0.019	0.024	0.031
Bid-ask spread - Control	0.044	0.032	0.023	0.024	0.031	0.038	0.048
Difference	**0.010**	**0.014**	**0.007**	**-0.006**	**-0.012**	**-0.014**	**-0.017**
T-test	**1.106**	**1.896**	**1.330**	**-1.783**	**-3.034**	**-3.197**	**-2.610**
p-value	**0.271**	**0.060**	**0.186**	**0.076**	**0.003**	**0.002**	**0.010**
Zero return - Treatment	0.424	0.417	0.379	0.358	0.230	0.236	0.241
Zero return - Control	0.386	0.385	0.351	0.340	0.299	0.313	0.358
Difference	**0.038**	**0.032**	**0.027**	**0.018**	**-0.069**	**-0.077**	**-0.117**
T-test	**0.707**	**0.607**	**0.527**	**0.404**	**-1.676**	**-1.935**	**-2.620**
p-value	**0.481**	**0.545**	**0.599**	**0.687**	**0.095**	**0.054**	**0.010**
Analyst following - Treatment	0.937	0.858	0.885	1.673	2.637	3.044	3.469
Analyst following - Control	1.441	1.381	1.319	1.637	2.027	2.035	1.833
Difference	**-0.505**	**-0.522**	**-0.434**	**0.035**	**0.611**	**1.009**	**1.635**
T-test	**-1.241**	**-1.401**	**-1.259**	**0.085**	**1.164**	**1.931**	**2.722**
p-value	**0.216**	**0.163**	**0.209**	**0.932**	**0.246**	**0.055**	**0.007**
Foreign ownership - Treatment	0.063	0.091	0.094	0.166	0.236	0.286	0.303
Foreign ownership - Control	0.082	0.083	0.113	0.139	0.168	0.209	0.227
Difference	**-0.020**	**0.008**	**-0.019**	**0.026**	**0.068**	**0.077**	**0.076**
T-test	**-0.835**	**0.319**	**-0.743**	**0.963**	**2.171**	**2.186**	**1.898**
p-value	**0.405**	**0.750**	**0.458**	**0.337**	**0.031**	**0.030**	**0.059**

This table tabulates the changes in bid-ask spread, zero return, analyst following and foreign ownership for the treatment and the control groups, 3-year, 2-year, 1-year before the adoption of an ARE, the year of the adoption, and 1-year, 2-year and 3-year after the adoption. The line difference is computed as the value for Treatment group minus the value for the Control group. T-statistics and p-value (2-sided) are also reported.

Table 2.9 reveals that for all our four variables of interest, control and treatment firms are indistinguishable until one year after the adoption: the differences in means between treatment and control firms are almost always statistically non-significant for years prior to the adoption.

From the adoption year, bid-ask spreads for treatment firms fall below those of control firms (0.018 vs. 0.024). Their difference (-0.006) is marginally significant (p-value of t-test = 0.076). In the following years the differences become even more significant (all p-values < 0.010).

The number of zero-return trading days for treatment firms becomes marginally smaller than for control firms in the first year after the adoption (difference = -0.069, p-value = 0.095). This effect becomes much more pronounced during the second and third year after the adoption (difference = -0.077, p-value = 0.054, and difference = -0.117, p-value = 0.010).

Until the first year after the adoption there is no significant difference in analyst following between treatment and control firms. However, two years after the change the difference (1.009) is significant (p-value = 0.055), and three years after it is even more pronounced (1.635, p-value = 0.007).

Concerning foreign ownership, the effect of ARE adoption is much more rapid. As early as one year after the change, a statistically significant increase in foreign owners is visible for treatment firms compared to control firms (difference = 0.068, p-value = 0.031). The effect tends to amplify slightly 2 and 3 years after the adoption.

Taken together, ARE adoption is associated with more foreign investors becoming aware of the existence of the firm. These investors are likely to be sophisticated owners and this translates into smaller bid-ask spreads. This demonstrates that companies can significantly reduce information asymmetries by communicating in English. This in turn creates more liquidity, as measured by the zero-return metric. Finally, this activity attracts more attention from analyst due to investor demands for analyst recommendations. Figure 2.1 illustrates the results of the analysis of the economic effects over time. We plotted the effects of ARE adoption. We find that most of the decrease in information asymmetry follows changes in ownership, and that changes in analyst following trail changes in information asymmetry. This suggests that the economic consequences of ARE adoption stem from changes in ownership.

Figure 2. 1 Analysis over Time

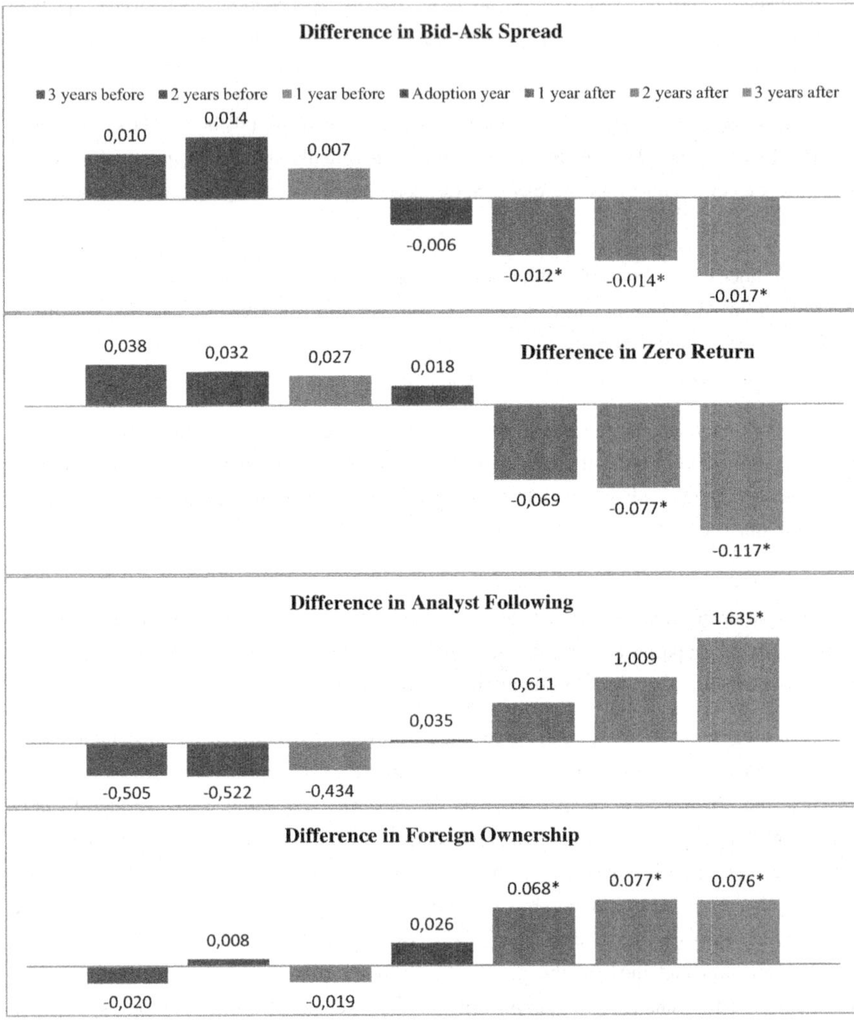

*Significant at the 0.05 level.

2.6 Conclusion

In this study, we argue that the annual report language is a crucial ingredient of a firm's visibility. Past literature has stressed the importance of accounting harmonization, suggesting that if the "language of business" is unified then information asymmetry should decrease. This view has received considerable attention from academics over the last twenty years (see Leuz and Verrecchia 2000; Covrig et al. 2007). Nonetheless, the association between accounting harmonization and positive economic consequences relies heavily on the assumption that market participants are able to read and understand any set of financial statements as long as they are governed by the same accounting rules. In practice, before we even reach the question of accounting standards, the first barrier to understanding and comparing financial statements and increasing transparency is the language barrier. Therefore, using English for external reporting purposes is the only way to address any outsider of the firm easily and directly, irrespective of their nationality, and reduce the costs of information acquisition by making the firm's financial statements more accessible for investors and analysts. In this study, we set out to analyze and assess the economic consequences of using English as an external reporting language for firms from non-English speaking countries. We test the relationship between publishing an annual report in English (ARE) and several measures of information asymmetry, and analysts' and investors' behavior.

We use a sample of "adopter" firms that issued an ARE for the first time. This sample is drawn from the Global Reports database, which states the language used by firms in their annual reports. From this initial database of 3,543 firms (11,338 observations), we identify 113 firms which published an ARE in addition to their local-language report.

Our findings are consistent with the idea that issuing an ARE in addition to the local-language report reduces information asymmetry, and increases analyst following and foreign investor ownership, after controlling for endogeneity. This study thus contributes to the literature on market participants' responses to firms' communication policy and disclosure patterns. While prior literature has identified the use of the English language as a possible explanation for various phenomena observed in capital markets (home bias, institutional ownership, trading behavior etc.), our study is the first to directly address the question of the possible economic consequences of issuing an annual report in English.

This study could be extended in a number of different directions. One possibility would be to study how financial analysts' forecast properties may be influenced by the language of the annual report. For instance, researchers could analyze whether the country-specialist analyst's superiority over industry specialists documented by Sonney (2009) holds for firms that publish an ARE. Second, researchers might extend examination of the "language barrier issue" beyond the annual report. Hales et al. (2011), for example, investigate the effect of vivid language on investor judgments. In the same vein, the following questions could be raised: Are CEOs who are non-native English speakers able to express themselves as clearly as native speakers in their roadshows? How do analysts respond to the information conveyed? Are analysts who share the language of the CEO/CFO better able to capture the subtleties of their discourse? Another interesting setting would be to analyze companies that stop publishing English annual reports in addition to their local language annual report. Do they experience any economic drawbacks?

Appendix to Chapter 2

Description of variables

Variable		Description	Source
Dependent variables			
Analyst following	=	ln(1+ # of analysts).	IBES through WRDS
Bid-ask spread	=	Yearly median value of the absolute value of the daily bid-ask spread scaled by the mid point between the bid and ask price.	Datastream (DS.Bidprice, DS.Askprice)
Foreign ownership	=	Number of "foreign" investors over the total number of investors, as identified in the database. We define a "foreign" investor as an investor from a country whose language is different from the one used in the firm's country of incorporation.	Thomson Ownership (Thomson Financial)
Zero return	=	Number of zero-return trading days over the firm's fiscal year divided by the total trading days of the fiscal year.	Datastream (DS.Bidprice, DS.Askprice)
Independent variables			
Closely held shares	=	(Number of closely held shares / Common shares outstanding) × 100	Worldscope (WS. CloselyHeldSharesPct)
Foreign sales	=	International sales / Net sales or revenues × 100 Firms with missing data are assumed not to have international sales.	Worldscope (WS.ForeignSalesPctSales)
Future debt increase	=	Dummy variable coded 1 if the firm has a debt increase superior to the median debt increase of the sample in the next two years, and 0 otherwise.	Worldscope (WS.TotalLiabilities)
Future equity increase	=	Dummy variable coded 1 if the firm shows an equity increase that is higher than the median equity increase of the sample in the next two years, and 0 otherwise.	Worldscope (WS.CommonStock)
Growth opportunities	=	(Market value + Total debts)/Assets (simplified version of the definition provided by (Klein 2002)). Data winsorized at 0.01.	Datastream: (DS.MarketValue),[17] Global (Standard and Poor's): (mnemonic: [MKVAL + DT]/AT), Infinancials: (Market capitalization: code 11937, Total debts: code 54022), Worldscope (Thomson Financial): (WS.TotalAssets, WS.TotalDebt).

[17] First source for Market value was *Datastream*. When data were not available, the other indicated databases were used (Global (S&P), Infinancials, Worldscope).

Industry	=	Dichotomous variables used to represent different industries at the two-digit SIC code level: Agriculture (01-09), Mining-construction (10-17), Manufacturing (20-39), Transportation (40-49), Trade (50-59), Finance-Insurance (60-67), Services (70-89), Public administration (91-99).	Infinancials (SIC sector code: code 20004), Worldscope (WS.PrimarySICCode). Classification: www.siccode.com
International standards	=	Dummy variable coded 1 if the firm adopts IAS/IFRS or US GAAP and zero otherwise.	Worldscope (WS.acctgstdfollowed)
Leverage	=	Total debt/total assets ratio at year-end. Data winsorized at 0.01.	Global: (mnemonic: [DT/AT]), Infinancials: (codes: 54022/53077), Worldscope: (WS.TotalAssets, WS.TotalDebt).
Quantity of information	=	ln(number of pages in the annual report in the local Language/ average number of pages in each country). We scale by the average number of pages in each country to control for "language efficiency" (certain languages need more words to express the same idea).	Hand collected from annual reports
Return on assets	=	Income before extraordinary items/Total assets. Data winsorized at 0.01.	Global: (mnemonic: ROA), Infinancials: (code: 5020), Worldscope: (WS.ReturnOnAssets),.
Return variability	=	Return variability is computed as the annual standard deviation of monthly stock returns. We compute return variability beginning in month -2 through month +10 relative to fiscal year end. We use the log transformation of this measure to mitigate the use of outliers.	Datastream (DS.index)
Size (Market value)	=	Natural logarithm of the market value of equity measured as the stock price times the number of shares outstanding (in US$ millions).	Worldscope (WS.marketcap)
Size (Sales)	=	Natural logarithm of the sales for the year.	Global: (mnemonic: SALE), Infinancials: (code: 53002), Worldscope: (WS.Sales).
Share turnover	=	Accumulated US$ trading volume during the year divided by market value of outstanding equity. We compute return variability beginning in month -2 through month +10 relative to fiscal year end. We use the log transformation of this measure to mitigate the use of outliers.	Datastream (DS.volume)

Chapter 3

Disclosure Incentives, Enforcement, and Culture: Impact on Corporate Risk Disclosure

3.1 Introduction

Disclosure practices differ widely not only across countries, but also within a country and between industries. There is an intense debate on how best to achieve transparency and international comparability of financial statements. The dominant approach is to harmonize accounting standards across countries. Despite the significant steps towards harmonization that have resulted from various regulatory changes in a large number of countries, it is clear that a single set of accounting standards *per se* is not sufficient for transparent and internationally comparable financial reporting and disclosure[18]. Apart from managerial

[18] Most work on corporate disclosure and reporting uses the terms "reporting" and "disclosure" interchangeable. To be more specific, however, corporate reporting originally stems from the mandate of a company to report on its ongoing business activities and future prospects to its shareholders. Reporting consists of, for instance, issuing (annual) reports and disclosing relevant and timely information. Corporate disclosure, therefore, is part of

incentives and markets' demand for information, a country's institutional environment, its strength of enforcement, as well as its cultural values are expected to affect corporate financial disclosure. In this study, we provide an in-depth analysis of the determinants of firms' disclosure behavior. We offer various explanations for why firms may not fully comply with mandatory disclosure rules. More specifically, we find that benefits associated with non-disclosure are greater than costs associated with non-compliance.

We focus on listed European firms that adopted International Financial Reporting Standards (IFRS) and analyze their 2007 annual reports with regard to mandatory and voluntary risk management and financial instruments disclosures. Our data set has several desirable features. First, we use very recent hand-collected data on disclosure rather than data from the 1992/1993 CIFAR index. Second, all firms in the sample are obliged to comply with IFRS. Consequently, there is no self-selection bias. It also follows that any heterogeneity in disclosure behavior has to be attributed to factors other than differences in reporting standards. Third, analyzing firms from 20 countries from within the European Union (including Switzerland and Norway) guarantees that all firms operate in the same environment in which goods and services, capital, and labor can almost freely move. We can therefore focus on the impact of various social-economic and institutional differences across countries. Fourth, there is significant variation in the cultural background of the European countries in our data set as documented by Hofstede (1991, 2001), Schwartz (1994, 1999, 2004) and the GLOBE project (House et al. 2004). We analyze whether disclosures across countries can partly be explained by these differences in cultural values. Finally, the data set allows us to directly tackle the disclosure behavior as determined by the most intensely debated accounting standards: IAS 32, IAS 39 and IFRS 7. Previously, IAS 32 and IAS 39 specified how firms had to report on risk management. IFRS 7 came into effect in 2007 and amended IAS 32. Disclosure and reporting requirements on corporate risk management activities, risk exposures and financial instruments based on these standards have been perceived to be particularly difficult to interpret.[19] We therefore conclude that if reporting standards are – at least to some degree – open for interpretation, the impact of other determinants on the actual disclosure is likely to be particularly pronounced. In case that these determinants differ across countries, harmonization of accounting standards is likely to be unable to lead to a consistent disclosure behavior of firms.

---

a firm's overall reporting. When specifically referring to disclosure instead of reporting, one typically emphasizes the revelation (or "disclosure") of information within a report to shareholders.

[19] The IASB states, for example, that "the requirements in IAS 39 were difficult to understand, apply and interpret."

We study three different disclosure indices as dependent variables: total, mandatory and voluntary disclosure. Prior studies draw their inferences from studying either a total disclosure index or focus on either the mandatory or voluntary index. We find a huge variation in corporate risk management disclosures. The mean (standard deviation) for the total disclosure index is 51.38% (0.1204), for the mandatory index it is 66.29% (0.1579), and for voluntary disclosure index it is 39.48% (0.1312). The finding that firms on average comply to only 66% with mandatory disclosure rules causes for concern, given that all firms are subjected to the same set of accounting standards.

This chapter is grouped into three sets of analyses, each of which focuses on various aspects and determinants of corporate disclosure behavior. The first set of analyses exploits the general determinants of corporate disclosure. The second set focuses on the role of enforcement for corporate disclosure behavior while the third set examines the role of culture for corporate disclosure practices.

To begin with, we classify the determinants of disclosure into four groups: *managers disclosure incentives'*, *accounting standards, business structure*, and *institutions*. We find that each group, both in separate regressions as well as in a full model, has a significant impact on each disclosure index. Controlling for country fixed effects does neither affect our main results nor the inferences. Instead, including country indicator variables increases the explanatory power of our models by at least 50%, depending on the disclosure index. This underlines the importance of country-specific effects for individual firm disclosures. Aggregating the disclosure indices on a per country basis corroborates our findings: We find that the country-level variables explain more than 60% of the average mandatory and more than 40% of the average voluntary disclosure index. If we extract country-fixed effects based on firm level regressions, we find similar results.

In the second set of analyses, we analyze the role of enforcement for corporate disclosure behavior. As expected, we find that the strength of enforcement generally has a positive impact on corporate disclosures indices. Furthermore, we expect and find that the perception of the strength of enforcement at the firm level is an important determinant of firms' disclosure practices. Assuming that outsiders' demand for information shape a firm's perception of enforcement, we find that the impact of enforcement is indeed much stronger the larger the information demands from outsiders. In an additional analysis, we focus on the interplay of enforcement and differences between IFRS and formerly applied local accounting standards. Whereas differences between local GAAP and IFRS have a large explanatory power for our disclosure indices, their influence is mitigated when strong enforcement mechanisms are in place.

The third set of analyses focuses on the direct impact of culture on firms' disclosure practices, as well as on the interaction of enforcement and culture. At a descriptive level, we perform a k-means cluster analysis of 20 different cultural values yielding five cultural clusters. We find that both the mandatory and voluntary disclosure indices vary significantly across these clusters. Via a multilevel regression analysis we further explore this finding. We find that cultural clusters (and cultural values) have an impact on firms' disclosure practices. The explanatory power of our models is twice as large as models that regress legal origins on disclosure indices. To explore the interaction effects of culture and enforcement on firms' disclosures, we create sub-samples based on selected cultural values. We find that the impact of enforcement varies significantly across these sub-samples, indicating that cultural values pre-determine the impact of enforcement. Finally, we predict a country's strength of enforcement based on its cultural attributes. We find that cultural values impact managers' disclosure practices directly and indirectly through the predicted enforcement variable. Alternative model specifications corroborate our findings.

Our study contributes to the literature in several ways. First, we directly address the debate on whether accounting standards alone are sufficient for transparent and comparable disclosure behavior. Prior literature has seen accounting standards as the primary input for high-quality reporting (Levitt 1998). Ball et al. (2003), however, state that disclosure quality is an endogenous function of managers' incentives, market demands and political influences. We corroborate their assertion and provide evidence that factors other than accounting standards have a significant impact on firms' disclosure practices. Prior studies have so far used indirect measures, such as the degree of earnings management (Leuz et al. 2003) or the extent of timely loss recognition (Ball et al. 2003), as proxies for firms' disclosure and reporting outcomes. Our study focuses on more straightforward disclosure measures, namely mandatory and voluntary disclosure indices. Hence, we emphasize the question *what* managers actually report to the public, rather than *how* they report it. We are the first to analyze the impact of disclosure incentives on recent disclosure indices using a large international data set of firms that have to follow the same set of accounting standards.[20] Our findings support the view that transparency and international comparability is unlikely to be achieved by accounting standards alone.

[20] Unlike Archambault and Archambault (2003), who focus mainly on cultural values and firm characteristics, we control for differences between previous and current accounting standards and the impact of country characteristics.

Second, we contribute to the literature on the role of differences between local GAAP and IFRS. Several studies find that accounting differences matter in various areas.[21] We extend these studies by analyzing the impact of differences in accounting standards on firms' actual disclosure behavior. Our results are in line with prior studies. We find that differences in accounting standards between previously relevant local GAAP and IFRS have a significant impact on firms' disclosure practices.

Third, we contribute to the growing literature on the impact of enforcement and institutions on disclosure practices and disclosure quality. While Djankov et al. (2003) and Shleifer (2005) have shown the importance of enforcement in a finance context, several accounting studies find that properly implemented and enforced accounting standards are key to the success of any accounting regulation[22]. These studies, however, focus on the impact of enforcement on various financial market outcomes (e.g. stock liquidity or information asymmetries), or on accounting quality (e.g. timely loss recognition or earnings quality). To our best knowledge, no study directly examines the influence of enforcement on (1) firms' compliance with mandatory accounting rules, and (2) firms' voluntary disclosure choices.

Fourth, we also contribute to the growing literature on the role of institutions in accounting and finance (La Porta et al. (1998); La Porta et al. (2006); Leuz et al. (2003); Leuz (2010); Christensen et al. (2011); Daske et al. (2013)). Existing evidence documents that institutional factors have a significant impact on managers, analysts and stakeholders. While the majority of all studies focuses on legal systems, the strength of enforcement, and shareholder protection rights as proxies for a country's institutional system, we employ rarely used variables from the *Heritage Foundation,* and *Transparency International* to proxy for institutional systems. First, we show that these factors impact firms' disclosure behavior. Second, we show that mandatory and voluntary disclosure choices are influenced by different institutional factors. This is the first study that provides a comprehensive overview of the impact of institutional factors on firms' disclosure practices.

Fifth, we also contribute to the growing literature on the role of culture in accounting. Existing evidence documents that cultural values have a significant impact on managers,

---

[21] Daske et al. (2008) find that IFRS adopters from countries with larger differences between local GAAP and IFRS exhibit larger liquidity increases compared to adopters from countries with smaller differences. Ding et al. (2007) explore how differences between local GAAP and IFRS have an impact on disclosure quality. Florou and Pope (2009) find that IFRS-related ownership-changes are likely to be more pronounced if local GAAP and IFRS do not deviate by a wide margin. Using a European sample of publicity traded companies, Byard et al. (2010) show that the effect of mandated IFRS adoption on analysts' forecast error is influenced by the difference between domestic GAAP and IFRS.

[22] See, for example, Joos and Lang (1994), Hope (2003a), Leuz et al. (2003), Bushman et al. (2004), Joos (2004), Bradshaw and Miller (2008), and Holthausen (2009).

analysts and stakeholders.[23] Hope (2003b) concludes that "it is too early to write off culture as an explanatory variable for annual report disclosure levels". We support his view in several ways and go on similar to our analyses on the impact of institutional factors on risk management disclosures: First, we show that cultural values impact firms' disclosure behavior. Second, we show that mandatory and voluntary disclosure choices are influenced by different cultural values. Third, we point out that cultural clusters have a much higher explanatory power than clusters of legal origins. Fourth, we analyze how the impact of enforcement on mandatory disclosure varies for various cultural values. We argue that it is optimal for managers to not deviate from a country's cultural value set to avoid negative effects on their reputation and compensation. This is the first study that provides a comprehensive overview of the impact of cultural values on firms' disclosure practices.

Finally, we also contribute to the literature on risk management and financial instruments disclosure. The use of derivative instruments for corporate risk management has grown dramatically over the past decades. Against this background, we test for the effectiveness of existing regulation of the accounting treatment and reporting of these instruments. Increasing the disclosures with regard to corporate risk management policies and financial instruments, as required by IAS 32, IAS 39, and IFRS 7, provides a better picture of the firm's underlying risk exposures and improves the informativeness of corporate earnings as a signal of management ability (DeMarzo and Duffie 1995). While prior research has found considerable heterogeneity in risk disclosures within countries, the existing literature suffers from two limitations. First, it provides only limited evidence on the attributes of risk disclosures by focusing either on specific disclosure items (Linsmeier et al. 2002), or on specific sections of the annual reports (Vielmeyer 2004). Second, there is no larger-scale cross-country study of risk management disclosure to date. Most recently, Dobler et al. (2011) conduct a content analysis of financial risk disclosures for 160 firms from four countries. They find that cross-country variation in risk disclosure attributes can only partly be linked to domestic disclosure regulation and accounting standards, suggesting that risk disclosure incentives play an important role. Following their call for further research on the determinants of risk

[23] Ding et al. (2005) find an association between accounting harmonization scores and cultural values. Kai et al. (2011) find that cultural attributes have a significant impact on corporate risk-taking and capital structure decisions. Stulz and Williamson (2003) show that investor protection is related to culture. Salter (2001) shows that national cultures affect managers' disclosure behavior. The findings of Jaggi and Low (2000) suggest that national culture has no significant influence on disclosure in common law countries. However, the influence of national culture in civil law countries is significant but not always in the expected direction. Hope (2003a) finds that cultural attributes have a significant impact on analysts' forecast accuracy.

disclosure[24], we extend prior analyses[25] insofar as we distinguish between mandatory and voluntary risk disclosure, and by analyzing the amount of risk disclosures under IFRS.

This study has the following drawbacks. First, the construction of a disclosure index involves some degree of subjectivity. We try to alleviate this problem by analyzing a mandatory and a voluntary disclosure index. The composition of the mandatory index is less prone to discretion. The voluntary index is based on recommendations in the corresponding IFRS standards. Second, we focus on risk management and financial instruments disclosure. Therefore, our results cannot easily be generalized to more comprehensive disclosure indices that cover other disclosure items. Third, we only analyze a cross section of firms' disclosure such that we cannot identify how disclosure evolves over time. Fourth, as we focus on the first year after the adoption of IFRS 7, a *learning effect* may affect our results. Firms typically comply more with disclosure rules if they are used to the disclosure requirements. This probably overstates the overall disclosure non-compliance for our sample firms. However, our main results are not affected by this caveat since all firms are equally affected by this *learning effect*. Moreover, focusing on the first adoption year provides a much better and more interesting model setup to analyze determinants of non-compliance, especially in times when compliance is more difficult to achieve.

This study is organized as follows: The next section develops our hypotheses, reviews the literature and introduces our variables. Section 3.3 presents the data. Section 3.4 examines the role of various disclosure incentives, as well as institutional country characteristics on firms disclosure practices. In Section 3.4 we also focus on the role of enforcement and the market's demand for accounting information. Section 3.5 investigates the role of country effects and institutional factors on disclosure indices. Section 3.6 concludes.

---

[24] "The lack of transparency and clarity in risk disclosure and the increasing complexity of business supported by constantly improving information technologies have created a need to conduct more research in accounting and related fields to study how public firms are (descriptive) and should be (prescriptive) disclosing information about their risk profile, tolerance levels, risk management, and monitoring processes." (Dobler et al. 2011, p1)

[25] Lopez and Rodriguez (2007) study the determinants of disclosure levels in the accounting for financial instruments of Portuguese listed companies. Hill and Short (2009) compare the risk disclosures of IPO companies with those of listed companies. Iatridis (2008) analyzes the financial characteristics of firms that provide extensive accounting information of financial instruments and hedging activities in UK firms. Most recently, Dobler et al. (2011) explore firms' risk disclosures based on a content analysis of annual reports of 160 manufacturing firms from the U.S., Canada, U.K., and Germany and find considerable heterogeneity in risk disclosures across these countries. Focusing on risk disclosures under IFRS, Shackleton et al. (2012) find that the implementation of hedge accounting rules under IFRS reduces the level of asymmetric information faced by derivative users. Rather than analyzing the effect of the mere existence of accounting standards, we focus on the amount of information disclosed under these standards.

3.2 Related Literature and Hypotheses

In this section, we provide a comprehensive literature review and develop our hypotheses. As we will outline in the following sections, there is an extant literature on the role of managers' incentives, accounting standards and firm-specific characteristics for companies' actual reporting behavior. Most of them analyze the impact of IFRS adoption on corporate behavior. This has to be put into perspective: Most research on IFRS Academics typically focus solely on an indicator variable that takes on the value of unity if the firm reports under IFRS, and zero otherwise. They then conduct two analyses: First, they model the choice of voluntarily IFRS adoption by employing a Logit model with the indicator variable as dependent variable. Some studies, however, do not control for a potential self-selection bias that comes with voluntarily IFRS adoption. Failing to take this possibility into account results in downward-biased standard errors overestimating the effects of IFRS adoption. Second, they analyze the consequences associated with IFRS adoption by regressing the indicator variable on various potential consequences they are interested in (timely loss recognition, measure for abnormal accruals, information asymmetry proxies, market valuation, cost of capital, foreign ownership, cross-border investment etc.). Both approaches are problematic since more recent research has found that companies have considerable discretion in implementing IFRS. Companies can use their discretion to "play the game" and use IFRS simply as a label, rather than to adapting to increased disclosures requirements. Such an analysis, therefore, cannot feasibly distinguish between serious adopters and label adopters. Moreover, large cross-country studies are relatively rare. In consequence, existing studies cannot draw meaningful conclusions of the impact of country-specific characteristics on reporting behavior.

This study, therefore, tries to improve on the above-mentioned drawbacks of prior literature. First, we do not focus on a binary variable that indicates a company's accounting standards. We, however, develop a much more comprehensive, directly observable, objective, and continuous measure that captures a company's compliance with IFRS. Instead of focusing on an indicator variable, we construct disclosure indices based on observed corporate behavior. This allows us to distinguish between serious adopters and label adopters and to identify the causes and consequences for being compliant with IFRS or not. Second, we do not focus on voluntary but on mandatory IFRS adoption. We therefore do not need to control for a potential self-selection bias. Third, by analyzing a large dataset from 20 European countries, we can focus on country-specific characteristics that are beyond the firm's control. We try to gauge the extent to which such country-given characteristics impact a firm's disclosure behavior and compliance with IFRS. One could interpret those country-given specifics as the non-diversifiable non-compliance with mandated accounting rules."

In this section, we successively focus on different sets of analyses and develop hypotheses in each section. We start with the determinants of firms' disclosure practices. Next, we focus on the role of enforcement for corporate disclosure before we turn to the literature review on the impact of a country's institutional system and its cultural values on corporate disclosure. Finally, we concentrate on the interplay of disclosure, enforcement, and culture.

3.2.1 Determinants of Firms' Disclosure Practices

The globalization of capital markets and other markets has increased the demand for high quality financial reporting and disclosure. Following this demand, regulators have tried to harmonize financial reporting standards in order to establish a set of reporting rules that is equal across countries. In 2002, the European Commission mandated the application of IFRS for all firms headquartered in the European Union for fiscal years starting on or after 01/01/2005.

Proponents of a unique set of accounting standards argue that IFRS reporting and disclosure increases transparency and improves comparability of financial reporting and disclosure across firms (e.g., EC regulation No. 1606/2002). Thus, even if the quality of financial disclosure does not improve per se, comparability of financial information is useful to investors (Armstrong et al. 2010a; Covrig et al. 2007). Various studies provide evidence that higher quality reporting and more extensive disclosures are negatively associated with firms' cost of equity capital, adverse selection problems in equity markets, and information asymmetries, and positively associated with market liquidity, earnings quality, and firm value.[26] In addition, higher comparability of financial statements can increase capital markets integration which, in turn, might result in positive externalities such as increased visibility of firms to investor (Merton 1987) and higher cross-border investment (Bradshaw et al. 2004).

Ball et al. (2003) take another view and argue that financial reporting and disclosure practices are highly sensitive to managers' incentives, country's enforcement efforts, and capital market development. They show that the interaction of accounting standards and managers' incentives may lead to lower quality financial reporting and disclosure. Their

[26] See, amongst others, Welker (1995), Botosan (1997), Leuz and Verrechia (2000), Verrechia (2001), Botosan and Plumlee (2002), Hail (2002), Hail and Leuz (2006), Lambert at al. (2007), Barth et al. (2008), Daske et al. (2008), Li (2010b), Lambert et al. (2011).

findings document that accounting standards *per se* are not sufficient to increase disclosure quality. Dobler et al. (2011) find that cross-country variation in risk disclosures can only partly be linked to domestic disclosure regulation and accounting standards, suggesting that risk disclosure incentives play an important role. In a similar spirit, Ball et al. (2000) point out that accounting standards do not address the level in detail of practice, and that there is considerable judgment involved in their implementation. They suggest that institutional differences across countries play an important role. In this line, Adelopo and Moure (2010) see firms as social actors that operate within a nexus of economic, legal, and cultural institutions which shape managers' incentives. Hence, differences in these institutions induce different accounting practices by firms (La Porta et al. 1998; Nobes 1998; Campbell 2006, 2007). Consequently, international comparability of accounting information will not be achieved through homogenization of accounting standards alone. Also, there are skeptical views on whether adopting international accounting standards will bring significant changes to information quality. Holthausen (2003) argues that accounting standards are complementary to the institutional environment, thus, it is unclear whether adopting a new standard will always provide better information to investors. Risk management and financial instruments disclosures allow for a considerable part of discretion due to its subjective and partly non-verifiable nature. In consequence, "a considerable part of corporate risk management disclosure observed empirically can be assumed to be (quasi-) voluntary and depends on disclosure incentives even in the presence of disclosure regulation" (Linsley and Shrives 2000; 2006; Dobler 2008; Dobler et al. 2011). Taken together, an (almost) identical set of managers' and auditors' incentives as well as harmonized institutional structures across countries would be necessary. This, in turn, would require a significantly higher level of worldwide integration of economic, legal and political systems. Absent such integration, the amount of disclosures in financial statements prepared under IFRS will still vary greatly across countries.

In this study, we provide evidence that a firm's (non-)compliance with mandatory disclosure rules as well as its amount of voluntary disclosure are a function of regulation and incentives with both factors linked to the institutional and cultural environment and the latter additionally depending on firm specific factors.[27] To give our empirical analyses sufficient structure, we categorize determinants of firms' disclosure practices into four groups: a *firm's business structure, managers' incentives, accounting standards*, and *countries' institutions*.

[27] Similar arguments are made by Ball and Shivakumar (2005), Ball (2006), Burgstrahler et al. (2006), Hail and Leuz (2006), and Daske et al. (2008).

Each group of disclosure determinants consists of several variables. In the following, we describe these variables in more detail and elaborate their expected direction of impact. When discussing our results in section 3.4, we use Wald tests to measure the explanatory power of each set of variables. Therefore, the emphasis is on the explanatory power of sets of variables representing various disclosure incentives.

Business structure

We proxy for a firm's *business structure* by *firm size, leverage, internationality, profitability, and growth opportunities*. All variables in this group are related to a firm's operational characteristics.

Firm size has been shown to be positively associated with disclosure (Adrem 1999; Raffournier 1995). One reason is the greater demand for information in larger firms (political cost argument). In addition, larger firms rely more on outside financing (Petersen and Rajan (1994); Berger and Udell (1998); Demirgüç-Kunt et al. (2002)). This increases the need for more extensive disclosures.

The role of *leverage* on firms' disclosure decisions is ambiguous. On the one hand, managers in high leveraged firms have incentives to increase disclosures to reduce agency costs of debt. On the other hand, debt can be used as a monitoring device (Jensen 1986) and therefore be negatively associated with disclosures (Vashishtha 2012). Ahmed and Courtis (1999) find in a meta-analysis of disclosure studies that disclosure increases with leverage. Jaggi and Low (2000) find the same relation between disclosures and leverage. Consistent with these studies, we expect a positive relation between the extent of mandatory and voluntary disclosures and *leverage*.

With regard to *internationality*, we expect a positive relation to firm disclosures. Companies with a larger exposure to foreign markets (measured by the proportion of foreign assets to total assets and foreign sales to total sales) are also likely to require larger foreign resources, such as labor and capital. They therefore have to disclose more to acquire these resources (Zarzeski 1996; Archambault and Archambault 2003).

Prior studies provide evidence that firms' *profitability* also affects firms' disclosures. The direction of its impact is, however, ambiguous. While Wallace and Naser (1995) find a negative relationship between *profitability* and disclosure levels, we expect a positive impact. Profitable firms do not hide risk management information from outsiders but signal that they can handle complex risk management tools successfully. Moreover, one can argue that highly profitable firms took *ex ante* risky investment decisions which turned out to be profitable *ex post*. They therefore disclose more (voluntarily) to reveal these risk factors. Therefore, they disclose more about their risk management strategies and underlying risk factors.

Finally, firms that have higher *growth opportunities* are expected to provide more disclosures, particularly more risk management disclosures. This is to put away investors' potential doubts relating to their financial conditions (Iatridis 2008). In addition, Myers (1977) notes that firms with abundant growth opportunities are more likely to be in need of external financing to fund current and future profitable projects. We therefore expect more disclosures for firms with larger growth opportunities.

Managers' incentives

To capture *managers' incentives* we use the following variables: *future financing needs*, *speculation* with derivatives, *future positive abnormal returns*, the degree of *competition* within an industry, the *number of analysts* following a firm, and a binary variable indicating whether the firm is audited by a *BIG4 auditor*. All variables included in this category focus either on forward-looking private information of firms' managers (*future financing needs,* future positive abnormal returns), or on outsiders which are expected to directly affect managers' incentives (*competition, number of analysts, BIG4 auditor*). *Speculation* is a within-firm variable which captures managers' risk attitudes. The variables are not directly related to a firm's day-to-day business activities and operational characteristics.

External financing needs are an important determinant of corporate disclosures (Healy and Palepu 2001). We capture *future financing needs* by indicator variables for future debt and equity issuances.[28] Following Beyer and Guttman (2011), we argue that managers are privately informed about the value of their firm and have incentives to disclose information and manipulate their disclosure decisions in order to obtain the best possible financing terms.[29] We therefore expect that future debt increases are accompanied by more disclosures to mitigate potential agency problems between debtholders and managers. On the other hand, we have no prediction on the effect of future equity increases on disclosures. Either managers

[28] Note the difference between our proxy for capital structure, *leverage*, and these two variables. *Leverage* is the actual amount of debt on the firm's balance sheet, whereas *future debt and equity increases* cannot be seen in the actual annual report. They can only be known in part by managers and insiders who may know about the need for future capital to fund investment opportunities. Note also the difference between these two proxies and the book-to-market ratio: The latter proxies for growth opportunities which does not necessarily result in raising debt or equity capital.

[29] Similarly, Thakor (2012) provides an economic rationale to withhold strategic information and to manipulate disclosure decisions. His model predicts that all firms voluntarily signal objective private information, but not all firms disclose additional subjective information about strategy that is prone to multiple interpretations and hence potential disagreement. He also predicts that an improvement in corporate governance leads to a decrease in information disclosure.

disclose less because equity holders have access to inside information, or managers disclose more to make equity offerings more attractive.[30]

The dummy variable *speculation* indicates whether a firm engages in speculative activities.[31] We expect firms trading with derivatives to be under greater scrutiny of auditors and investors. Hence, they comply more with mandatory disclosure rules and provide more voluntary disclosures. Moreover, we assume that managers aim to weaken investors' doubts about possible negative outcomes related to speculation. This should lead to more risk management disclosures.

The variable *positive future abnormal returns* indicates whether a firm performs better than the market (whereas the market in our setting consists of all non-financial firms in the DJSTOXX 600) in the following year. Firms with positive future abnormal returns are likely to be less risky and to have superior investment opportunities. Consequently, these firms need to rely less on external financing. Moreover, as Jung and Kwon (1988) and Dye (1998) point out, informed managers are more likely to disclose when outsiders' prior beliefs about the firms' future performance are less favorable. Hence, if outsiders expect a favorable development in the future, managers will disclose less today. We therefore expect a negative impact of positive future abnormal returns on mandatory and voluntary disclosures.

We proxy for *competition* by the Herfindahl index. It is calculated over total sales and two-digit SIC codes. Theoretical models as well as empirical studies have ambiguous predictions regarding the effect of competition on disclosure (Jin 2005). Firms face a trade-off between the benefits of reducing information asymmetry with capital market participants and the costs of aiding competitors by revealing proprietary information (Ellis et al. 2012). These costs are expected to be smaller if proprietary information has less value to the firm, i.e. if the firm operates in more competitive markets. Moreover, following Board (2009), we argue that competitive pressures between firms promote mandatory and voluntary disclosures. Higher competition forces firms to differentiate from each other by disclosing more, even if disclosure is costly. Hence, we expect a positive impact of *competition* on firm disclosure.

We proxy for a firm's outside information environment by the *number of analysts* following the firm. The interplay between mandatory and voluntary disclosures and analyst

[30] Against the background of the 2008 financial crisis, one can also argue that firms which disclosed more in 2007 had easier access to debt capital in 2008 and 2009. Consequently, firms that disclosed less in 2007 had to rely more often on equity capital in 2008 and 2009.

[31] We identify only a small number of speculators in our sample. Allayannis and Ofek (2001) and Jin and Jorion (2006) suggest that the use of derivatives by non-financial firms is associated with lower levels of risk. This is consistent with firms using derivatives to hedge rather than to speculate. We classified a firm as a speculator if it has disclosed explicitly in its annual report to use derivatives not only for hedging purposes.

following is unclear. On the one hand, firms' may disclose more to meet analysts' information needs. In addition, firms are expected to comply more with mandatory disclosure rules as they are under greater scrutiny of analysts. On the other hand, a firm's disclosure amount may be smaller in the presence of lots of analysts. Both provide information to outsiders and thus may serve as substitutes. Moreover, in the special case of risk disclosures managers may want to withhold information to not attract analysts' attention on risk disclosures. Taken together, we expect a positive impact of analyst following on the mandatory disclosure index and a negative impact on the voluntary index.

We expect a positive influence of *BIG4 audit firms* on disclosure. Theory predicts that larger audit firms provide better audit quality (DeAngelo 1981; Fama and Jensen 1983); their reputation is diminished if client firms provide low quality annual reports (Ali and Hwang 2000; Chalmers and Godfrey 2004). Empirical studies, however, have insofar provided mixed results of the impact of auditors on firm disclosures. Whereas Wallace and Naser (1995) and Lopes and Rodriguez (2007) found that auditor size is positively related to firm level disclosures, Ali and Hwang (2000) and Hassan et al. (2007) find no significant association. Following the notion that *BIG4* audit firms also serve as a proxy for enforcement at the firm level, we expect a positive correlation between disclosure and *BIG4*.

Accounting standards

The third group of disclosure determinants, *accounting standards*, proxies for differences in formerly applied local GAAP and IFRS. Daske et al. (2008) find that mandatory and voluntary IFRS adopters exhibit larger increases in liquidity around IFRS adoption if local GAAP differs more from IFRS. We use the *absence* and *divergence* measures as developed by Ding et al. (2005) to proxy for differences in accounting standards. They measure differences between national GAAP ad IFRS using two measures. The first measure, *divergence,* indicates to which degree national GAAP and IFRS differ from each other. It scores higher if both national GAAP and IFRS cover a specific accounting topic, but they prescribe different methods. The second measure, *absence*, indicated to which degree national GAAP do not cover accounting issues that are, however, regulated by IFRS. We expect firms to disclose less under IFRS if formerly applied local GAAP was 'underdeveloped' compared to IFRS, indicated by a large *absence* index. We argue that the absence of accounting standards under local GAAP resulted in greater flexibility and opacity in firms' accounting practices and disclosure levels, to which managers are more accustomed to. On the contrary, we expect a positive influence of *divergence* on firms' disclosure practices. Managers are already aware of the existence of similar, but diverging accounting standards under local GAAP and engage more in applying them correctly under IFRS. Taken together, we interpret *absence* and *divergence* as proxies for a firms' commitment to mandatory and voluntary disclosures. In case of a high *absence* index, we expect a negative impact on disclosure. The firm's costs with non-disclosure are smaller since it has not committed itself to such disclosure under local GAAP. On the other hand, *divergence* stands for a greater commitment of disclosing information under local GAAP, although there are inconsistencies with IFRS. Therefore, the impact is expected to be positive.

Countries' institutions

The last group of determinants, *countries' institutions*, tries to capture a country's institutional structure, with a particular focus on enforcement. It includes a country's strength of *enforcement*, a country's *business sophistication*, and a country's *equity market development*.

We expect the level of *enforcement* to be positively related to both mandatory and voluntary disclosures. We capture enforcement via a factor score of a principal component factor analysis with rotated factor matrix of the following four variables: (i) rule of law, (ii) regulatory quality, (iii) government effectiveness, and (iv) corruption index (all variables are taken from Kaufmann et al. (2009)). We postpone the discussion on the role of enforcement to section 3.2.2.

We proxy for the development of a country's capital market by two variables: *business sophistication* and *equity market development*. A country's *business sophistication* is an aggregated index composed of three factors from The Heritage Foundation (2007); a country's *equity market development* is the ratio of a country's traded stocks market capitalization to the country's GDP. We do not have a prediction of the impact on disclosures. On the one hand, both variables can be negatively related to firms' disclosure indices. A more developed capital market provides easy access to capital and information, mitigating the role of direct information flows between the firm and its outsiders. In addition, a more developed capital market is likely to be accompanied by greater strength and pressure of monitoring groups, such as labor unions and consumer bodies. These groups seek to ensure an equitable distribution of benefits derived from enhanced economic wealth, which may result in less firm disclosures to protect firms' "wealth" from these monitoring groups. On the other hand, a country's capital market development may promote firm disclosures since it provides the necessary infrastructure to transmit information to the public.

We summarize our first hypothesis as follows (see also Figure 3.1):

> **Hypothesis 1:** *A firm's level of mandatory disclosure compliance as well as its voluntary disclosure index are affected by four groups of determinants: the firm's business structure, managers' incentives, differences between local GAAP and IFRS, as well as a country's institutional system.*

Figure 3. 1 Determinants of Financial Disclosure Practices

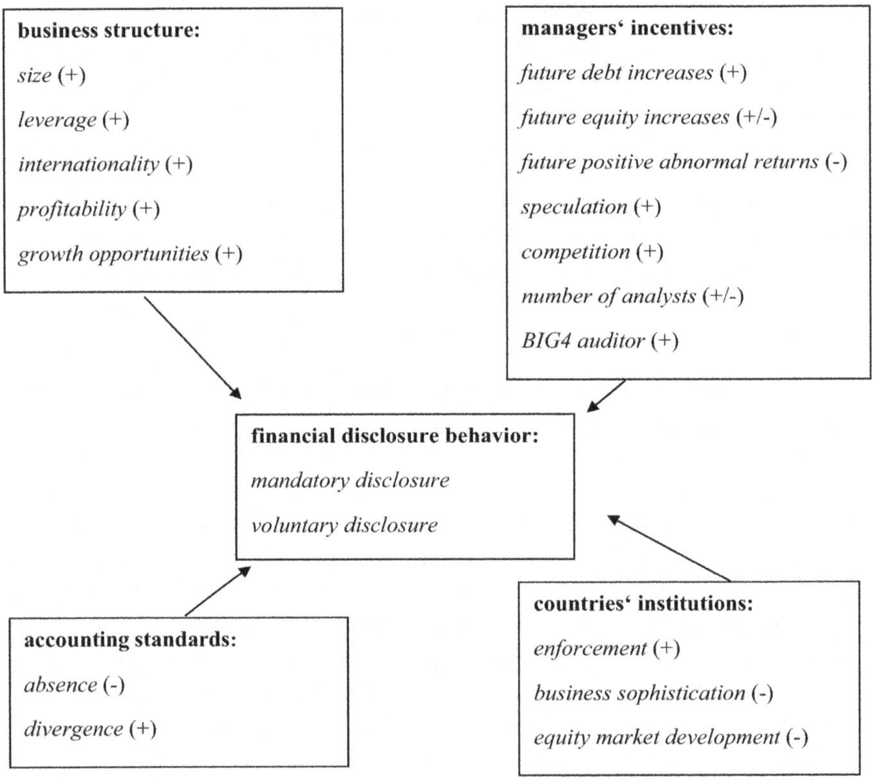

This figure illustrates our first set of Hypotheses (H1, H1a-H1d): firms' financial disclosure practices are an endogenous function of four groups of determinants: *operational characteristics, managers' incentives, accounting standards,* and *countries institutions.* "+" and "-" symbols in parentheses denote the expected direction of impact of each variable on firms' disclosure scores. All variables are calculated as defined in the Appendix to Chapter 3.

3.2.2 Enforcement and the Demand for Accounting Information

Effective financial reporting and disclosure convergence requires consistent implementation and enforcement of accounting standards (Ball 1995, 2006; Daske et al. 2008). Since the IFRS mandate in 2005, there is a growing literature on the role of enforcement on accounting outcomes. Bae et al. (2008b) highlight that an appropriate set of accounting standards in one country need not to be appropriate in another country, as long as lax and inconsistent enforcement is in place. In the same vein, Leuz (2010) points out that enforcement differences are going to play a larger and more important role in firms' disclosure practices, given that more and more countries adopt IFRS. Supporting Leuz' conclusion, Armstrong et al. (2010a) find an incrementally negative reaction to the adoption of IFRS in Europe for countries which are thought to have a weaker enforcement of accounting standards. In their study about the economic consequences of mandatory IFRS adoption, Daske et al. (2008) conclude that capital market benefits occur only in countries where firms have incentives to be transparent and where legal enforcement is strong. Corroborating evidence is provided by Li (2010b), who finds that mandatory IFRS adoption significantly reduces the cost of equity, but only in countries with strong legal enforcement. This brief overview clearly indicates that differences in enforcement across countries have been subject to various studies on financial market outcomes and accounting quality.[32] However, there is – to our best knowledge – no study that directly tests the impact of enforcement on firms' disclosure levels. We aim to fill this gap by analyzing the role of enforcement for firms' disclosure behavior.

Consistent with prior studies, we expect enforcement to have a positive impact on firms' mandatory and voluntary disclosure levels. However, the mechanisms *how* enforcement affects disclosure outcomes is far from being trivial. Holthausen (2009, 453-456) opines "At this point, I do not think we have very strong evidence to help us fully *understand* the importance of enforcement with respect to financial disclosure outcomes" (pp. 456). In addition, Guay and Verrechia (2006) state that links between enforcement and accounting information are critical to our understanding of how disclosure practices are influenced by managers' incentives and outsiders demand for information. They call for more research

[32] Other important studies include the following: Burgstrahler et al. (2006) show that strong legal enforcement on public equity markets provides incentives to report earnings that reflect the true economic performance of the firm. Hail (2011) expects voluntary disclosures to be more effective, and hence more likely to exist, if a country has rigorous enforcement mechanisms. Christensen et al. (2011) find that the benefits of securities regulation in the European Union in terms of higher market liquidity ultimately depend on their implementation and enforcement. Florou and Pope (2009) show that the legal context determining compliance and enforcement are important determinants of institutional demand for equities. La Porta et al. (1997; 1998; 2000, 2002) , Leuz et al. (2003), and La Porta et al. (2006) also focus on a country's institutional environment and enforcement mechanisms.

along this line. We directly address this issue and offer one possible explanation why enforcement is critical for firms' disclosure practices. In particular, we expect the impact and importance of enforcement to be conditional on outsiders' demand for accounting information. We expect that enforcement has a much more pronounced effect on mandatory disclosures if the (contracting) demand for accounting information from outsiders is high. Our reasoning is as follows: Although the strength of enforcement is constant for firms within each country, the perceived strength of enforcement is much higher for firms with a greater demand for accounting information. This 'perception' leads managers to be more compliant with existing disclosure rules since they perceive (and actually are) under greater scrutiny of outsiders. To explore this issue, we assume that the demand for accounting information is more pronounced in firms that (i) rely more on debt financing (i.e. have a higher leverage ratio), (ii) are more internationally oriented (i.e. have a higher foreign assets/foreign sales ratio), (iii) are under greater scrutiny of financial analysts (i.e. have more analysts following the firm), (iv) have higher future equity needs (i.e. there is an above sample median equity increase in the next two years) , and (v) have higher future debt needs (i.e. there is an above sample median debt increase in the next two years). This leads to our next hypothesis:

> **Hypothesis 2a:** *The impact of enforcement on firms' mandatory disclosure index is stronger for firms with a greater demand for accounting information.*

In addition, we analyze the interaction of enforcement and differences between formerly applied local GAAP and IFRS and its effect on mandatory and voluntary disclosure. We expect these differences to matter less if accounting rules are properly enforced since a firm's prior commitment to disclosure plays a smaller role in case actual accounting standards are properly enforced. Given that enforcement is strong, the impact of *absence* and *divergence* on disclosure is attenuated. Our next hypothesis therefore is:

> **Hypothesis 2b:** *The impact of differences between local GAAP and IFRS on firms' disclosure indices are less pronounced if enforcement is strong.*

Figure 3.2 illustrates our second set of hypotheses.

Figure 3. 2 Demand for Accounting Information and Enforcement

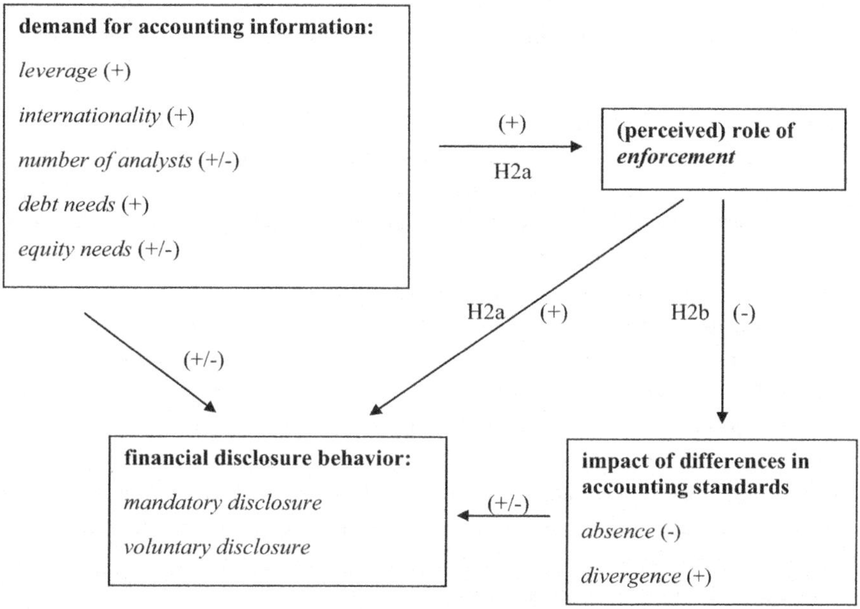

This figure illustrates our second set of Hypotheses (H2a and H2b): outsiders' demand for (accounting) information has an impact on firms' *perceived* strength of enforcement. The higher outsiders demand for information, the more pronounced is a country's strength of enforcement on firms' disclosure practices (H2a). Moreover, the impact of differences in accounting standards on firms' disclosure practices is less pronounced if enforcement is strong (H2b). "+" and "-" symbols in parentheses denote the expected direction of impact of each variable on firms' disclosure scores. All variables are calculated as defined in the Appendix to Chapter 3.

3.2.3 Disclosure and Culture

Recent literature in finance and economics has shown that culture is an important determinant of institutions (Greif 1994; Landes 2000; Stulz and Williamson 2003; Kwok and Solomon 2006). Besides, national culture also plays a crucial role in shaping managers' internal and external disclosure choices, and determines how outsiders react to firms' disclosures (Gray 1988; Hope 2003a). In the accounting domain, a growing literature focuses on the role of culture. Nabar and Boonlert-U-Thai (2007) find and conclude that culture is an important determinant of accounting choice, measured by the degree of earnings management. Antia et al. (2007) find a negative relationship between firm valuation and cultural distances between countries with U.S. foreign subsidiaries and the U.S. Breuer et al. (2009) find that the level of corporate debt financing is affected by cultural values. Ding et al. (2005) find that cultural factors have power in explaining differences between national GAAP and IFRS. Li et al. (2011) find that national culture is associated with firm-level riskiness and firm risk-taking.

There have also been various attempts to shed more light on the role of culture with regard to disclosure practices. Adelopo and Moure (2010) find that corporate social disclosures by big European banks are affected by cultural attributes. On the contrary, Jaggi and Low (2000) conclude that cultural values do not predict disclosure levels once legal origin is considered. In this study, we argue that legal systems are influenced and pre-determined by cultural attributes. We do not believe that there may be any reverse causality: legal systems are anchored in national culture; they are part of the culture and emerged from cultural habits. Therefore, it is straightforward to analyze the impact of national culture on disclosure levels directly, rather than looking on indirect summary measures such as legal origins. In support of our argument, Hope (2003b) concludes that "there is no support for the argument that culture is unimportant in explaining firm disclosures after controlling for legal origin" (p. 2). Hope further calls for more research on the relation between culture and disclosures. Our study directly picks up his call for future research. We provide insights into the relation between national culture and disclosures. We use a recent data set and focus on countries with uniform accounting standards.

We proxy for cultural values using three different data sources: Hofstede (1991, 2001), Schwartz (1994, 1999, 2004) and the GLOBE project (House et al. 2004). Hofstede (1991, 2001) identifies five cultural dimensions along one can compare and contrast cultural attributes: *uncertainty avoidance, power distance, masculinity, individualism.*[33] Hofstede's framework has been commonly accepted as standard for the description of cultural differences in the finance, accounting, and economics literature. Schwartz' (1994, 1999, 2004) model of cultural values overcomes some difficulties of Hofstede's approach. Schwartz uses more recent data; his model is theoretically derived; it is more comprehensive, and it was derived from more diverse regions. Schwartz proposes seven different cultural dimensions: *conservatism, intellectual autonomy, affective autonomy, hierarchy, mastery, egalitarian commitment,* and *harmony.* Finally, the GLOBE project (House et al. 2004) measures both cultural practices as well as cultural values. It provides nine cultural dimensions: *power distance, uncertainty avoidance, humane orientation, institutional collectivism, in-group*

[33] *Long term orientation* is also a cultural value in the Hofstede framework. We exclude this variable from our analyses since it is only for a few countries in our sample available.

collectivism, assertiveness, gender egalitarianism, future orientation, and *performance orientation.* [34]

In this study, we do not attempt to analyze the impact of each cultural value on firms' disclosure practices separately. Instead, we pool several cultural values into groups and examine their joint impact on firms' disclosure practices, while at the same time controlling for (other) disclosure incentives. In addition, we perform a k-means cluster analysis over all cultural values to obtain five cultural clusters. We hypothesize that firms' disclosure practices vary significantly across these five cultural clusters. Taken together, our third set of hypothesis is as follows:

> **Hypothesis 3a:** *Firms' disclosure practices differ across cultural clusters.*

> **Hypothesis 3b:** *Cultural values influence the amount of mandatory and voluntary risk management disclosures.*

Figure 3.3 illustrates hypothesis 3a.

[34] In our main analyses we solely focus on the Hofstede variables and analyze the impact of the Schwartz and GLOBE variables in robustness checks.

Figure 3. 3 Financial Disclosure Practices and Culture

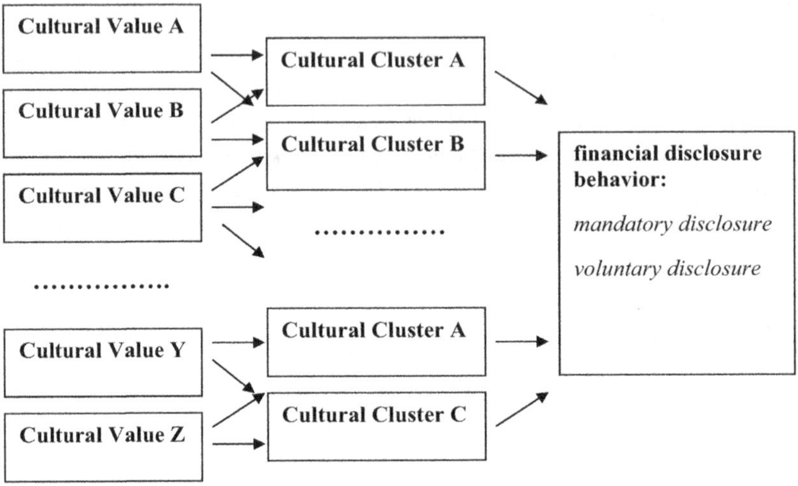

This figure illustrates Hypotheses 3a (H3b is illustrated in Figure 3.4.). Firms' financial disclosure practices are an endogenous function of a country's cultural value set. All variables are calculated as defined in the Appendix to Chapter 3.

3.2.4 Disclosure and the Interplay of Culture and Enforcement

In this section, we briefly elaborate on the interaction of enforcement and cultural attributes. To our best knowledge, there exists up till today no study that analyzes the interplay of cultural values and enforcement and their effects on firms' disclosure practices. As already pointed out in section 3.2.3, we see culture as the dominating and underlying ground on which institutions evolved. Hence, every institution has inherent cultural roots. With regard to our empirical analyses, this means that every institutional variable captures some underlying cultural characteristic. Therefore, one should not only observe a direct influence of culture on disclosure practices, but also an indirect influence via institutional variables. In this study, we focus on *enforcement* as the mediator variable for cultural values and analyze its interaction with the Hofstede cultural values.[35] We therefore perform two different analyses.

First, we examine how the impact of enforcement on mandatory disclosures varies between countries with a high vs. low emphasis on (i) *power distance*, (ii) *individualism*, (iii) *uncertainty avoidance*, and (iv) *masculinity*. We expect the following effects:

> (i) In societies with a strong emphasis on *power distance*, accounting systems are often seen as a tool to justify decisions of the top management to present a desired image. Thus, it is more likely for managers to circumvent and override existing controls (Chan et al. 2003). We therefore expect a negative influence of power distance on firm disclosures. We also expect that the role of enforcement on firm disclosures is much more pronounced in high power distance societies. A better enforcement in these countries is necessary to protect outsiders of the firm from opportunistic behavior by insiders and to mitigate the downsides of huge power distance.
>
> (ii) Individualistic countries place less weight and reliance on accounting numbers. Individualistic people form their own opinion and mistrust collective disclosed information. Moreover, managers in countries with a strong emphasis on individualism have more incentives to manipulate accounting numbers and disclosures to pursuit their own goals. Therefore, we expect a negative relation between *individualism* and disclosures. With regard to enforcement, we expect that the impact of enforcement is less pronounced in individualistic countries.
>
> (iii) We expect high uncertainty avoidant cultures to comply more with disclosure rules to reduce the amount of uncertainty. Hence, *uncertainty avoidance* is expected to have a positive impact on mandatory disclosures. The role of enforcement in high uncertainty avoidant countries is expected to be weaker compared to low uncertainty avoidant societies, since insiders and outsiders of the firm have already internalized uncertainty avoidant behavior. They both act as complements, rather than substitutes. Hence, there is no need for an emphasized role of enforcement in these cultures.
>
> (iv) *Masculinity* is not expected to have a significant impact on disclosures. Prior studies have found masculine vs. feminine societies to not differ in their disclosure practices.

Second, we analyze the direct versus the indirect influences of culture on disclosures by predicting the level of enforcement which can be attributed to cultural attributes. We are thus

[35] Consequently, we solely analyze the mandatory disclosure index since *enforcement* has proven to have no direct and significant impact on voluntary disclosures.

able to separate the cultural part of enforcement from the pure enforcement part. We expect both the direct and indirect part to have a significantly positive impact on disclosure practices.

Taken together, our final set of hypotheses is as follows:

> **Hypothesis 4a:** *The impact of enforcement on firms' mandatory* disclosure *practices is conditional on a country's cultural values.*

> **Hypothesis 4b:** *Cultural values have an indirect impact on firms' mandatory* disclosure *practices via a country's strength of enforcement.*

Figure 3.4 illustrates our fourth set of hypothesis and hypothesis 3b.

Figure 3. 4 Cultural Values, Enforcement and Financial Disclosure Practices

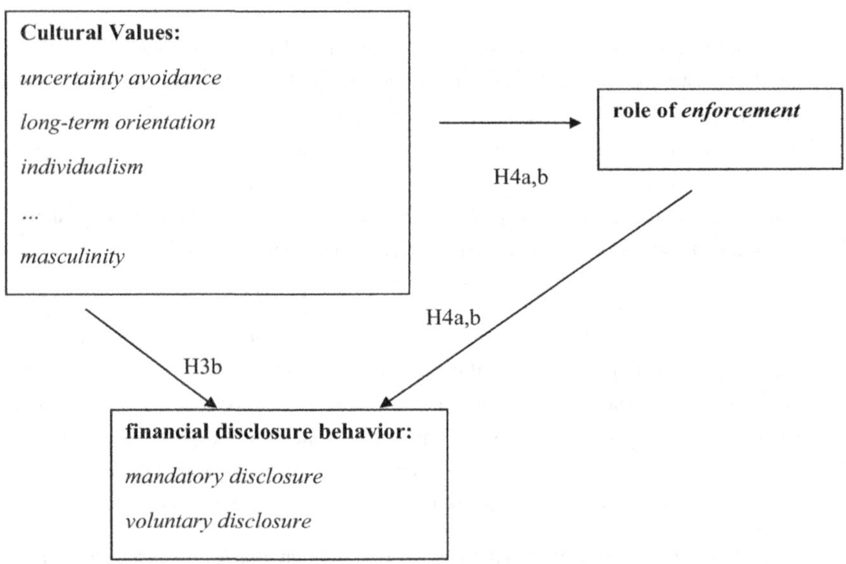

This figure illustrates Hypotheses 4a and 4b, and Hypothesis 3b: A country's strength of enforcement is conditional on a country's set of cultural values (H4a). This also implies an indirect impact of cultural values on firm's financial reporting practices (H4b). Moreover, cultural values have a direct impact on firms' disclosure practices. All Hypotheses are non-directional. All variables are calculated as defined in the Appendix to Chapter 3.

3.3 Sample and Descriptive Statistics

3.3.1 Sample

We analyze non-financial companies from 18 EU countries, Norway and Switzerland. Our objective was to have at least ten firms headquartered in each country. We therefore selected companies in a two-stage process: In the first stage, we randomly choose 300 non-financial firms from the DJ STOXX 600 (as at 05/31/2009) that comprises firms from 17 European countries including Norway and Switzerland. In the second stage, we increased the number of firms per country to at least ten. Therefore, we manually added firms from the respective countries and listed in the DJ STOXX 600 to our sample (in total, we added 26 companies to the initial sample of 300 randomly selected companies). In addition, we added 35 firms from three other EU countries (Czech Republic, Hungary and Poland), selected by population. For these three countries and in case a country is represented by less than ten firms in the DJ STOXX 600, we selected firms from the respective leading national stock index by market capitalization and subject to the availability of annual reports in English (this increased our sample by additional 24 companies). Our final sample comprises 385 firms from 20 countries.[36] Panel A of Table 3.1 presents the sample selection process and shows the distribution of firms per country. Panel B shows the industry distribution based on one-digit SIC codes of our sample firms.

[36] As Norway is a member of the European Economic Area, Norwegian firms have to use IFRS for financial years starting in 2005. In Switzerland, firms listed at the Swiss Exchange's main board (Hauptsegment) are required to use IFRS or US-GAAP, again for financial years starting in 2005. All Swiss firms in our sample use IFRS. Although the 4th and 6th EU directives introducing IFRS were not implemented in full conformity across all EU countries, the differences are negligible for the purpose of this study.

Table 3. 1 Sample Selection and Distribution of Firms

Panel A: Sample selection and distribution of firms per country

Country name	DJ STOXX 600 randomly selected	DJ STOXX 600 filled-up	DJ STOXX 600 total	national stock indices filled-up	final sample	% of final sample
Austria	4	3	7	4	11	2.9%
Belgium	6	4	10	0	10	2.6%
Czech Republic	0	0	0	10	10	2.6%
Denmark	12	0	12	0	12	3.1%
Finland	13	0	13	0	13	3.4%
France	42	0	42	0	42	10.9%
Germany	45	0	45	0	45	11.7%
Greece	4	2	6	5	11	2.9%
Hungary	0	0	0	11	11	2.9%
Ireland	3	4	7	3	10	2.6%
Italy	13	0	13	0	13	3.4%
Luxemburg	1	3	4	6	10	2.6%
Netherlands	19	0	19	0	19	4.9%
Norway	2	6	8	3	11	2.9%
Poland	0	0	0	14	14	3.6%
Portugal	3	4	7	3	10	2.6%
Spain	21	0	21	0	21	5.5%
Sweden	15	0	15	0	15	3.9%
Switzerland	18	0	18	0	18	4.7%
United Kingdom	79	0	79	0	79	20.5%
Total	**300**	**26**	**326**	**59**	**385**	**100.0%**

Panel B: Distribution of firms per industry

SIC code	industry	N	%
SIC code 1	Mining-Construction	43	11.2%
SIC codes 2 & 3	Manufacturing	192	49.9%
SIC code 4	Transportation	77	20.0%
SIC code 5	Trade	35	9.1%
SIC code 7	Services	27	7.0%
SIC code 9	Public administration	11	2.9%
Total		**385**	**100.0%**

Panel A presents the country distribution of the sample firms. In the first stage, we randomly choose 300 non-financial firms from the DJ STOXX 600. In the second stage, we increased the number of firms per country to at least 10. Therefore, we manually added firms from the respective countries and listed in the DJ STOXX 600 to our sample. In addition, we added firms from three other EU countries (Czech Republic, Hungary and Poland), selected by population. In this case and in case a country is represented by less than ten firms in the DJ STOXX 600, we selected firms from the respective leading national stock index by market capitalization and subject to the availability of annual reports in English. Panel B presents the industry distribution of all sample firms.

About 43% of all firms are headquartered in the three biggest European economies (France, Germany, United Kingdom). The remaining 57% of our sample firms are roughly equally distributed among all other countries (minimum of 2.6% for Belgium, Czech Republic, Ireland, Luxemburg and Portugal; maximum of 5.5% for Spain). The majority of firms have their main operating segment in the manufacturing industry (49.9%), followed by the transportation industry (20%) and the mining and construction industry (20%). Only 2.9% of our sample firms operate in the public administration industry.

All our firm data is taken from audited financial statement. We therefore think that the quality of this data is significantly higher than in survey-based studies such as Bodnar et al. (1995; 1996, 1998) and Bodnar et al. (2012). In relation to other studies based on audited data such as Judge (2006) and Magee (2009), we collected a larger number of items for each firm. In sum, we use a large, very detailed set of recent audited data.

Annual reports were obtained from *Infinancials*, accounting data from *Worldscope* and *Compustat*, stock market data from *Datastream,* analyst data from *I/B/E/S*, and country data from Hofstede (1991, 2001), the Schwartz Value Survey (1994, 1999, 2004), the GLOBE project (House et al. 2004), Kaufmann et al. (2009), Ding et al. (2005), and the Heritage Foundation (2007).

3.3.2 Disclosure Indices

We follow Cooke (1989) and measure disclosure by three main indices. Each index is calculated on the basis of hand-collected data items from financial statements, notes and management reports. We compute each index by adding up the scores of all items without weighting them. This is the norm in annual report disclosure studies (Ahmed and Courtis 1999; Chavent et al. 2006). An item scores one if it is disclosed and zero otherwise. Each index is a ratio of the actual level of disclosure over the possible level. All indices are calculated such that non-disclosure of irrelevant items is not penalized.[37] We distinguish a mandatory disclosure index (*mand*), a voluntary disclosure index (*volun*) and a total disclosure index (*total*). The latter equals the sum of the former two indices. The main indices are as follows: The index on mandatory disclosure (*mand*) consists of up to 25 disclosure items. The *mand* index is based on current regulation such that there is very limited space for discretion when constructing the index. The index on voluntary disclosure (*volun*) consists of up to 64 disclosure items. Here, we have set a relatively high hurdle by including 74 items. If

[37] For example, if a firm clearly states in its annual report that it is not affected by foreign exchange risks, all disclosure items which relate to foreign exchange risks are not included in the mandatory and voluntary disclosure scores. For an excellent overview of disclosure studies, see Chavent et al. (2006)

we had included fewer items, the index figures would have been accordingly higher. We selected voluntary disclosure items based on recommendations in *IAS 32, IAS 39*, and *IFRS 7*. The total disclosure index (*total*) has a maximum of 89 disclosure items and does not distinguish between mandatory and voluntary disclosures. All indices are naturally bounded by 0 and 1.

Both the mandatory as well as the voluntary disclosure index adhere to disclosure requirements and recommendations from *IAS 32, IAS 39* and *IFRS 7*. We analyze financial statements and annual reports for the first financial year starting on or after 1 January 2007. Since then, *IFRS 7* has to be mandatorily adopted by all sample firms. Besides *IFRS 7*, two other standards have to be followed by all sample firms for financial instruments and risk management disclosures: *IAS 32* and *IAS 39*. Both are effective for all financial years starting on or after 1 January 2005. This setting allows us to control for *learning effects* associated with the adoption of certain accounting standards. While the accounting principles and disclosure requirements outlined in *IFRS 7* are "new" for all sample firms, we expect a lower compliance rate with *IFRS* 7 compared to the compliance rate with *IAS 32* and *IAS 39*. The latter two standards were already adopted two times prior to 2007. Hence, firms are more used to the requirements outlined in *IAS 32* and *IAS 39*.

Table 3.2 presents the main constituents and disclosure vs. non-disclosure statistics of our disclosure indices. Panel A focuses on the mandatory disclosure index whereas Panel B focuses on the voluntary disclosure index.

Table 3. 2 Constituents of Disclosure Indices and Disclosure Rates

Panel A: Constituents of mandatory disclosure index and compliance rates

	# firms to disclose	disclosure (%)	non-discl. (%)
material risks	385	20	80
credit risk exposure	385	35	65
use of fair value option	385	45	55
impact of financial instruments on P&L	385	48	52
operational risk management strategy	385	48	52
fair value of liabilities	385	60	40
computation of derivatives' fair values	351	61	39
liquidity risk exposure	385	62	38
categories of financial instruments	385	63	37
derivatives in hedge accounting relationship (by hedge type)	302	78	22
foreign exchange gains&losses	385	79	21

treatment of hedge accounting	302	88	12
impact of derivatives on P&L	351	89	11
financial risk management strategy	385	92	8
maturity of debt	385	97	3
fair values of derivatives	351	98	2
commodity sensitivity analysis (SA) or VaR analysis	138	59	41
commodity SA or VaR: detailed element 1	138	55	45
commodity SA or VaR: detailed element 2	138	33	67
foreign exchange sensitivity analysis (SA) or VaR analysis	369	85	15
foreign exchange SA or VaR: detailed element 1	369	83	17
foreign exchange SA or VaR: detailed element 2	369	54	46
interest rate sensitivity analysis (SA) or VaR analysis	363	88	12
interest rate SA or VaR: detailed element 1	363	86	14
interest rate SA or VaR: detailed element 2	363	41	59

Panel B: Constituents of voluntary disclosure index and disclosure rates

	# firms to disclose	disclosure (%)	non-discl. (%)
fair value of foreign debt	248	8	92
notional value of foreign debt	248	20	80
debt interest rate fixed	385	22	78
debt interest rate floating	385	22	78
credit rating	385	28	72
debt interest rate fixed & floating together	385	35	65
impact of financial instruments on equity	385	44	56
interest bearing liabilities	385	45	55
exchange rates	385	48	52
floating portion of debt	385	56	44
impact of derivatives on P&L (in derivatives note)	351	60	40
foreign debt book value	385	65	35
foreign sales	385	65	35
notional value of derivatives	351	71	29
maturities of derivatives	351	80	20
derivatives by type	351	81	19
commodity risk (CO) additional SA or VaR analysis, CO risk = 1	138	4	96
CO additional SA or VaR, CO risk = 0	247	1	99
foreign exchange risk (FX) additional SA or VaR, FX risk= 1	369	3	97
FX additional SA or VaR, FX risk = 0	16	19	81
interest rate risk (IR) additional SA or VaR, IR risk =1	363	3	97
IR additional SA or VaR, IR risk = 0	22	18	82
CO SA additional voluntary item 1 (SA=1 & VAR = 0 & CO risk = 1)	71	91	9
CO SA additional voluntary item 2 (SA=1 & VAR = 0 & CO risk = 1)	71	46	54

CO VaR additional voluntary item (SA = 0 & VAR = 1 & CO risk = 1)	10	70	30
FX SA additional voluntary item 1 (SA=1 & VAR = 0 & FX risk = 1)	299	95	5
FX SA additional voluntary item 2 (SA=1 & VAR = 0 & FX risk = 1)	299	50	50
FX VaR additional voluntary item (SA = 0 & VAR = 1 & FX risk = 1)	15	47	53
IR SA additional voluntary item 1 (SA=1 & VAR = 0 & IR risk = 1)	312	96	4
IR SA additional voluntary item 2 (SA=1 & VAR = 0 & IR risk = 1)	312	39	61
IR VaR additional voluntary item (SA = 0 & VAR = 1 & IR risk = 1)	7	57	43
CO SA additional voluntary item 1 (SA = 1 & VAR = 1 & CO risk = 1)	5	40	60
CO SA additional voluntary item 2 (SA = 1 & VAR = 1 & CO risk = 1)	5	40	60
CO SA additional voluntary item 3 (SA = 1 & VAR = 1 & CO risk = 1)	5	20	80
FX SA additional voluntary item 1 (SA = 1 & VAR = 1 & FX risk = 1)	9	44	56
FX SA additional voluntary item 2 (SA = 1 & VAR = 1 & FX risk = 1)	9	33	67
FX SA additional voluntary item 3 (SA = 1 & VAR = 1 & FX risk = 1)	9	22	78
IR SA additional voluntary item 1 (SA = 1 & VAR = 1 & IR risk = 1)	8	38	62
IR SA additional voluntary item 2 (SA = 1 & VAR = 1 & IR risk = 1)	8	38	62
IR SA additional voluntary item 3 (SA = 1 & VAR = 1 & IR risk = 1)	8	25	75
CO exposure	138	6	94
CO exposure additional item	8	87	13
CO exposure after hedging	8	87	13
CO exposure before hedging	8	50	50
CO exposure hedged	8	75	25
CO exposure last year	8	87	13
CO exposure time horizon	8	25	75
FX exposure	369	36	64
FX exposure additional item	133	78	22
FX exposure after hedging	133	84	16
FX exposure before hedging	133	70	30
FX exposure hedged	133	65	35
FX exposure last year	133	74	26
FX exposure time horizon	133	18	82
FX exposure transaction	133	33	67
FX exposure translation	133	20	80
FX exposure translation & transaction	133	12	88
IR exposure	363	23	77
IR exposure additional item	83	60	40
IR exposure after hedging	83	92	8
IR exposure before hedging	83	68	32
IR exposure hedged	83	64	36
IR exposure last year	83	73	27
IR exposure time horizon	83	22	78

Panel A presents the constituents of the mandatory disclosure index in column 1. Column 2 lists the number of firms that (mandatorily) have to disclose the information. We do not penalize for non-disclosure of irrelevant items. Column 3 gives the percentage of firms that actually disclose the relevant information, based on the number of firms listed in column 2. Column 4 displays the percentage of non-compliant firms which do not disclose relevant information. Panel B presents the constituents of the voluntary disclosure index in column 1. Column 2 lists the number of firms that (voluntarily) could disclose the information. Column 3 gives the percentage of firms that actually disclose the voluntary information, based on the number of firms listed in column 2. Column 4 displays the percentage of firms that do not disclose the voluntary information.

As can be seen from Panel A, the item which is least often disclosed is *material risks*: only 77 companies (20% of total sample firms) disclose a comprehensive narrative summary of materials risks affecting the company in the near future. The mandatory disclosure of *credit risk exposures* is also considerably low: only 35% of our sample firms disclose their credit risk exposure, although they are obliged to do so according to *IFRS 7*. The *impact of financial instruments on the profit and loss account* is disclosed by only 48% of all sample firms; the same is true for the narrative description of firms' *operational risk management* activities. Firms' that use derivatives have to disclose how they compute the fair values of their derivative holdings. However, 39% of all sample firms withhold this information. On the other hand, the *fair values* themselves are disclosed by 98% of all sample firms. The *maturity structure of corporate debt* is also disclosed by the large majority of all firms: only 3% of our sample firms do not disclose debt maturities.

Panel B focuses on firms' voluntary disclosure patterns. Disclosures related to firms' *foreign debt* holdings as well as *debt interest rates* are among the items which are least often disclosed by all sample firms. Moreover, only 28% of all firms which bonds are rated by rating agencies disclose their rating in the annual report. Disclosures related to firms' derivative holdings are relatively common: 71% of all sample firms disclose derivatives' *notional values*, 80% disclose derivatives' *maturity structures*, and 81% disclose their different *types of derivatives*. Concerning risk exposure disclosures, only 6% out of the 138 sample which are affected by commodity risks voluntarily disclose their *commodity risk exposure*. For *interest rate* and *foreign exchange exposures*, the disclosure rate increases to 23% for all firms with interest rate risks (363 firms), and to 36% for all firms with foreign exchange risks (369 firms). However, there is a huge variation in the level of detail regarding exposure disclosures.

Key characteristics of the disclosure indices as our dependent variable are presented in Table 3.3, Panel A.

Table 3. 3 Descriptive Statistics of Disclosure Indices

Panel A: Descriptive statistics of main disclosure indices

	total	*mand*	*volun*
N	385	385	385
mean	0.5138	0.6629	0.3948
sd	0.1204	0.1579	0.1312
min	0.0952	0.0909	0.0000
p5	0.2941	0.3636	0.1852
p25	0.4468	0.5789	0.3103
p50	0.5135	0.6818	0.3793
p75	0.5962	0.7727	0.4826
p95	0.7016	0.8800	0.6207
max	0.8431	1.0000	0.7931

Panel A presents descriptive statistics of our main disclosure indices (total, mandatory, and voluntary disclosure index).

Panel B: Descriptive statistics of disclosure sub-indices

	FX index	*IR index*	*CO index*	*Derivative index*
N	385	385	138	351
mean	0.5547	0.4927	0.3349	0.6756
sd	0.1537	0.1706	0.3022	0.1789
min	0.0000	0.1111	0.0000	0.0000
p5	0.2857	0.2222	0.0000	0.3636
p25	0.4550	0.3846	0.0000	0.5555
p50	0.5556	0.4615	0.4000	0.7273
p75	0.6667	0.6153	0.6000	0.8182
p95	0.7778	0.7692	0.7500	0.9091
max	0.9333	0.9444	1.0000	1.0000

Panel B presents descriptive statistics of four sub-indices of disclosure. Each sub-index focuses on a specific risk or aspect: the FX index focuses on foreign exchange risk related disclosure, the IR index focuses on interest rate risk related disclosures, the CO index focuses on commodity risk related disclosures, and the derivative index focuses on disclosures particularly related to derivatives.

Panel C: Constituents of disclosure sub-indices

	FX index	**IR index**	**CO index**	**Derivative index**
material risks				
credit risk exposure				
use of fair value option				
impact of financial instruments on P&L				
operational risk management				
fair value of liabilities		x		
computation of derivatives' fair values				x
liquidity risk exposure				
categories of financial instruments				
derivatives in hedge accounting relationship (by hedge type)				x
foreign exchange gains&losses	x			
treatment of hedge accounting				x
impact of derivatives on P&L				x
financial risk management				x
maturity of debt		x		
fair values of derivatives				x
commodity sensitivity analysis (SA) or VaR analysis			x	
commodity SA or VaR: detailed element 1			x	
commodity SA or VaR: detailed element 2			x	
foreign exchange sensitivity analysis (SA) or VaR analysis	x			
foreign exchange SA or VaR: detailed element 1	x			
foreign exchange SA or VaR: detailed element 2	x			
interest rate sensitivity analysis (SA) or VaR analysis		x		
interest rate SA or VaR: detailed element 1		x		
interest rate SA or VaR: detailed element 2		x		
fair value of foreign debt	x			
notional value of foreign debt	x			
debt interest rate fixed		x		
debt interest rate floating		x		
credit rating		x		
debt interest rate fixed & floating together		x		
impact of financial instruments on equity				
interest bearing liabilities		x		
exchange rates	x			
floating portion of debt		x		
impact of derivatives on P&L (in derivatives note)				x
foreign debt book value	x			
foreign sales	x			
notional value of derivatives				x
maturities of derivatives				x
derivatives by type				x
commodity risk (CO) additional SA or VaR analysis, CO risk = 1			x	
CO additional SA or VaR, CO risk = 0			x	
foreign exchange risk (FX) additional SA or VaR, FX risk= 1	x			

FX additional SA or VaR, FX risk = 0	x		
interest rate risk (IR) additional SA or VaR, IR risk =1		x	

Panel C: Constituents of disclosure sub-indices(continued)

IR additional SA or VaR, IR risk = 0		x	
CO SA additional voluntary item 1 (SA=1 & VAR = 0 & CO risk = 1)			x
CO SA additional voluntary item 2 (SA=1 & VAR = 0 & CO risk = 1)			x
CO VaR additional voluntary item (SA = 0 & VAR = 1 & CO risk = 1)			x
FX SA additional voluntary item 1 (SA=1 & VAR = 0 & FX risk = 1)	x		
FX SA additional voluntary item 2 (SA=1 & VAR = 0 & FX risk = 1)	x		
FX VaR additional voluntary item (SA = 0 & VAR = 1 & FX risk = 1)	x		
IR SA additional voluntary item 1 (SA=1 & VAR = 0 & IR risk = 1)		x	
IR SA additional voluntary item 2 (SA=1 & VAR = 0 & IR risk = 1)		x	
IR VaR additional voluntary item (SA = 0 & VAR = 1 & IR risk = 1)		x	
CO SA additional voluntary item 1 (SA = 1 & VAR = 1 & CO risk = 1)			x
CO SA additional voluntary item 2 (SA = 1 & VAR = 1 & CO risk = 1)			x
CO SA additional voluntary item 3 (SA = 1 & VAR = 1 & CO risk = 1)			x
FX SA additional voluntary item 1 (SA = 1 & VAR = 1 & FX risk = 1)	x		
FX SA additional voluntary item 2 (SA = 1 & VAR = 1 & FX risk = 1)	x		
FX SA additional voluntary item 3 (SA = 1 & VAR = 1 & FX risk = 1)	x		
IR SA additional voluntary item 1 (SA = 1 & VAR = 1 & IR risk = 1)		x	
IR SA additional voluntary item 2 (SA = 1 & VAR = 1 & IR risk = 1)		x	
IR SA additional voluntary item 3 (SA = 1 & VAR = 1 & IR risk = 1)		x	
CO exposure			x
CO exposure additional item			x
CO exposure after hedging			x
CO exposure before hedging			x
CO exposure hedged			x
CO exposure last year			x
CO exposure time horizon			x
FX exposure	x		
FX exposure additional item	x		
FX exposure after hedging	x		
FX exposure before hedging	x		
FX exposure hedged	x		
FX exposure last year	x		
FX exposure time horizon	x		
FX exposure transaction	x		
FX exposure translation	x		
FX exposure translation & transaction	x		
IR exposure		x	
IR exposure additional item		x	
IR exposure after hedging		x	
IR exposure before hedging		x	
IR exposure hedged		x	
IR exposure last year		x	
IR exposure time horizon		x	

Panel C presents the constituents of each sub-index (FX-, IR-, CO-, and Derivative-sub-index).

The mean of the mandatory disclosure index *mand* is 66.29%. Hence, firms on average disclose only two thirds of what they are obliged to disclose. The minimum of the mandatory disclosure index is surprisingly low at 9.09%. However, 75% of all firms disclose 58.00% or more. In our sample, there is only one single firm that discloses everything (*mand*=100.00%). With respect to voluntary disclosure, the mean on *volun* is at 39.48%. (By construction of the *volun* index, this figure is not directly comparable to the *mand* figure.) With the 25% percentile at 31.03% and the 75% percentile at 48.27%, most firms' voluntary disclosure lies within a relatively narrow range. The mean of the total disclosure index *total* is at 51.38%, its maximum is at 84.31%, its minimum at 9.52%.

Panel B of Table 3.3 presents descriptive statistics for each sub-index. In general, firms provide the most disclosures on foreign exchange related risks (mean of 55.47%), followed by interest rate related risks (49.27%), and commodity related risks (33.49%). The maximum disclosures with regard to foreign exchange and interest rate related risks lie both at about 94%, whereas the maximum for the commodity sub-index is 100%. The descriptive statistics of the derivative sub-index are pretty similar to the statistics of the mandatory disclosure index (see Panel A). This is not surprising since IFRS 7, IAS 32 and IAS 39 mainly refer to financial instruments disclosure. The mean of the derivative index is at 67%, its maximum value lies at 100%.

Panel C of Table 3.3 presents the constituents of four disclosure sub-indices. Each index focuses on one specific aspect of disclosure: foreign exchange risk related disclosure (*FX_index*), interest rate risk related disclosure (*IR_index*), commodity risk related disclosure (*CO_index*), and disclosure with regard to derivatives (*deriv_index*). Each index is constructed based on disclosures with regard to FX, IR, CO and derivatives, no matter of whether the disclosure is mandatory or voluntary.[38]

The particularly low mandatory disclosure index calls for attention. It reflects firms' reluctance to comply with mandatory disclosure requirements. This can be for at least three reasons: First, as it is the case for any imposed regulation, some companies may not find it beneficial to reveal sensitive information with regard to its risk management strategies and risk exposures. If they would, they would have disclosed the information even in the absence

[38] Although we think it is interesting to present some descriptive statistics for each sub-index, we decided to not using these sub-indices in the course of our analyses. The scope of this chapter is to analyze firms' general risk management and financial instruments disclosures. We aim at providing a comprehensive determinant study for mandatory and voluntary disclosures, which will be particular important for standard setters and regulators. For this purpose, it is not necessary to analyze firms' disclosure patterns (with regard to foreign exchange, interest rate, or commodity risks) in detail. However, we think that it is worth looking at this aspect in future work.

of any regulation. Second, the regulatory disclosure requirements may fall short of companies' interests. As already discussed above, IAS 32, IAS 39 and IFRS 7 are the most intensively debated accounting standards. It took years to revise the disclosure requirements due to ongoing resistance and exertion of influence by companies to prevent increased disclosures. Following this line, standard setters would need to focus more on companies' needs and to give them more flexibility when deciding what to disclose. Third, the enforcement mechanisms do not work well. As outlined in the next section, companies are rarely fined or prosecuted when not complying with IFRS. In light of our findings, better governance and enforcement mechanism should be implemented to ensure compliance. These tasks could be carried out in part by government sponsored entities, but also by firm committees.

To put our descriptive statistics in context, we now briefly elaborate on the IFRS enforcement mechanism set out in the European Union.

3.3.3 Enforcement Mechanisms in the EU[39]

The enforcement system in Europe was firstly regulated in 2002 by the European Regulation No 1606/2002 ("IAS regulation (EU 2002)"), where it is written:

"A proper and rigorous enforcement regime is key to underpinning investors' confidence in financial markets. Member States [...] are required to take appropriate measures to ensure compliance with international accounting standards. The [European] Commission intends to liaise with Member States, notably through the *Committee of European Securities Regulators (CESR)*, to develop a common approach to enforcement."

Following European Regulation No 1095/2010, the *European Securities and Market Authority (ESMA)* superseded *CESR* with effect from 1 January 2011. When reviewing financial statements, *ESMA* aims to promote a high level of consistency amongst different national enforcers. A review may either be a full review (a company's full set of financial statements is covered) or only a partial review (only certain parts are covered). Each Member State within the European Economic Area designates a "Competent Authority" for enforcement of financial information. Other bodies are allowed to carry out enforcement either in their own right or on behalf of the competent administrative authorities, providing that these bodies are supervised by, and responsible to, the relevant competent administrative authority. Only Germany and Sweden made use of that option to delegate enforcement from

[39] The following elaborations in section 3.3.3 are entirely taken from ESMA (2011) and CESR (2010).

the competent authority. In most countries enforcement is carried out by one single authority. In the United Kingdom and Ireland two authorities are involved: one authority deals with periodic financial reports; the other with financial information in prospectuses. In Denmark there is one authority which deals with financial information in prospectuses as well as periodic financial information of financial entities and one authority which deals with periodic financial disclosure by non-financial entities. Irrespective of the different structures adopted by national enforcers which can lead to different processes and scopes of activity, all national enforcers serve a common objective, namely to promote market confidence and protect investors. Table 3.4 lists all European enforcers as of 31.12.2010.

Table 3. 4 List of European Enforcers

Country	Competent Authority	
Austria	Financial Market Authority	FMSA
Belgium	Financial Services and Markets Authority	FSMA
Czech Republic	Czech National Bank	CNB
Denmark	Danish Financial Services Authority	Finanstilsynet
	Danish Commerce and Companies Agency	DCCA
Finland	Finish Financial Supervisory Authority	FIN-FSA
France	Financial Markets Authority	AMF
Germany	German Federal Financial Supervisory Authority	BaFin
	Financial Reporting Enforcement Panel	FREP
Greece	Hellenic Capital Market Commission	HCMC
Hungary	Hungarian Financial Supervisory Authority	HFSA
Ireland	The Central Bank of Ireland	CBI
	Irish Auditing and Accounting Supervisory Authority	IAASA
Italy	Companies and Securities National Commission Consob	Consob
Luxembourg	Financial Markets Supervisory Commission	CSSF
Netherlands	Netherlands Authority for the Financial Markets	AFM
Norway	Norway Financial Supervisory Authority	NFSA
Poland	Polish Financial Supervision Authority	PFSA
Portugal	Securities National Commission	CMVM
	Bank of Portugal	BP
	Insurance Portugal Institute	ISP
Spain	Spanish Securities Market Commission	CNMV
Sweden	Swedish Financial Supervisory Authority	Finansinspektionen
	The Nordic Growth Market	NGM AB
	Nasdaq OMX Stockholm	Nasdaq OMX
United Kingdom	Financial Services Authority	FSA
	Financial Reporting Review Panel	FRRP

Source: CESR (2010) and ESMA (2011)

Via a combination of a risk-based approach together with random selection or rotation, issuers whose accounts are subject to a full review are selected. This approach depends on both the probability of a material misstatement in the financial statements and the potential impact of such a misstatement on market confidence and investor protection. When performing only a partial review, not all areas of the financial statements are analyzed for compliance with the disclosure requirements by the enforcers. Partial reviews might be prompted by a number of considerations including known areas of non-compliance by issuers in previous years, first time application of mandatory standards or areas of particular focus given the economic climate or trading conditions. In case any potential infringement of the disclosure framework are identified, they are brought to the attention of the issuer. Before taking a decision whether or not the accounting treatment adopted by the issuer complies with the relevant disclosure framework, the enforcer may ask for additional information or explanation by the issuer. After taking into account the materiality of the issue and in case the enforcer concludes that the treatment is not acceptable, the infringement may result in one or more of the following enforcement actions.

If the infringement is considered material:

- *Issuance of new financial statements accompanied by a new audit opinion (where applicable):* this action entails the withdrawal of the original accounts and issuance of revised financial statements which may be subject to a new audit opinion;
- *Public corrective note or other type of communication to the public:* this may mean a press release either by the issuer or the enforcer informing the market of the error and the effect of the corrective action in advance of the issuance of the next annual or interim financial statements; *or*
- *Correction in the next financial statements*: the issuer adopts an acceptable treatment in the next accounts and corrects the prior year by restating the comparative amounts through applying IAS 8 – *Accounting Policies, Changes in Accounting Estimates and Errors* or otherwise includes additional disclosures not requiring the restatement of comparatives.

If the infringement is found not to be material:

- *Notification of the issuer of the infringement* but normally no information is published to the market.

Since 2005, approximately 7,500 – 8,000 listed companies have been identified by European regulators as IFRS users and are under supervision of authorities. In 2010, European enforcers performed a full review of around 1,000 companies (compared to 1,200 in 2009), covering at about 15% of listed entities in Europe. In addition, some 700 accounts (compared to 900 in 2009) were subject to partial review. Around 800 (900 in 2009) enforcement actions were taken by the enforcers as a result of their reviews, split as follows:

- Issuance of revised financial statements: 22 (19 in 2009);
- Public corrective notes or other public announcement: 220 (160 in 2009);
- Corrections in future financial statements: 380 (560 in 2009);
- Notice to the issuer without requiring any corrective action or public announcement: 150 (170 in 2009).[40]

These figures highlight that nearly 50% of all accounts under review did not fully comply with IFRS. Moreover, the main lack of compliance was found with regard to financial instruments and risk management disclosures according to IAS 32, IAS 39, and IFRS 7. The ESMA report for 2010 states that "there are still issuers that have not achieved a satisfactory level of transparency, mainly because of their continued use of boiler-plate disclosures rather than attempting to accurately describe facts specific to the issuer and/or transaction." The enforcers particularly emphasize lack of information with regard to a) impairment of financial assets available for sale, b) fair value hierarchy, and c) disclosure of risks arising from financial instruments (in particular information related to price risk, sensitivity analysis and counterparty risk disclosures). Hence, our findings of low mandatory and voluntary disclosure indices corroborate the findings of the European enforcers. It seems that companies do not want to – or cannot – fully comply with mandatory disclosure rules as given by IFRS.

3.3.4 Why do Firms not Fully Comply with IFRS?

In the following, we try to offer some explanations why firms do not fully comply with mandatory disclosure rules. We classify our explanations into "*practical*", "*theoretical*", and "*project specific*" considerations.

From a "*practical*" point of view, Dobler (2008) developed three arguments why firms may withhold information. Firstly, the manager does not know the information, and hence, cannot report it. Secondly, the manager cannot credibly report the information since it is not verifiable by external parties. Thirdly, the manager does not report the information because he fears creating disadvantages for the firm. The first argument relates to models of uncertainty of *information availability*, the second argument is mainly captured by *cheap talk models*, particularly in connection with forecasts, while the third argument relates to the *cost factor,* which is formalized in both discretionary disclosure and cheap talk models. We do not go into

[40] All data is from CESR (2010) and ESMA (2011).

more detail and refer to the existing literature on disclosure models (see, for an excellent review, (Verrecchia 2001)). However, each of the arguments outlined above does hinder full disclosure compliance and may lead to our observed low level of disclosure compliance.

There also exist various *theoretical* reasons why firms prefer less disclosure. First, they may want to protect insiders' information advantages (Vashishtha 2012). Second, they may try to withhold information which is valuable for competitors (proprietary costs argument, see (Board 2009). Third, firms may want to manipulate external financing conditions by being very selective on their risk disclosures (Beyer and Guttman 2011). Fourth, firms may want to retain risk management disclosures to avoid negative external effects and disclosure costs (Dobler et al. 2011).

With regard to the *project-specific* reasons for non-disclosure, we note that huge parts of risk management and financial instruments disclosure can be assumed to be (quasi-) voluntary (Linsley and Shrives 2000). Risk management and financial instruments disclosures allow for a considerable part of discretion due to its subjective and partly non-verifiable nature. Hence, the actual amount of information disclosed depends on disclosure incentives even in the presence of disclosure regulation. Imposing mandatory risk disclosure does not necessarily change the present disclosure equilibrium if there are sufficient incentives for non-disclosure. Moreover, our findings can certainly be explained to a large extent by the composition of our sample. We do not solely focus on countries with well-developed capital markets such as Germany or the U.K. (as it is typically the case in prior studies), but include a large number of firms from Eastern and Southern European countries. Their business practices, as well as their institutions and cultural habits are very different from those in Western European countries. In the course of this study we will focus on these cross-country differences. They are able to explain a huge fraction of the variety in disclosure indices, emphasizing that a country's culture and its institutional system are important determinants of firms' disclosure practices. Hence, regulators and EU institutions should focus more on country-specific factors such as cultural values, a country's business sophistication, and its enforcement regime in place when imposing a unique set of rules on different countries at the same time. Finally, *IFRS 7* was adopted for the first time in 2007. Hence, issuers of financial statements have not yet developed significant experience in the application of *IFRS 7*. We expect the compliance rate to increase after 2007 and label this effect a "*learning effect*". Since all companies in our sample have to apply IFRS 7 from the same point in time onwards, this learning effect is not expected to have an impact on our results. Although the learning curve may differ across firms over time, all firms are starting from the same "origin" with regard to the application of IFRS 7. Moreover, this opens up new opportunities for analyzing firm-specific and – in particular – country-specific determinants of disclosure (non-) compliance. We are able to focus on the impact of institutional and cultural country characteristics on disclosure compliance apart from differences in companies' learning curves. The following Table 3.5 illustrates how mandatory and voluntary disclosure differs across countries.

Table 3. 5 Per-Country Statistics of Dependent Variables

Panel A: Descriptive statistics of the disclosure indices per country

country	***total***	***mand***	***volun***
Austria	0.5636	0.7553	0.4134
Belgium	0.5085	0.6267	0.4109
Czech Republic	0.4720	0.5910	0.3705
Denmark	0.4763	0.6093	0.3719
Finland	0.5846	0.7841	0.4220
France	0.5493	0.6750	0.4528
Germany	0.5343	0.7476	0.3587
Greece	0.4480	0.5810	0.3392
Hungary	0.4050	0.5331	0.3052
Ireland	0.5746	0.6760	0.4988
Italy	0.4900	0.6433	0.3673
Luxemburg	0.5145	0.6494	0.4037
Netherlands	0.5225	0.6979	0.3808
Norway	0.5773	0.7088	0.4807
Poland	0.5598	0.6597	0.4779
Portugal	0.4977	0.6155	0.4050
Spain	0.4484	0.5940	0.3327
Sweden	0.4414	0.5932	0.3232
Switzerland	0.4750	0.6390	0.3411
United Kingdom	0.5177	0.6458	0.4178
Total (mean)	**0.5138**	**0.6629**	**0.3948**
Total (std)	**0.12**	**0.16**	**0.13**

Panel A displays the average disclosure scores for the total, mandatory, and voluntary disclosure index per country.

Panel B: ANOVA analysis

total

source	*SS*	*df*	*MS*	*F*	*p-value*
beetween groups	0.6243	19	0.0329	3.21	0.0000
within groups	3.7347	365	0.0102		
total	4.3591	384	0.0114		

mand

source	*SS*	*df*	*MS*	*F*	*p-value*
beetween groups	1.2473	19	0.0656	3.76	0.0000
within groups	6.3648	365	0.0174		
total	7.6122	384	0.0198		

volun

source	*SS*	*df*	*MS*	*F*	*p-value*
beetween groups	0.8696	19	0.0458	3.75	0.0000
within groups	4.4519	365	0.0122		
total	5.3216	384	0.0139		

Panel B presents an analysis of variance (ANOVA) analysis of *total, mand,* and *volun*. We analyze the variance of each disclosure index both between and within countries.

Panel A presents descriptive statistics of our disclosure indices per country. The mean of total disclosure is highest for Finnish (58.46%), Norwegian (57.73%), and Irish (57.46%) firms and lowest for Spanish (44.84%), Greek (44.80%) and Hungarian (40.50%) firms. Mandatory disclosure is highest for firms headquartered in Finland (78.41%), Austria (75.53%) and Germany (74.76%) and lowest for firms from the Czech Republic (59.10%), Greece (58.10%) and Hungary (53.31). Voluntary disclosure is highest for Irish (49.88%), Norwegian (48.07%) and Polish (47.79%) firms and lowest for Hungarian (30.52%), Swedish (32.32%), and Spanish (33.27%) firms. In total, firms which comply least with mandatory disclosure rules are headquartered in the countries from East and South Europe (Czech Republic, Greece, Hungary, Spain). Firms which disclose most are headquartered in Central and North Europe (Austria, Finland, Germany, Norway). The same applies in essence also for voluntary disclosures. Panel B presents results of standard analysis of variance techniques. They demonstrate that the means for *total, mand*, and *volun* differ significantly between countries (all p-values of the corresponding F-statistics are 0.0000).

3.3.5 Independent Variables

Country-level variables

In the following we describe our independent variables. To proxy for enforcement at the country level, we use data from Kaufmann et al. (2009). This data is available for all our 20 sample countries.[41] We perform a principal component factor analysis with four input factors: *government effectiveness, regulatory quality, rule of law,* and *corruption.* We obtain one factor with an eigenvalue above 1 and use this factor as our proxy for enforcement. This approach is fairly standard in the literature (Hail and Leuz (2006), Larcker et al. (2007), Laksmana (2008)). For robustness-checks we also computed the average score from the four input factors and use this average score as our enforcement proxy. Our results do not alter when using this proxy. (the correlatin between both proxies is 0.999 and significant at t he 1%-level).

We use sub-indices of the *Index of Economic Freedom* from the *Heritage Foundation (2007)* to proxy for *business sophistication* and free capital flow within a country. We take the mean of the following three sub-indices: *Investment Freedom, Financial Freedom,* and *Business Freedom. Investment Freedom* measures the extent to which there are no constraints on the flow of investment capital. Individuals and firms would be allowed to move their resources into and out of specific activities both internally and across the country's borders without restriction. Such an ideal country would receive a score of 100 on the investment freedom index. *Financial freedom* is a measure of banking efficiency as well as a measure of independence from government control and interference in the financial sector. Financial institutions provide various types of financial services to individuals and companies. Banks are free to extend credit, accept deposits, and conduct operations in foreign currencies. Foreign financial institutions operate freely and are treated the same as domestic institutions. Such a country would receive a score of 100 on the financial freedom index. Finally, *Business freedom* is a quantitative measure of the ability to start, operate, and close a business that represents the overall burden of regulation as well as the efficiency of government in the regulatory process. The *business freedom* score for each country is a number between 0 and 100, with 100 equaling the freest business environment. A higher score of our aggregate index generally translates into greater business sophistication and more free capital flows within a country.

[41] Some other studies use data on enforcement from La Porta et al. (1998). However, their data is only available for 16 of our 20 sample countries. Our main results do not change if we estimate our regressions based on only these 16 countries and use data provided by LaPorta et al. (1998) to proxy for enforcement.

We proxy for a country's *equity market development* via the percentage of a country's traded stocks' market capitalization of GDP. This data comes from the *World Bank*.[42]

Data for differences between local GAAP and IFRS are taken from Ding et al. (2005) and Ding et al. (2007). They define two indices: An *absence* index, and a *divergence* index. *Absence* measures the extent of absent rules in local GAAP compared to IFRS on recognition/measurement or disclosure. *Divergence* measures the extent of divergent rules in local GAAP compared to IFRS in the sense that there exists inconsistencies between IFRS and local GAAP.

The *Financial Development Report* captures a variety of factors characterizing a financial and economic system using 134 variables. These are grouped into the following seven major pillars: *institutional environment, business environment, financial stability, banks, nonbanks, financial markets,* and *size, depth and access.* In addition to these pillars, we also use selected individual variables and sub-pillars (as calculated by the *World Economic* Forum) as proxies for financial development and political and economic factors.

We proxy for national culture by using different concepts based on the work of Hofstede (1991, 2001), Schwartz (1994, 1999, 2004) and the GLOBE project (House et al. 2004). Hofstede (1991, 2001) identifies four cultural dimensions: *power distance, individualism, uncertainty avoidance,* and *masculinity.*[43] *Power distance* is the extent to which the less powerful members of organizations and institutions accept and expect that power is distributed unequally. *Individualism* measures the degree to which individuals are integrated into groups. On the individualist side we find societies in which the ties between individuals are loose except within the nuclear family. On the collectivist side are societies in which people are integrated into strong, cohesive in-groups, which continue protecting them in exchange for unquestioning loyalty. *Masculinity* versus its opposite, *femininity*, refers to the distribution of roles between the genders. Masculine societies stress achievement, heroism, assertiveness and material success. Feminine societies stress relationships, modesty, caring for the weak and quality of life. *Uncertainty avoidance* deals with a society's intolerance for uncertainty and ambiguity. It indicates to what extent a culture affects its members' preferences towards unstructured situations. Uncertainty avoiding cultures try to minimize the possibility of such situations by strict laws and rules, safety and security measures.

---

[42] Our results do not change when we use other proxies for capital market development such as data from the World Economics' Forum *Financial Development Report (2008)*.

[43] Hofstede also identifies *long-term orientation* as an additional cultural value. We do not use *long-term orientation* as this data is available only for eight out of the 20 countries in our study.

Schwartz (1994, 1999, 2004) developed a more comprehensive set of cultural dimensions, so far available for 73 countries. Schwartz (1994, 1999, 2004) derived his model from three basic problems that confront all societies: the nature of the relation between the person and the group, the securing of responsible behavior to preserve the social fabric and the management of relationships between the natural and social world. Schwartz (1994, 1999, 2004) considers the following variables: intellectual autonomy, affective autonomy, embeddedness (conservatism), hierarchy, mastery, egalitarianism, harmony. *Autonomy* puts an emphasis on the person as an autonomous entity that is entitled to pursue his or her individual interests. More specifically, *intellectual autonomy* emphasizes self-direction and flexibility of thoughts whereas *affective autonomy* stresses stimulation and hedonism. *Embeddedness* emphasizes the maintenance of the status quo and relies on social order, respect for tradition, moderation and wisdom. *Egalitarianism* relates to sharing basic interests and showing concern for the welfare of others and bears on the values equality, social justice, loyality and honesty. *Hierarchy* corresponds to the legitimacy of an unequal distribution of power and resources and applies to values such us authority, wealth and humbleness. *Harmony* points to accepting the world as it is and relates to unity with nature, protecting the environment, world in peace and world of beauty. *Mastery* supports the idea of getting ahead through active self-assertion and refers to values such as influence, competence, daring and ambition.

The GLOBE project (House et al. 2004) consists of data from 62 cultures representing all major regions throughout the world. GLOBE measures both cultural practices (as is) and cultural values (should be). We make use of the cultural practices measures. They consist of nine different dimensions. *Power distance* is the degree to which members of a collective expect power to be distributed equally. *Uncertainty avoidance* is the extent to which a society, organization, or group relies on social norms, rules and procedures to alleviate unpredictability of future events. *Humane Orientation* is the degree to which a collective encourages and rewards individuals for being fair, altruistic, generous, caring and kind to others. *Institutional Collectivism* reflects the degree to which individuals are integrated into groups within the society. *In-Group Collectivism* focuses on the degree to which individuals have strong ties to their small immediate group. *Assertiveness* represents the degree to which individuals are assertive, dominant & demanding in their relationships with others. *Gender Egalitarianism* is the degree to which a collective minimizes gender inequality. *Future Orientation* measures the extent to which a collective encourages and rewards future-oriented behaviors such as delaying gratification, planning and investing in the future. *Performance Orientation* proxies for the degree to which a collective encourages and rewards group members for performance improvement and excellence. In our main analyses we focus on the Hofstede (1991, 2001) variables.

Panel A of Table 3.6 presents the per-country descriptive statistics of our country-level variables. Panel B presents descriptive statistics of all firm-level variables. Firm size, as measured by the log of total assets, ranges between USD 32mn and USD 253bn. All other variables reveal significant variation in the data. Panel C shows Pearson-correlation among all variables. All correlation coefficients are smaller than 0.35, indicating that multi-collinearity should not be an issue in the empirical analysis.

Table 3. 6 Descriptive Statistics of Independent Variables

Panel A: Descriptive statistics of country-level variables

country	*absence*	*divergence*	*enforcement*	*business sophistication*	*equity market development*	*Hofstede UA*	*Hofstede PD*	*Hofstede IND*	*Hofstede MAS*	*law*
Austria	34	36	0.59	73.90	32.76	70	11	55	79	german
Belgium	22	32	0.00	87.53	55.78	94	65	75	54	french
Czech Republic	44	20	-1.53	70.37	24.07	74	57	58	57	german
Denmark	31	21	1.22	88.27	77.94	23	18	74	16	scand.
Finland	22	31	0.93	81.77	221.12	59	33	63	26	scand.
France	21	34	-0.54	65.73	131.80	86	68	71	43	french
Germany	18	38	0.33	76.30	101.19	65	35	67	66	german
Greece	40	28	-1.93	53.23	48.90	112	60	35	57	french
Hungary	40	26	-1.49	66.73	34.23	82	46	80	88	french
Ireland	0	34	0.54	90.70	52.61	35	28	70	68	common
Italy	27	37	-2.07	69.00	109.32	75	50	76	70	french
Luxemburg	54	17	0.86	82.30	0.45	70	40	60	50	french
Netherlands	10	25	0.76	86.13	231.71	53	38	80	14	french
Norway	7	17	0.74	63.70	121.77	50	31	69	8	scand.
Poland	23	30	-2.32	51.77	19.88	93	68	60	64	german
Portugal	29	22	-1.09	66.20	64.74	104	63	27	31	french
Spain	28	29	-0.86	76.00	205.58	86	57	51	42	french
Sweden	10	26	0.91	81.40	209.47	29	31	71	5	scand.
Switzerland	42	22	0.98	74.70	409.55	58	34	68	70	german
United Kingdom	0	35	0.64	90.40	368.86	35	35	89	66	common
Total (mean)	**25.10**	**28.00**	**-0.17**	**74.81**	**126.09**	**67.65**	**43.40**	**64.95**	**48.70**	

Panel A: Descriptive statistics of country-level variables (ctd.)

country	*Schwartz aut*	*Schwartz egl*	*Schwartz mas*	*Schwartz hie*	*Schwartz emb*	*Schwartz har*	*Globe UA*	*Globe FO*	*Globe PD*	*Globe IC*	*Globe HO*	*Globe PO*	*Globe IGC*	*Globe GE*	*Globe AS*
Austria	4.64	5.02	3.96	1.81	3.22	4.48	5.16	4.46	4.95	4.30	3.72	4.44	4.85	3.09	4.62
Belgium	4.67	5.16	4.12	1.95	3.38	4.21	4.77	4.07	4.93	4.02	3.51	4.20	4.11	3.41	4.36
Czech Republic	4.44	4.45	4.12	2.40	3.70	4.22	4.44	3.63	3.59	3.60	4.17	4.11	3.18	3.79	3.69
Denmark	4.75	5.30	4.14	2.06	3.56	4.48	5.22	4.44	3.89	4.80	4.44	4.22	3.53	3.93	3.80
Finland	4.38	5.15	3.81	2.15	3.82	4.51	5.02	4.24	4.89	4.63	3.96	3.81	4.07	3.35	3.81
France	4.19	5.33	3.55	2.22	3.97	4.68	4.43	3.48	5.28	3.93	3.40	4.11	4.37	3.64	4.13
Germany	4.82	5.25	4.17	2.05	3.32	4.84	5.19	4.11	5.39	3.68	3.29	4.17	4.27	3.08	4.64
Greece	3.96	4.63	4.08	1.64	3.21	4.17	3.39	3.40	5.40	3.25	3.34	3.20	5.27	3.48	4.58
Hungary	4.03	4.42	3.63	1.84	3.49	4.24	3.12	3.21	5.56	3.53	3.35	3.43	5.25	4.08	4.79
Ireland	4.35	4.83	4.06	2.13	3.32	3.68	4.30	3.98	5.15	4.63	4.96	4.36	5.14	3.21	3.92
Italy	4.33	5.23	4.06	1.89	3.55	4.45	3.79	3.25	5.43	3.68	3.63	3.58	4.94	3.24	4.07
Luxemburg	4.45	5.08	3.95	2.12	3.50	4.37	4.77	4.07	4.93	4.02	3.51	4.20	4.11	3.41	4.36
Netherlands	4.75	5.32	4.23	2.19	3.54	4.32	4.70	4.61	4.11	4.46	3.86	4.32	3.70	3.50	4.32
Norway	4.51	5.34	4.18	1.78	3.68	4.59	5.19	4.36	4.54	4.88	4.17	3.92	3.75	3.71	3.66
Poland	3.86	4.53	3.79	2.59	3.96	4.08	3.62	3.11	5.10	4.53	3.61	3.89	5.52	4.02	4.06
Portugal	4.00	5.03	3.95	1.83	3.37	4.23	3.91	3.71	5.44	3.92	3.91	3.60	5.51	3.66	3.65
Spain	4.31	5.25	3.81	1.96	3.41	4.46	3.97	3.51	5.52	3.85	3.32	4.01	5.45	3.01	4.42
Sweden	4.41	5.07	3.76	2.12	3.71	4.52	5.32	4.39	4.85	5.22	4.10	3.72	3.66	3.84	3.38
Switzerland	5.16	5.42	4.05	2.36	3.36	4.63	5.37	4.73	4.90	4.06	3.60	4.94	3.97	2.97	4.51
United Kingdom	4.36	4.87	3.95	2.28	3.31	3.85	4.65	4.28	5.15	4.27	3.72	4.08	4.08	3.67	4.15
Total (mean)	4.42	5.03	3.97	2.07	3.52	4.35	4.52	3.95	4.95	4.16	3.78	4.02	4.44	3.50	4.15
Total (std)	0.32	0.31	0.19	0.24	0.23	0.28	0.68	0.50	0.54	0.51	0.43	0.39	0.74	0.34	0.40

Panel A presents descriptive statistics of all country-level variables. The sample consists of 385 firms from 20 European countries. All variables are calculated as defined in the Appendix to Chapter 3.

Panel B: Descriptive statistics of firm-level variables

	N	mean	sd	p50	min	max
business structure						
size	385	8.7632	1.6799	8.7411	3.4927	12.7443
leverage	385	0.2571	0.1899	0.2321	0.0000	0.9395
internationality	385	0.3306	0.3002	0.3102	0.0000	0.9969
profitability	385	0.1100	0.4320	0.0786	-0.7240	0.5294
growth opportunities	385	6.5226	39.9557	2.9142	0.7250	240.08
managers' incentives						
future debt increases	385	0.5065	0.5006	1.0000	0.0000	1.0000
future equity increases	385	0.5013	0.5006	1.0000	0.0000	1.0000
speculation	385	0.0623	0.2421	0.0000	0.0000	1.0000
pos. future abnormal returns	385	0.4961	0.5006	0.0000	0.0000	1.0000
competition	385	0.0705	0.0319	0.0818	0.0399	0.1809
analyst following	385	26.5403	14.5102	25.0000	0.0000	84.0000
BIG4	385	0.9143	0.2803	1.0000	0.0000	1.0000
accounting standards						
absence	20	25.1000	14.8639	25.0000	0.0000	54.0000
divergence	20	28.0000	6.6491	28.5000	17.0000	38.0000
countries' institutions						
enforcement	20	-0.1659	1.1878	0.4332	-2.3189	1.2245
business sophistication	20	74.8067	11.5037	75.3500	51.7667	90.7000
equity market development	20	126.0862	114.8688	89.5662	0.4480	409.5474

Panel B presents descriptive statistics of all firm-level variables. The sample consists of 385 firms from 20 European countries. All variables are calculated as defined in the Appendix to Chapter 3.

Panel C: Pearson-correlation matrix

	total	mand	volun	size	leverage	internat.	profit	growth opp.
total	1.0000							
mand	0.8546***	1.0000						
volun	0.8547***	0.4646***	1.0000					
size	0.2787***	0.2932***	0.1797***	1.0000				
leverage	0.1580***	0.0903*	0.1832***	0.1518***	1.0000			
internationality	0.1624***	0.1667***	0.1199**	0.2227***	0.0822	1.0000		
profitability	0.0980*	0.0084	0.1521***	0.0204	0.0760	-0.0687	1.0000	
growth opportunities	-0.0418	-0.0135	-0.0530	-0.1402***	0.1002**	-0.0290	-0.0090	1.0000
future debt increases	0.0988*	0.0954*	0.0675	-0.0474	-0.1574***	0.0240	-0.0254	-0.0618
future equity increases	-0.0033	-0.0239	0.0253	-0.0158	0.1449***	0.1699***	0.0257	0.0515
speculation	0.1127**	0.1791***	0.0096	0.2552***	-0.0354	-0.0713	0.0229	-0.0244
future abnormal returns	-0.1198**	-0.1365***	-0.0748	0.0385	-0.0976*	-0.0133	-0.0322	-0.0670
competition	-0.1073**	-0.1346***	-0.0479	-0.1431***	0.0052	0.1375***	-0.0512	0.0399
analyst following	-0.1189***	-0.1837*	-0.0093	0.4845***	-0.0058	0.1391***	-0.0605	-0.0802
BIG4	0.1204**	0.1151**	0.0921*	0.1852***	0.0643	0.1192**	-0.1610***	-0.1508***
absence	-0.1361***	-0.0883*	-0.1509***	-0.1755***	-0.0432	-0.2076***	0.0174	0.1279**
divergence	0.1294**	0.1681***	0.0498	0.2259***	0.0297	0.0071	0.0062	-0.1362***
enforcement	0.0865*	0.1420***	0.0090	0.1219**	-0.0716	0.3518***	-0.0317	-0.0446
business sophistication	-0.0042	-0.0240	-0.0144	0.0948*	0.0031	0.2778***	-0.0583	-0.0070
equity market	-0.0284	-0.0294	-0.0130	0.1764***	-0.0005	0.2435***	0.0017	-0.0689

Panel C: Pearson-correlation matrix (ctd.)

	debt inc.	Equity inc.	Specul.	*Abn. Ret.*	Competition	analyst	BIG4	absence	divergence	enforcement	bus. Soph.
Future debt increases	1.0000										
future equity increases	0.0857*	1.0000									
speculation	0.0611	0.0208	1.0000								
future abnormal returns	0.1378***	-0.0701	0.0450	1.0000							
competition	0.0613	0.0898*	-0.0803	0.0266	1.0000						
analyst following	-0.0249	-0.0944*	0.0719	0.1182**	-0.1131**	1.0000					
BIG4	0.0133	-0.0642	0.0406	0.0069	-0.0067	0.1497***	1.0000				
absence	-0.0764	-0.2131***	0.0169	-0.0549	-0.1229**	-0.1861***	-0.1801***	1.0000			
divergence	0.0375	0.2001***	-0.0217	0.0857*	-0.0419	0.2220***	-0.0100	-0.4837***	1.0000		
enforcement	0.0271	0.1189**	0.0214	0.0290	0.0033	0.2022***	0.2038***	-0.3881***	-0.0375	1.0000	
business sophistication	0.0445	0.1605***	-0.0106	0.1193**	0.0800	0.1201**	0.2620***	-0.4329***	0.1550***	0.4518***	1.0000
equity market	0.0113	0.1140**	-0.0203	0.1692***	0.1202**	0.1819***	0.2210***	-0.3161***	0.1230**	0.4932***	0.5654***

Panel C presents Pearson-correlations of all main firm-level and country-level variables. *** denotes significance at the 1%-level, ** denotes significance at the 5%-level, and * denotes significance at the 10%-level. All variables are defined a described in the Appendix to Chapter 3.

Firm-level variables

We use the following firm-level variables: *size, leverage, internationality, profitability, growth opportunities, future debt* and *future equity increases, speculation, future positive abnormal returns,* the *Herfindahl* index, *number of analysts* following a firm, and being audited by a *BIG4* auditor. *Size* is measured by the natural logarithm of total assets in USD. *Leverage* is defined as total debt over total assets. *Internationality* is measured as foreign assets over total assets. *Profitability* is measured as net income normalized by sales. *Growth opportunities* is the ratio of the firm's market capitalization to the book value of common equity. *Future debt* [*equity*] *increase is a* dummy variable coded 1 if the firm has a debt [equity] increase superior to the median debt [equity] increase of firms in the DJ STOXX 600 in the next two years, and 0 otherwise. *Speculation* is a dummy variable coded 1 if the firm states in its annual report that it uses derivatives not only to hedge its operational activities but also to speculate on capital markets. *Future positive abnormal returns* is a dummy variable coded 1 if the firm's market (DJ STOXX 600) adjusted raw return over the next fiscal year is positive, and 0 otherwise. The *Herfindahl index* is an indicator for the amount of competition in an industry. It is defined as the sum of the squares of the market shares, measured by sales, within an industry. It ranges from 0 to 1 whereas a higher value indicates smaller competition. The *number of analysts* following a firm are taken from *I/B/E/S.* Finally, *BIG4* is a dummy variable equal to 1 if the firms' financial statements are audited by a BIG4 audit firm. Panel B of Table 3.6 provides descriptive statistics of our firm-level variables, whereas Panel C presents Pearson correlation of each dependent and independent variable.

3.3.6 Univariate Analyses

Before turning to the multilevel analyses, we now focus on firm and country characteristics subject to corporate disclosure patterns and a country's strength of enforcement. We split the total sample into two sub-samples based on the median values of total disclosure, mandatory disclosure, voluntary disclosure, and a country's strength of enforcement, respectively. Table 3.7 presents t-tests for differences in means for our explanatory variables across these subsamples. As a robustness check, we also tested for differences between groups via a Mann-Whitney-U-test. Differences are statistically significant at roughly the same significance levels.

Table 3. 7 Pairwise Comparisons across Disclosure Practices and Enforcement

	total				***mand***				***volun***			
	low *n=192*	*high* *n=193*	*t-test of difference*	*ranksum-test of difference*	*low* *n=189*	*high* *n=196*	*test of difference*	*ranksum-test of difference*	*low* *n=180*	*high* *n=205*	*test of difference*	*ranksum-test of difference*
size	8.3871	9.1374	**0.0000**	**0.0000**	8.4408	9.0742	**0.0001**	**0.0006**	8.4741	9.0171	**0.0004**	**0.0019**
leverage	0.2328	0.2812	**0.0061**	**0.0044**	0.2408	0.2728	**0.0490**	**0.0246**	0.2233	0.2867	**0.0003**	**0.0007**
internationality	0.2883	0.3763	**0.0023**	**0.0065**	0.2863	0.3769	**0.0018**	**0.0027**	0.2918	0.3681	**0.0036**	**0.0202**
profitability	0.0934	0.1265	0.2261	0.5902	0.0881	0.1311	0.1647	0.3996	0.0864	0.1307	**0.0492**	**0.3039**
growth opportunities	0.0878	0.0428	0.1350	**0.0275**	0.0865	0.0447	0.1530	**0.0370**	0.0887	0.0446	**0.0702**	**0.0624**
future debt increases	0.4635	0.5492	**0.0466**	**0.0931**	0.4603	0.5510	**0.0378**	**0.0755**	0.4833	0.5268	**0.0989**	0.3950
future equity increases	0.5104	0.4922	0.3610	0.7215	0.5079	0.4949	0.3994	0.7984	0.4889	0.5122	0.1623	0.6486
speculation	0.0365	0.0881	**0.0182**	**0.0364**	0.0370	0.0867	**0.0220**	**0.0440**	0.0667	0.0585	0.1857	0.7423
future abnormal returns	0.5417	0.4508	**0.0375**	**0.0749**	0.5450	0.4490	**0.0300**	**0.0600**	0.5167	0.4780	0.1127	0.4501
competition	0.0723	0.0688	0.1404	**0.0958**	0.0739	0.0672	**0.0207**	**0.0011**	0.0708	0.0702	0.2151	0.5795
analyst following	0.2894	0.3423	**0.0013**	**0.0028**	0.2922	0.3389	**0.0040**	**0.0154**	0.3130	0.3186	0.1876	0.4980
BIG4	0.8802	0.9481	**0.0086**	**0.0173**	0.8889	0.9388	**0.0404**	**0.0809**	0.8889	0.9366	**0.0479**	**0.0957**
absence	0.1940	0.1668	**0.0190**	**0.0333**	0.1904	0.1707	**0.0673**	**0.0614**	0.1897	0.1721	**0.0907**	0.2720
divergence	0.2701	0.2814	**0.0255**	**0.0610**	0.2671	0.2842	**0.0015**	**0.0006**	0.2742	0.2772	0.3006	0.9996
enforcement	-0.0895	0.0891	**0.0399**	0.3454	-0.0927	0.0894	**0.0037**	**0.3960**	-0.0361	0.0317	0.1269	0.7741
business sophistication	0.7628	0.7718	0.2098	0.4270	0.7655	0.7690	0.3781	0.6674	0.7619	0.7720	0.1832	0.3321
equity market	1.7273	1.6955	0.4031	0.8355	1.7524	1.6718	0.2669	0.8190	1.7165	1.7068	0.4701	0.7432
total	0.4187	0.6084	0.0000	0.0000	0.4290	0.5957	0.0000	0.0000	0.4311	0.5864	0.0000	0.0000
mand	0.5550	0.7702	0.0000	0.0000	0.5378	0.7836	0.0000	0.0000	0.6086	0.7105	0.0000	0.0000
volun	0.3078	0.4815	0.0000	0.0000	0.3404	0.4473	0.0000	0.0000	0.2850	0.4913	0.0000	0.0000

Table 3.7 Pairwise Comparisons across Disclosure Practices and Enforcement (ctd.)

	enforcement			
	low *n=197*	*high* *n=188*	*test of difference*	*ranksum-test of difference*
size	8.7416	8.7759	0.4237	0.3612
leverage	0.2812	0.2430	**0.0285**	**0.1357**
internationality	0.2114	0.4031	**0.0000**	**0.0000**
profitability	0.1565	0.0828	**0.0531**	0.1981
growth opportunities	0.0846	0.0539	0.2340	0.1664
future debt increases	0.4648	0.5309	0.1059	0.2115
future equity increases	0.4155	0.5514	**0.0050**	**0.0101**
speculation	0.0634	0.0617	0.4743	0.9485
future abnormal returns	0.5282	0.4774	0.1687	0.3367
competition	0.0698	0.0709	0.3627	0.1502
analyst following	0.2886	0.3320	**0.0086**	**0.0796**
BIG4	0.8451	0.9547	**0.0001**	**0.0002**
absence	0.2521	0.1385	**0.0000**	**0.0000**
divergence	0.2710	0.2786	0.1047	**0.0001**
enforcement	-1.1530	0.6738	0.0000	0.0000
business sophistication	0.6718	0.8231	**0.0000**	**0.0000**
equity market	0.9798	2.1388	**0.0000**	**0.0000**
total	0.4990	0.5225	**0.0325**	**0.0939**
mand	0.6268	0.6840	**0.0003**	**0.0013**
volun	0.3973	0.3934	0.3880	0.7116

This Table presents means of all dependent and independent variables for two sub-samples. We split the total sample of 385 firms based on the median of *total, mand* , *volun*, and *enforcement* into two sub-samples, respectively. The column "*low*" ("*high*") presents mean values of each variable listed in column 1 for all firms for which *total, mand, volun*, or *enforcement* is below (above or equal) the sample median. The column "*test of difference*" presents one-sided p-values of t-tests for differences in *low* and *high* of all variables. The column "*ranksum-test of difference*" presents one-sided p-values of the Wilcoxon ranked tests for differences in *low* and *high* of all variables. Figures in **bold** indicate a 10%-significance level. All variables are defined a described in the Appendix to Chapter 3.

Results for the total disclosure index are as follows: Firms that disclose less than the median of total disclosure are smaller in size (p = 0.0000), have a smaller fraction of foreign sales (p = 0.0023), a smaller leverage ratio (p = 0.0061), and have fewer analysts following (p=0.0013). On the other hand, firms that disclose more have to a lesser extent positive future abnormal returns (p = 0.0375), have more often future debt increases (p = 0.0466), are more often audited by a *BIG4* auditor (p = 0.0086), and are speculating more with derivatives (p = 0.0182).

Taking a closer look at these findings, we find that firms disclosing more mandatorily than the sample median are larger (p = 0.0001), more international (p = 0.0018), more leveraged (p = 0.0490), have more often future debt increases (p = 0.0378), more analysts following (p = 0.0040), speculate more often (p = 0.0220), and operate in more competitive industries (p = 0.0207). Focusing on voluntary disclosure, we find that firms which disclose more voluntarily than the sample median differ significantly only in size (p = 0.0004), leverage (p = 0.0003), internationality (p = 0.0036), profitability (p = 0.0492), and BIG4 auditors (p = 0.0479).

Finally, splitting the sample based on a low and high level of enforcement, we find that firms in countries with a strong enforcement regime are more international (p = 0.0000), less leveraged (p = 0.0285), have larger future equity increases (p = 0.0050), and more analyst following (p = 0.0086). Not surprisingly, the level of mandatory disclosure is also significantly higher in strong enforcement countries (p = 0.0003). However, the strength of enforcement does not have any impact on the level of voluntary disclosure (p = 0.3880).

3.4 Disclosure Practices, Disclosure Incentives and Enforcement

3.4.1 Disclosure Incentives and Disclosure Practices

In this section, we analyze how various disclosure incentives affect firms' disclosure practices. Specifically, we test our Hypothesis 1 by estimating the following OLS regression model ("basic model"):

$$disclosure\ index_i = \alpha + \beta_i\, OC_i + \gamma_i\, MI_i + \delta_i AR_i + \vartheta_i INS_i + \varepsilon_i \qquad (E3.1)$$

whereas *disclosure index* is either *total, mand,* or *volun; OC* represents the set of variables capturing a firm's business structure (*size, leverage, internationality, profitability, growth opportunities*); *MI* is the set of variables proxying for managers disclosure incentives' (*future debt/equity increases, speculation, future positive abnormal returns, competition, analyst following, BIG4*); *AR* is the set of variables capturing accounting rules (*absence and divergence scores*), and *INS* is the set of variables proxying for institutional influences (*enforcement, business sophistication, equity market development*).

We use White (1980) heteroscedasticity-consistent standard errors. [44] Wald tests are used to measure the explanatory power of each set of variables. Therefore, the emphasis is on the explanatory power of sets of variables representing various disclosure incentives. To control for potential effect of outliers, regressions have been run with all continuous independent variables winsorized at 1% top and bottom. In this case, results (not tabulated) are similar to those presented in the tables. We standardized all continuous independent variables to ease the interpretation of regression coefficients. Multicollinearity is no concern in *all* regressions; the corresponding variance inflation factors are all below 3.02.

Table 3.8 presents our results. In model (1) we explain the total disclosure index; in model (2) the mandatory disclosure index, and in model (3) the voluntary index. We focus in our discussion only on models (2) and (3), since the total disclosure index is simply a combination of the mandatory and voluntary index. All three models are well specified; the F-statistics range from 11.98 for the voluntary disclosure model to 7.19 for the mandatory model.

[44] Clustering standard errors is not appropriate as the number of clusters (at country or industry level) is too small and as clusters are highly unbalanced.

Table 3. 8 Multilevel Analysis of Disclosure Incentives

Panel A: Multilevel analysis

		(1) *total*		(2) *mand*		(3) *volun*	
business structure	*size*	0.0318	**3.83**	0.0315	**2.83**	0.0339	**3.70**
	leverage	0.0151	**3.14**	0.0130	**2.08**	0.0173	**3.14**
	internationality	0.0140	**2.30**	0.0196	**2.46**	0.0108	1.59
	profitability	0.0113	**6.26**	0.0014	0.59	0.0188	**8.02**
	growth opportunities	0.0040	1.12	0.0103	**3.61**	-0.0005	-0.09
managers' incentives	*future debt increases*	0.0337	**2.90**	0.0427	**2.89**	0.0258	**2.00**
	future equity increases	-0.0215	-1.78	-0.0346	**-2.18**	-0.0101	-0.74
	speculation	0.0245	1.34	0.0844	**3.12**	-0.0263	-1.16
	future pos. abnormal returns	-0.0232	-1.92	-0.0435	**-2.74**	-0.0081	-0.62
	competition	-0.0086	-1.55	-0.0120	-1.56	-0.0065	-1.01
	analyst following	-0.0011	**-2.05**	-0.0006	-0.81	-0.0017	**-2.74**
	BIG4	0.0414	**2.19**	0.0470	**2.06**	0.0382	1.60
accounting standards	*absence of acc. standards*	-0.0174	**-2.11**	-0.0002	-0.02	-0.0337	**-3.44**
	divergence of acc. standards	0.0128	1.95	0.0360	**4.40**	-0.0069	-0.81
countries' institutions	*enforcement*	0.0260	**2.68**	0.0498	**3.97**	0.0072	0.65
	business sophistication	-0.0250	**-2.44**	-0.0343	**-2.65**	-0.0191	-1.60
	equity market development	-0.0169	**-2.39**	-0.0181	-1.69	-0.0157	**-2.18**
	constant	0.5087	**21.22**	0.6470	**21.09**	0.4030	**13.38**
	N	385		385		385	
	F	9.28		7.19		11.98	
	R^2	0.2102		0.2349		0.1584	

Panel B: Tests of joint significances for disclosure incentives

	total F-statistic	*total* p-value	*mand* F-statistic	*mand* p-value	*volun* F-statistic	*volun* p-value
business structure	20.17	0.00	6.38	0.00	28.74	0.00
managers' incentives	3.83	0.00	5.20	0.00	2.24	0.02
accounting standards	8.43	0.00	11.30	0.00	7.13	0.00
countries' institutions	5.13	0.00	6.95	0.00	3.08	0.03
firm-level variables	10.12	0.00	6.95	0.00	14.76	0.00
country-level variables	4.97	0.00	7.67	0.00	3.27	0.01

Panel A presents results of OLS estimation and t-statistics based on robust standard errors. The dependent variables are *total* in model (1), *mand* in model (2), and *volun* in model (3). For the regression analysis, statistical significance is based on two-sided t-tests. The cut-off-values for significance levels are: 2.58 for significance at the 1%-level, 1.96 for the 5%-level, and 1.65 for the 10%-level; t-values in bold indicate significances at the 5%-level. Panel B reports F-statistics and two-sided p-values from Wald tests to test the joint significances of each group of variables in regressions on the disclosure indices. All continuous independent variables are standardized and calculated as defined in the Appendix to Chapter 3.

In general, our results reveal that mandatory and voluntary disclosures are driven by different factors. Solely *size, leverage,* and *future debt increases* are statistically and economically significant determinants of both indices; their impacts are positive, as expected.

Business structure

Focusing on the first set of variables which proxy for a firms' business structure, we find that *firm size* and *leverage* are positively correlated with both the mandatory as well as the voluntary disclosure index. Larger firms are expected to follow better disclosure practices in well-developed countries and are exposed to greater political costs. Highly leveraged firms have incentives to increase disclosures in order to reduce the agency costs of debt. Moreover, highly leveraged firms incur more monitoring costs which they seek to decrease by disclosing more information (Ahmed and Courtis 1999). The coefficient on *internationality* is positive and significant solely in the mandatory disclosure model. Depending on the industry, having a larger exposure to foreign markets requires more foreign resources such as labor and capital. Some firms, therefore, disclose more to acquire these resources (Zarzeski 1996; Archambault and Archambault 2003). *Profitability* is insignificant in the mandatory disclosure model, but highly significant in the voluntary model. This is consistent with Singhvi and Desai (1971) who argue that higher profitability motivates management to provide more voluntary information since an increase in investors' confidence translates into an increase in managers' compensation. Wallace and Naser (1995) argue that highly profitable firms likely signal their superior performance to the market by disclosing more. *Growth opportunities* has a positive and significant impact only on the mandatory disclosure index. This is in line with Myers (1977) who note that firms with large growth opportunities are more likely to be in need of external financing to fund current and future profitable projects.

Managers' incentives

The second set of variables, *managers' incentives*, focuses either on forward-looking private information of firms' managers, or on outsiders who affect managers' incentives. All variables are not directly related to a firm's day-to-day business activities and its operational characteristics.

Future financing needs play a major role in managers' disclosure decisions. *Future debt increases* proxies for a firm's (long-term) relationship to its debtholders. In contrast, *future equity increases* proxies for a more short-term oriented relationship between the firm and its equityholders. Since debtholders are generally better protected by law than the firm's equity holders, we expect *future debt increases* to be positively related to disclosures. Firms disclose more in anticiapation of future debt issuances, as detailed and transparent information is required to raise capital on the debt market. Indeed, the coefficient on *future debt increases* is positive and significant in both models. On the contrary, the influence of *future equity increases* on firm disclosures with regard to firms' risk management is expected to be negative. We follow Beyer and Guttman (2011) and postulate that managers manipulate their disclosure practices by selectively disclosing and withholding information to obtain better financing conditions on the equity market. As expected, managers tend to hold back information from shareholders in case the firm issues equity in the near future. Given that we analyze risk management and financial instruments disclosures, managers' intent is probably to dampen the risk premium required by equity holders for inherent business risks. The less risk-related disclosures managers make, the smaller the probability that future equity holders assume the firm to be a risky investment.

Speculation has – as expected – a significantly positive impact on mandatory disclosure compliance.[45] We offer two possible explanations. First, managers' intent is to signal they have everything under control, even though they take risky positions on the market. Second, firms engaging in speculative activities are under greater scrutiny of outsiders and hence, comply more with mandatory disclosure rules. *Speculation* has no statistically significant impact on voluntary disclosures.

Firms experiencing *positive future abnormal returns* disclose less mandatorily and voluntarily. We expected a negative impact on disclosures since these firms need to rely less on external financing and are considered to be less risky. Our results are also consistent with Dye (1998). He expects managers to disclose more when outsiders' prior beliefs are less favorable. In return, if outsiders expect a favorable development of the firm in the near future, managers disclose less.

As expected, the coefficient on *competition* is negative (but insignificant at conventional levels). Firms disclose more when they operate in competitive industries to differentiate from other firms in the same industry (Board 2009).

The *number of analysts* following a firm has a negative impact on disclosures. Hence, financial disclosure and analyst following seem to be substitutes, rather than complements. However, the effect is economically insignificant in the mandatory and voluntary disclosure model.

---

[45] Note that it is not mandatory to disclose whether a firm engages in speculative activities. Moreover, speculating firms are not subject to stricter disclosure rules than non-speculating firms.

Finally, the dummy variable indicating a BIG 4 auditor loads positive in both models. Theory predicts that larger audit firms provide better audit quality (DeAngelo 1981; Fama and Jensen 1983). The reputation of larger audit firms is impaired if their clients provide low quality annual reports. The larger the firm, the greater is the expected loss in reputation (Ali and Hwang 2000; Chalmers and Godfrey 2004). Hence, BIG 4 audit firms are anxious in enforcing the correct application of accounting standards. Hence, we interpret the BIG 4 indicator variable as proxy for enforcement at the firm level. Its positive and significant coefficient is therefore in line with existing theory.

Accounting standards

Concerning the effect of differences between formerly applied local GAAP and IFRS on firm disclosures, we obtain reciprocal results for the mandatory and voluntary disclosure indices. For mandatory disclosure, the coefficient on *absence* is insignificant, whereas it is negative and highly significant in the voluntary disclosure model. The coefficient on *divergence* is positive and highly significant in the mandatory disclosure model, and negative, but insignificant, in the voluntary disclosure model. These results are in line with our hypotheses. *Absence* measures the extent of absent rules in local GAAP compared to IFRS on recognition, measurement, and disclosure. Firms disclose less if the formerly applied local accounting standards were 'underdeveloped' compared to IFRS. Managers are more accustomed to prior accounting standards which allow for a more flexible and more opaque disclosure regime. The impact of *absence* on disclosure therefore has to be negative. Our results confirm this hypothesis, although the impact is statistically significant only in the voluntary disclosure model.

The opposite applies for *divergence*. It measures the extent of divergent rules in local GAAP compared to IFRS in the sense that there exist inconsistencies. We interpret a high *divergence* index as a strong commitment of a firm to comply with mandatory disclosure rules (whereas a high *absence* index is interpreted as a 'complimentary ticket' for non-disclosure). Hence, we expect and find a positive relationship between *divergence* and mandatory disclosure. Managers are already aware of the existence of similar, but diverging accounting standards under local GAAP and have a higher commitment to apply the new rules correctly.

Countries' institutions

Enforcement is positively related to disclosures. Its coefficient is statistically and economically highly significant for the mandatory disclosure index, whereas it is insignificant for the voluntary disclosure index. These results confirm our hypothesis. *Enforcement* generally has a large impact on mandatory disclosure. In fact, the coefficient on *enforcement* is the second largest in our regression model (after *speculation*). This highlights the importance of having effective enforcement mechanisms in place to ensure compliance with mandatory disclosure rules.

The effect of *business sophistication* (*equity market development*) on the mandatory (voluntary) disclosure index is statistically and economically negative. Prior literature has found inconclusive results concerning the effect of capital market development on disclosures. On the one hand, one can argue that highly developed equity and capital markets may promote firm disclosures since they provide the necessary infrastructure to transmit information. In addition, a high pressure from outsiders may force firms to disclose more. On the other hand, a highly developed capital market is naturally accompanied by a growth in the number and strength of pressure of monitoring groups, such as consumer bodies or labor unions. These bodies may seek to ensure an equitable distribution of benefits derived from enhanced economic wealth. Firms may want to protect against these wealth extractions by disclosing less and withholding information. Moreover, more developed capital markets provide easy access to information, and hence mitigate the role of direct information flows between the firm and its outsiders. Our results support the second view. A high degree of business sophistication and equity market development has a negative impact on disclosure.

General overview and joint F-tests

In total, we found that mandatory and voluntary disclosure practices are driven by different factors from four groups of determinants. Researchers would draw misleading inferences by analyzing only a total disclosure index, instead of analyzing mandatory and voluntary disclosures separately.

Overall, the economically largest impacts on the mandatory disclosure index stem from *speculation* (coeff = 0.0844), *enforcement* (0.0498), *BIG4* (0.0470), *positive future abnormal returns* (-0.0435), *future debt increases* (0.0427), and *divergence* (0.0360). The strong enforcement mechanism in Denmark is responsible for a nearly 15% larger mandatory disclosure index compared to Poland, where the strength of enforcement is smallest for our sample countries. The largest economical impacts on voluntary disclosure stem from *BIG4* (coeff = 0.0382), *size* (coeff = 0.0339), and *absence* (-0.0337). In common law countries, where *absence* is smallest, the voluntary disclosure index is more than 12% larger compared to Luxemburg, where *absence* is largest.

We now turn to the explicit tests of Hypothesis 1. Panel B of Table 3.8 presents the results. We show test statistics for the joint significances (Wald tests) of each group of variables. The F-statistics and corresponding p-values indicate that each set of variables is highly significant in explaining the total and mandatory disclosure index (p-values = 0.0000). Concerning the voluntary disclosure index, all groups are highly significant as well. However, a firm's business structure seems to be more important for voluntary disclosure decisions than a country's institutional systems or managers' incentives. Overall, Hypothesis 1 is confirmed; mandatory and voluntary disclosures are endogenously determined by factors reflecting a firm's *business structure, managers' incentives, accounting standards,* and *countries' institutions*.

The models we present in Table 3.8 contain all variables as explanatory variables at the same time. For robustness checks, we also estimated the model separately for our four sets of variables, *business structure*, *managers' incentives, accounting rules*, and *countries' institutions*. Table 3.9 presents the results. [46]

[46] As an additional robustness check, we also included industry fixed effects. Again, all inferences remain the same. We do not include industry fixed effects in our main model since we want to analyze the impact of *competition* within an industry on firms' disclosure practices.

Table 3. 9 Multilevel Analysis of Disclosure Incentives per Group of Incentives

		mand								volun							
		(1)		(2)		(3)		(4)		(5)		(6)		(7)		(8)	
business structure	*size*	0.042	**4.96**							0.017	**2.52**						
	leverage	0.006	1.85							0.020	**3.48**						
	internationality	0.017	**2.21**							0.012	1.78						
	profitability	0.001	0.64							0.019	**10.00**						
	growth opportunities	0.004	1.47							-0.006	-1.55						
managers' incentives	*future debt increases*			0.038	**2.52**							0.021	1.53				
	future equity increases			-0.006	-0.40							0.006	0.46				
	speculation			0.102	**3.59**							-0.001	0.00				
	future pos. abnormal ret.			-0.057	**-3.61**							-0.022	-1.62				
	competition			-0.016	**-2.01**							-0.007	-1.04				
	analyst following			0.002	**3.39**							0.000	0.07				
	BIG4			0.046	**1.96**							0.043	1.64				
accounting standards	*absence of acc. standards*					-0.001	-0.15							-0.022	**-2.94**		
	divergence of acc. stand.					0.026	**2.80**							-0.004	-0.50		
countries' institutions	*enforcement*							0.047	**3.63**							0.006	0.57
	business sophistication							-0.024	-1.75							-0.006	-0.50
	equity market development							-0.015	-1.48							-0.002	-0.20
	constant	0.663	86.2	0.577	19.8	0.663	83.4	0.663	83.8	0.395	61.4	0.352	12.2	0.395	59.6	0.395	58.9
	N	385		385		385		385		385		385		385		385	
	R^2	0.0991		0.1192		0.0383		0.0417		0.0853		0.0232		0.0235		0.0012	

This table presents results of OLS estimation and t-statistics based on robust standard errors. The dependent variables are *mand* in models (1)-(4), and *volun* in models (5)-(8). For the regression analysis, statistical significance is based on two-sided t-tests. The cut-off-values for significance levels are: 2.58 for significance at the 1%-level, 1.96 for the 5%-level, and 1.65 for the 10%-level; t-values in bold indicate significances at the 5%-level. All continuous independent variables are standardized and calculated as defined in the Appendix to Chapter 3.

3.4.2 Enforcement and the Demand for Accounting Information

In this section, we test Hypotheses 2a and 2b. We expect that the (perceived) strength of enforcement on firms' mandatory disclosure practices is conditional on outsiders' demand for accounting information. Specifically, we expect that a higher demand for accounting information emphasizes the role of enforcement at the firm level. We assume that information demand is pronounced in firms that (i) rely more on debt financing (i.e. have a higher leverage ratio), (ii) are more internationally oriented (i.e. have al larger exposure to foreign markets), (iii) are under greater scrutiny of financial analysts (i.e. have more analysts following the firm), (iv) have larger external financing (equity) needs (i.e. there is an above sample median equity increase in the next two years) , and (v) have larger external financing (debt) needs (i.e. there is an above sample median debt increase in the next two years). We therefore add to our basic model presented in equation 3.1 (E3.1) interaction terms of *enforcement* and a dummy variable equal to 1 if a firm has above sample median (i) *leverage*, (ii) *foreign assets*, (iii) *number of analysts*, (iv) *future equity increase*, and (v) *future debt increases*. We include industry fixed effects (and drop the *competition* variable); our model is estimated with robust standard errors. We focus only on the mandatory disclosure index since enforcement does not have a significant influence on voluntary disclosures. Table 3.10, Panel A presents our results.

Table 3. 10 Enforcement and the Demand for Accounting Information

Panel A: Enforcement and the demand for accounting information

	(1) *leverage*		(2) *internationality*		(3) *analysts*		(4) *equity needs*		(5) *debt needs*	
enforcement	0.0345	**2.46**	0.0435	**3.27**	0.0418	**3.08**	0.0450	**3.37**	0.0396	**3.09**
conditional variable	0.0113	1.77	0.0209	**2.49**	-0.0141	-1.13	-0.0338	**-2.16**	0.0175	0.82
*enforcement * conditional variable*	0.0326	**2.09**	0.0404	**2.16**	0.0283	**2.10**	0.0151	0.88	0.0449	**2.41**
size	0.0225	**2.00**	0.0243	**2.11**	0.0253	**2.83**	0.0216	1.91	0.0216	1.93
leverage			0.0113	1.76	0.0118	**2.11**	0.0109	1.68	0.0101	1.62
internationality	0.0230	**2.80**			0.0241	**3.03**	0.0243	**2.94**	0.0248	**2.99**
profitability	0.0005	0.23	0.0007	0.30	-0.0010	-0.45	0.0001	0.02	0.0002	0.08
growth opportunities	0.0108	**3.58**	0.0103	**3.27**	0.0099	**3.41**	0.0109	**3.65**	0.0095	**3.05**
future debt increases	0.0367	**2.48**	0.0329	**2.22**	0.0349	1.58	0.0358	**2.39**		
future equity increases	-0.0354	**-2.29**	-0.0263	-1.66	-0.0316	**-2.47**			-0.0308	**-1.98**
speculation	0.0755	**3.05**	0.0793	**2.93**	0.0741	**3.02**	0.0753	**2.93**	0.0772	**3.01**
future abnormal returns	-0.0528	**-3.47**	-0.0397	**-2.43**	-0.0468	**-2.79**	-0.0485	**-3.13**	-0.0487	**-3.18**
analyst following	0.0000	-0.04	-0.0002	-0.25			-0.0001	-0.11	-0.0001	-0.20
BIG4	0.0387	1.70	0.0388	1.62	0.0310	1.34	0.0297	1.28	0.0334	1.42
absence of acc. standards	0.0031	0.28	0.0035	0.32	0.0027	0.30	0.0010	0.09	0.0025	0.23
divergence of acc. standards	0.0382	**4.87**	0.0398	**4.93**	0.0404	**5.49**	0.0385	**4.89**	0.0364	**4.62**
business sophistication	-0.0396	**-3.10**	-0.0418	**-3.22**	-0.0384	**-3.01**	-0.0397	**-3.04**	-0.0365	**-2.89**
equity market development	-0.0102	-0.96	-0.0145	-1.36	-0.0122	-1.41	-0.0120	-1.12	-0.0124	-1.17
constant	0.6369	**17.81**	0.6006	**15.81**	0.6428	**25.48**	0.6380	**17.84**	0.6223	**16.41**
industry fixed effects	yes		yes		yes		yes		yes	
N	385		385		385		385		385	
R^2	0.2912		0.2724		0.2879		0.2834		0.2897	

Panel B: Enforcement and accounting standards

	mand				*volun*			
	divergence		*absence*		*divergence*		*absence*	
strong enforcement	0.0581	**2.26**	0.0736	**2.96**	0.0023	0.61	0.0303	1.30
conditional variable	0.0581	**4.10**	-0.0069	-0.25	-0.0107	-0.66	-0.0726	**-3.06**
*conditional variable * str. enforcement*	-0.0252	-1.85	0.0187	0.67	0.0195	1.63	0.0499	**2.15**
N	385		385		385		385	
F	6.46		7.48		10.02		10.19	
R^2	0.2629		0.2816		0.1666		0.1731	

Panel A presents results of OLS estimation and t-statistics based on robust standard errors. In all models, *mand* is the dependent variable. We measure the demand for accounting information via five different variables: *leverage, internationality, analyst following, equity needs,* and *debt needs.* We assign the *conditional variable* a value of 1 if the firm has above sample median *leverage, foreign assets, analyst following, future equity increases,* and *future debt increases,* respectively, and 0 otherwise. Industry fixed effects are included in the models as indicated. For the regression analysis, statistical significance is based on two-sided t-tests. The cut-off-values for significance levels are: 2.58 for significance at the 1%-level, 1.96 for the 5%-level, and 1.65 for the 10%-level; t-values in bold indicate significances at the 5%-level. Panel B reports results of OLS estimation and t-statistics based on robust standard errors. In model (1), *mand* is the dependent variable; in model (2), *volun* is the dependent variable. *Strong enforcement* is an indicator variable taking the value of 1 if a country's strength of enforcement is above the sample median strength of enforcement, and 0 otherwise. *Conditional variable* is either *divergence* or *absence* (continuous variable). Industry fixed effects are included in the models. We only show coefficients and t-statistics of the variables of interest. All continuous independent variables are standardized and calculated as defined in the Appendix to Chapter 3.

Models (1) to (5) focus on different proxies for the demand for accounting information. The first three rows in Table 3.10 present the base and interaction effects. *Enforcement* is highly significant in every model (t-values ≥ 2.46). The coefficients on three out of the five conditional variables are comparable to those in Table 3.8, Panel A. Their magnitudes, signs, and statistical significances are essentially the same.[47] The coefficients on the interaction terms of *enforcement* and *leverage* (model (1)), *internationality* (model (2)), *analyst following* (model (3)), and *debt needs* (model (5)) are all positive and highly significant (t-values = 2.09, 2.16, 2.10 and 2.41, respectively). This provides clear evidence that managers' perceived strength of country-level enforcement is much stronger if outsiders' demand for accounting information is high. The coefficient on the interaction term of enforcement and *equity needs* is statistically insignificant (model (4), t = 0.88): future equity issuances do not significantly increase managers' perceived strength of enforcement. In summary, enforcement plays a much more crucial role when the demand for accounting information is high. Its impact on managers' mandatory disclosure practices is approximately twice as large as compared to settings with below median demands for accounting information.[48] Hypothesis 2a is therefore supported by the data.

We now turn to Hypothesis 2b and examine whether the impact of the *absence* and *divergence* indices on mandatory and voluntary disclosure are less pronounced in strong enforcement regimes. Panel B of Table 3.10 presents the results. We only show the coefficients on the main and interaction effects. All other coefficients and t-statistics are essentially the same as in Panel A when we included industry controls. In the mandatory model, the main effects of *divergence* and *strong enforcement* (indicator variable taking the value of unity if *enforcement* is above the sample median level of *enforcement*) are positive. As expected, the interaction effect of strong *enforcement* and *divergence* is negative and significant at conventional levels (t = -1.85). Hence, our hypothesis that strong enforcement mitigates the impact of *divergence* on mandatory disclosure is supported. The main and interaction effects on *absence* are insignificant, as it is also the case in Table 3.8, Panel A. Note, however, that the signs go in the opposite direction, lending support for our hypothesis that strong enforcement mitigates the impact of *absence* on mandatory disclosures.[49] In the voluntary model, the main effect of *strong enforcement* is insignificant in both models, as it is

[47] The only exemptions are the coefficients on *analyst following* in model (3) and *debt needs* in model (5). The main effect for analyst following -0.0141 and statistically insignificant in model (3), but only -0.0006 and statistically insignificant in Table 3.8. The main effect for debt needs is statistically insignificant in model (5), whereas it is highly significant in Table 3.8.

[48] Concerning all other variables in models (1) to (5) we point out that each coefficient is similar in magnitude and significance to the basic model specification. The only exemption is *BIG4,* which is now statistically, but not economically, insignificant.

[49] Testing for the null hypothesis that the sum of both coefficients is equal to zero cannot be rejected.

also the case in Table 3.8. The main effect of *divergence* is insignificant, too. The effect of *absence* is negative and significant. The interaction effects are positive and significant. This shows that *enforcement* has a statistically and economically significant impact on voluntary disclosures. The effect, however, solely comes via the *absence* and *divergence* indices. There is still no direct effect of enforcement on voluntary disclosure (*enforcement per se* is statistically and economically insignificant for voluntary disclosures). In lieu thereof, *enforcement* is statistically and economically significant via its impact on *absence*. Whereas a weak level of enforcement leads to strong impacts of *absence* and *divergence*, a strong enforcement regime attenuates these impacts.

3.4.3 Disclosure and Country Effects

Country-fixed effects

As outlined in section 3.2.1, institutional characteristics at the country level play an important role for firms' disclosure practices. We have so far explicitly controlled for *enforcement, business sophistication,* and *equity market development* at the country level. However, by restricting our analyses only on these three measures we certainly miss a lot of other relevant institutional characteristics. We therefore estimate the basic model (1) with country fixed effects to control for unobservable time-invariant variables beyond *enforcement* and *capital market development.*

Panel A-1 of Table 3.11 presents summary statistics of our results, whereas Panel A-2 presents the detailed regression estimates. We will focus on Panel A-1 for the sake of clarity.

Table 3. 11 Disclosure and Country Effects

Panel A-1: Corporate disclosure and country fixed effects

	total			mand			volun		
	(1)	(2)	(3)	(1)	(2)	(3)	(1)	(2)	(3)
firm-level variables	yes	yes	yes	yes	yes	yes	yes	yes	yes
country-level variables	no	**yes**	**no**	no	**yes**	**no**	no	**yes**	**no**
industry fixed effects	yes	yes	yes	yes	yes	yes	yes	yes	yes
country fixed effects	no	no	**yes**	no	no	**yes**	no	no	**yes**
N	385	385	385	385	385	385	385	385	385
F	9.17	7.85	7.17	6.32	7.38	5.70	11.60	9.94	10.41
R^2	0.1931	0.2404	0.3235	0.2181	0.2814	0.3313	0.1339	0.1718	0.2713
Vuong p-value (1) vs. (2)		**0.0043**			**0.0007**			**0.0233**	
Vuong p-value (2) vs. (3)		**0.0009**			**0.0045**			**0.0004**	
Vuong p-value (1) vs. (3)		**0.0000**			**0.0000**			**0.0000**	

Panel A-2: Corporate disclosure and country fixed effects

	total				mand				volun			
	(1)		(2)		(3)		(4)		(5)		(6)	
size	0.0245	**2.63**	0.0303	**3.43**	0.0230	1.94	0.0310	**2.72**	0.0274	**2.59**	0.0310	**3.05**
leverage	0.0122	**2.25**	0.0186	**4.01**	0.0086	1.19	0.0175	**2.71**	0.0157	**2.70**	0.0197	**3.76**
internationality	0.0185	**3.00**	0.0190	**3.01**	0.0249	**3.09**	0.0245	**2.91**	0.0147	**2.20**	0.0159	**2.23**
profitability	0.0103	**5.71**	0.0097	**4.91**	0.0009	0.41	0.0009	0.36	0.0176	**7.26**	0.0162	**7.06**
growth opportunities	-0.0007	-0.21	0.0014	0.38	0.0042	1.53	0.0080	**2.19**	-0.0041	-0.90	-0.0029	-0.59
future debt increases	0.0309	**2.62**	0.0300	**2.68**	0.0369	**2.43**	0.0353	**2.38**	0.0256	1.94	0.0252	**2.04**
future equity increases	-0.0121	-1.02	-0.0215	-1.78	-0.0206	-1.33	-0.0335	**-2.11**	-0.0042	-0.32	-0.0108	-0.79
speculation	0.0172	0.90	0.0100	0.54	0.0791	**2.87**	0.0707	**2.68**	-0.0351	-1.53	-0.0414	-1.87
future abnormal returns	-0.0347	**-2.97**	-0.0262	**-2.10**	-0.0539	**-3.56**	-0.0413	**-2.57**	-0.0205	-1.58	-0.0156	-1.15
analyst following	-0.0003	-0.60	-0.0003	-0.51	0.0006	0.82	0.0000	0.00	-0.0013	-1.94	-0.0007	-0.99
BIG4	0.0214	1.13	0.0308	1.53	0.0147	0.69	0.0296	1.18	0.0286	1.18	0.0335	1.42
constant	0.4995	**17.07**	0.5591	**15.15**	0.6196	**16.78**	0.7386	**14.43**	0.4073	**11.26**	0.4206	**8.95**
industry fixed effects	yes		yes		yes		yes		yes		yes	
country fixed effects	no		yes		no		yes		no		yes	
N	385		385		385		385		385		385	
F	9.17		7.17		6.32		5.70		11.60		10.41	
R^2	0.1931		0.3235		0.2181		0.3313		0.1339		0.2713	
Vuong Z-statistic		-3.99				-4.19				-3.93		
Vuong p-value (1-sided)		0.0000				0.0000				0.0000		

Panels A-1 and A-2 present results of OLS estimation and t-statistics based on robust standard errors. The dependent variables are *total*, *mand*, and *volun*, respectively. Firm-level and country-level variables, as well as industry and country fixed effects are included in the models as indicated. We present one-sided p-values of Vuong-tests to compare R^2s of different model specifications. P-values in bold indicate significance at the 1%-level. All continuous independent variables are standardized and calculated as defined in the Appendix to Chapter 3.

Panel B: Country-level regressions (OLS & 2SLS)

	total				mand				volun			
	(1)		(2)		(3)		(4)		(5)		(6)	
enforcement	0.0354	**3.66**	0.0454	**3.05**	0.0585	**4.85**	0.0743	**4.79**	0.0181	1.59	0.0225	1.35
business sophistication	-0.0255	**-2.65**	-0.0317	**-2.74**	-0.0377	**-3.42**	-0.0480	**-4.05**	-0.0171	-1.35	-0.0194	-1.38
absence of acc. standards	-0.0191	**-2.02**	-0.0178	**-2.46**	-0.0050	-0.53	-0.0030	-0.38	-0.0327	**-2.79**	-0.0322	**-3.44**
divergence of acc. standards	0.0157	**2.12**	0.0184	**2.57**	0.0346	**3.68**	0.0390	**4.16**	0.0000	0.00	0.0010	0.11
constant	0.4076	**14.25**	0.3818	**9.27**	0.4869	**13.61**	0.4442	**10.37**	0.3411	**10.22**	0.3315	**7.01**
N	20		20		20		20		20		20	
R^2	0.4938		0.4799		0.6034		0.5791		0.4246		0.4229	

Panel B reports OLS estimation in models (1), (3), and (5). Models (2), (4), and (6) are estimated using 2SLS. We use on robust standard errors.

Panel C: Country-level regressions with extracted fixed effects (OLS & 2SLS)

	total				mand				volun			
	(1)		(2)		(3)		(4)		(5)		(6)	
enforcement	0.0283	**2.18**	0.0338	**2.42**	0.0472	**3.37**	0.0542	**3.57**	0.0144	1.03	0.0175	1.12
business sophistication	-0.0248	-1.76	-0.0289	-1.91	-0.0355	**-2.40**	-0.0407	**-2.65**	-0.0180	-1.16	-0.0203	-1.21
absence of acc. standards	-0.0125	-1.19	-0.0117	-1.39	0.0015	0.15	0.0025	0.29	-0.0260	**-2.14**	-0.0255	**-2.62**
divergence of acc. standards	0.0133	1.52	0.0151	1.89	0.0332	**3.14**	0.0354	**3.75**	-0.0027	-0.25	-0.0017	-0.18
constant	-0.0534	**-4.06**	-0.0532	**-4.78**	-0.0905	**-6.37**	-0.0903	**-7.62**	-0.0256	-1.72	-0.0255	**-2.01**
N	20		20		20		20		20		20	
R^2	0.3158		0.3104		0.4195		0.4131		0.3388		0.3374	

For Panel C, we first estimate firm-level regressions using the full set of firm-specific controls plus country-fixed effects. We subsequently regress these country-fixed effects on country-level variables. Models (1), (3), and (5) present OLS regressions. Models (2), (4), and (6) are estimated using 2SLS. We use robust standard errors. Instrumental variables for a country's legal enforcement are the country's real per capita GDP averaged from 1997 to 2006, and three binary variables indicating an English, German, French, or Scandinavian legal origin. For Panels B and C the cut-off-values for significance-levels are 2.86 for significance at the 1%-level, 2.09 for the 5%-level, and 1.72 for the 10%-level; t-values in bold indicate significances at the 5%-level. All continuous independent variables are standardized and calculated as defined in the Appendix to Chapter 3.

Models (1) are estimated with firm-level variables and industry-fixed effects (for *total, mand*, and *volun*, respectively). Models (2) are estimated with firm-level, country-level variables, and industry-fixed effects. Finally, models (3) are estimated with firm-level variables, industry-fixed effects, and country-fixed effects. Our results are as follows: First, the explanatory power increases significantly from models (1) to (2), from models (2) to (3), and from models (1) to (3). For example, the R^2 in a regression on *total* increases from 0.1931 in model (1) to 0.2404 in model (2) to 0.3235 in model (3). According to the Vuong test-statistics, these differences are statistically highly significant ($p < 0.01$). The same is true for regressions on *mand* and *volun*. Second, the inclusion of country-fixed effects does not alter our previous findings on the determinants of disclosure. The coefficients on almost all variables do not loose statistical and economic significance (see Panel A-2).[50] Third, an ANOVA analysis further corroborates our findings (see Table 3.5, Panel B). A significant part of the variations in the disclosure indices can be attributed to cross-country differences (all p-values of the ANOVA analysis are smaller than 0.0001). To sum up, country-fixed effects explain large parts of mandatory and voluntary disclosure indices, emphasizing that it is not appropriate to solely take firm-level variables into account when analyzing disclosure behavior. This also indicates that standard setters and regulators should be more aware of existing differences between country's historical roots and cultural conditions. Standard setters are already aware that companies operating in specific industries and companies of different sizes need to have industry and size specific disclosure standards. However, there seems to be no discernment in taking a country's institutional system, historical roots, and cultural values into account when setting up reporting standards. We therefore suggest to consider country specifics by standard setters – at least when setting up appropriate enforcement mechanisms across countries. Having one enforcement system across multiple countries may not address their needs sufficiently. It would be better to have country-tailored supervisory and enforcement authorities that adapt to each country's specific needs.

Country-level analysis and endogeneity

To complement our analyses, we next aggregate our disclosure indices at the country level. We regress the country-mean of each disclosure index on our five country-level variables (*enforcement, business sophistication, equity market development, absence*, and *divergence*). This approach has the advantage that each country enters the regressions only once and receives equal weight. The models labeled "OLS" in Table 3.11, Panel B present our

[50] Note that multicollinearity is still not an issue; the largest variance inflation factor in these models is 3.10 (on *size*).

findings based on simple OLS regressions with robust standard errors. In general, all previously found results are corroborated. The coefficient on *enforcement* is highly significant and positive for mandatory disclosure and less significant for voluntary disclosure. *Business sophistication* has a negative and significant impact on disclosures. The coefficient on the *absence* index is negative and significant for the voluntary disclosure index; the *divergence* index loads positive and is significant for the mandatory disclosure index. The coefficient on *equity market development* is negative and significant for both indices. The explanatory power of the models lies between 0.4246 for the voluntary disclosure model and 0.6034 for the mandatory disclosure model. The coefficient on *enforcement* in the mandatory model is by far the largest compared to all other coefficients. This clearly emphasizes that a country's enforcement is particularly important for disclosure compliance. Besides, a country's market development, and its accounting standards are systematically related to cross-country differences in disclosure levels.

The multiple regressions assume, however, that *enforcement* is an exogenous variable. If, on the other hand, enforcement and disclosure levels are simultaneously determined, our results suffer from a possible endogeneity bias. We address this concern by performing a 2SLS regression. We use a country's legal origin and its wealth as instruments for the enforcement variable as suggested by Levine (1999) and Leuz et al. (2003). While related to the level of enforcement, a country's legal origin can be considered as predetermined and exogenous to our disclosure indices. The origins of most legal systems are several centuries old and many countries obtained their legal system through occupation and colonization. We use four indicator variables for English, French, German, and Scandinavian legal origins as instrumental variables. In addition, we use a country's average per capita GDP — measured prior to our sample period, 1997 to 2006 — as an instrument because an effective legal infrastructure is costly to create and maintain, and hence a country's wealth potentially influences the level of legal enforcement.[51] All columns labeled with "2SLS" in Panel B of Table 3.11 report the second stage results of the 2SLS regression. Again, our results are robust to the potential endogeneity of enforcement. Disclosure increases in the strength of a country's enforcement and decreases in a country's capital market development. Hence, our results are not driven by a potential endogeneity bias.

[51] We show in Section 3.5 that our instruments fulfill the exclusion restriction, i.e. are not significantly related to disclosure levels.

Extracted country-fixed effects and endogeneity

Finally, we follow Hail and Leuz (2006) and extract country-fixed effects based on firm-level regressions and then regress the country-fixed effects on the country-level variables. This approach exploits firm-level information and controls for differences in country economic heterogeneity. We estimate country-fixed effects using the basic model but exclude country-level variables. Our findings are very similar in case we also include country-level variables. Panel C of Table 3.11 reports the results. As before, all columns labeled "OLS" report results of simple OLS regressions with robust standard errors, whereas columns labeled "2SLS" present the results using a 2SLS approach using the same instruments for enforcement as explained above. The coefficients in the total and mandatory regressions are generally smaller and less significant compared to the findings in Panel B. The explanatory powers are also smaller (0.4195 (0.3388) in the mandatory (voluntary) disclosure model). However, our basic findings are corroborated and robust to different model specifications (OLS, 2SLS).

3.5 Disclosure, Culture, and Enforcement

3.5.1 Descriptive Cluster Analysis

In this section, we focus on the explanatory role of cultural values on managers' disclosure practices. We begin with a cluster analysis to provide descriptive evidence on systematic disclosure patterns across groups of countries with similar cultural characteristics. The analysis is based on eleven cultural variables from Hofstede (1991, 2001) and Schwartz (1994, 1999, 2004).[52] All variables are standardized to z-scores, and a k-means cluster analysis with five distinct country clusters is conducted.[53] Panel A of Table 3.12 presents the cluster membership of our sample countries.

[52] We do not use the cultural values of the GLOBE Project (House et al. 2004) because values for Belgium and Luxembourg are missing. The inclusion of all nine GLOBE cultural variables leads to comparable clusters.

[53] We had chosen five distinct cultural clusters to allow for a more subtle classification than clusters based on legal origins.

Table 3. 12 Disclosure and Cultural Clusters

Panel A: Cluster membership of countries

	cluster 1	cluster 2	cluster 3	cluster 4	cluster 5
countries	Austria Germany Switzerland	Denmark Finland Netherlands Norway Sweden	Ireland U.K.	Belgium France Italy Luxemburg Poland	Czech Republic Greece Hungary Portugal Spain
N	84	70	79	89	63
% of sample	21.82	18.18	20.52	23.12	16.36

Panel B: Mean values of cultural variables, country variables and disclosure scores by cultural clusters

	cluster 1	cluster 2	cluster 3	cluster 4	cluster 5
cultural values					
Hofstede PD	31.64	31.04	34.11	61.89	56.56
Hofstede IND	65.64	72.16	86.59	69.21	50.57
Hofstede MAS	68.56	13.70	66.25	52.27	53.29
Hofstede UA	64.15	43.36	35.00	84.60	90.79
HAR	4.75	4.47	3.83	4.47	4.30
EMB	3.32	3.65	3.31	3.79	3.43
HIE	2.09	2.08	2.26	2.19	1.93
MAS	4.12	4.03	3.96	3.77	3.90
AFF AUT	4.55	4.27	4.16	3.77	3.75
INT AUT	5.19	4.87	4.55	4.71	4.58
EGL	5.26	5.23	4.87	5.14	4.84
Globe UA	5.22	5.06	4.61	4.25	3.78
Globe FO	4.29	4.43	4.24	3.52	3.49
Globe PD	5.23	4.44	5.15	5.19	5.19
Globe IC	3.84	4.78	4.32	4.01	3.66
Globe HO	3.41	4.08	3.87	3.49	3.56
Globe PO	4.37	4.02	4.12	4.02	3.72
Globe IGC	4.28	3.74	4.22	4.58	5.03
Globe GE	3.05	3.65	3.61	3.59	3.50
Globe AS	4.61	3.83	4.12	4.16	4.27
institutions and accounting standards					
enforcement	0.5035	0.9021	0.6290	-0.8241	-1.2982
business sophistication	0.7564	0.8115	0.9044	0.6832	0.6796
equity market development	1.5831	1.8134	3.2883	0.8761	0.9714
absence	0.2274	0.1384	0.0000	0.2343	0.3143
divergence	0.3091	0.2197	0.3142	0.2854	0.2321
disclosure scores					
total	0.53	0.52	0.52	0.53	0.45
mand	0.73	0.68	0.65	0.66	0.58
volun	0.36	0.39	0.43	0.43	0.35

Panel C: Differences in mandatory and voluntary disclosures across clusters

	cluster 1	cluster 2	cluster 3	cluster 4	volun cluster 5
cluster 1		0.0871	**0.0003**	**0.0003**	0.2261
cluster 2	**0.0279**		**0.0301**	**0.0233**	**0.0247**
cluster 3	**0.0009**	0.1180		0.3822	**0.0000**
cluster 4	**0.0022**	0.2129	0.3254		**0.0001**
cluster 5	**0.0000**	**0.0005**	**0.0079**	**0.0019**	
	mand				

This table presents results and descriptive statistics from a k-means cluster analysis using five distinct clusters and eleven cultural variables from Hofstede (1991, 2001) and Schwartz (1994, 1999, 2004). The variables are standardized to z-scores. Hofstede UA/PD/IND/MAS denote the *uncertainty avoidance / power distance / individualism / masculinity* cultural values introduced by Hofstede (1991, 2001). HAR, EMB, HIE, MAS, AFF AUT, INT AUT, and EGL denote the *harmony, embeddedness, hierarchy, mastery, affective autonomy, intellectual autonomy,* and *egalitarianism* cultural values introduced by Schwartz (1994, 1999, 2004). Globe UA/FO/PD/IC/HO/PO/IGC/GE/AS denote the *uncertainty avoidance, future orientation, power distance, institutional collectivism, human orientation, performance orientation, in-group collectivism, gender egalitarianism,* and *assertiveness* cultural values introduced by the GLOBE Project (2004). Panel A reports the cluster membership for the 20 sample countries based on the cluster analysis performed on all Hofstede (1991, 2001) and Schwartz (1994, 1999, 2004) cultural variables. Panel B reports the means of the cultural variables, the institutional variables, and the disclosure scores by cluster. Panel C presents one-sided p-values for tests of differences in the means of the mandatory (below the diagonal) and the voluntary (above the diagonal) disclosure indices across clusters using a t-test. P-values in bold indicate significances at the 5%-level. All variables are calculated as defined in the Appendix to Chapter 3.

Groupings are to some extent consistent with the common- and code-law classification, as well as geographic grouping used in prior research (see, e.g., Ball et al. (2000); Ball et al.(2003), Leuz et al. (2003)). All countries in the first cluster (c1) have a German-law tradition; it consists of Austria, Germany, and Switzerland. We label it the "German cluster". The second cluster (c2) contains all Scandinavian countries (Denmark, Finland, Norway, Sweden) and the Netherlands; we label it the "Scandinavian cluster". The countries (Ireland, U.K.) in the third cluster (c3) are the only two countries with a common-law tradition. All countries in the fourth cluster (c4) have a French-law tradition and have a common border with France (with the exemption of Poland; c4 consists of Belgium, France, Italy, Luxembourg, Poland). The fifth cluster (c5) contains two east European countries (Czech Republic and Hungary) as well as Portugal, Spain, and Greece.

Panel B of Table 3.12 reports the means of all cultural values, the institutional variables, and the disclosure scores for each cluster. The German cluster (c1) is characterized by small values of *power distance*, and high values of *masculinity*, *autonomy*, *uncertainty avoidance*, *harmony*, and *assertiveness*. The Greece cluster (c5) is characterized by the opposite dimensions of cultural values. The second (Scandinavian), third cluster (U.K.), and fourth (French) cluster lie in between the first and the fifth. The level of *uncertainty avoidance* (*Globe_UA, Hofstede_UA*) declines almost monotonically from the German cluster (c1) to the Greece cluster (c5). The same is true for *future orientation* (*Globe_FO*). Values for *performance orientation* (*Globe_PO*), *autonomy* (*AFF_AUT*), and *harmony* (*HAR*) decrease between c1 and c5 as well.

Focusing on the means of the institutional variables, we find that *enforcement* is strongest in the Scandinavian cluster (c2) and weakest in the Greece cluster (c5), *business sophistication* is highest in the U.K. cluster (c3) and smallest in the Greece cluster (c5), and the *absence* index is lowest in the U.K. cluster (c3) and highest in the Greece cluster (c5).

The average of the mandatory disclosure index is highest in the German cluster (c1) followed by the Scandinavian cluster (c2), the U.K. and French clusters (c3 and c4), and the Greece cluster (c5). The mean of voluntary disclosures is highest in the French and U.K. clusters (c4 and c3), followed by the Scandinavian cluster (c2), the German cluster (c1), and the Greek cluster (c5). This reveals that in countries with similar cultural values mandatory and voluntary disclosures are substitutes, rather than complements. The German cluster (c1), for example, complies the most with mandatory disclosure rules, but provides (nearly) the least voluntary disclosures. The only exemption is the Greece cluster in which mandatory and voluntary disclosures fall short of disclosure indices in any other cluster.

Panel C of Table 3.12 confirms that most differences between the clusters' average disclosure scores are statistically significant. The p-values presented in the upper half of the matrix refer to t-tests of differences in means between voluntary disclosures across cultural clusters. The p-values presented below the diagonal refer to tests of differences in means in mandatory disclosures across cultural clusters.

3.5.2 The Role of Culture: Multilevel Analysis

The results presented in the previous section suggest that there are systematic differences in mandatory and voluntary disclosure indices across cultural clusters. We now analyze the impact of cultural clusters and cultural values on disclosures via multilevel regression analyses.

Impact of cultural clusters on disclosure

We first focus on the impact of cultural clusters on mandatory and voluntary risk management disclosure and test for Hypothesis 3a. We therefore include indicator variables for each cultural cluster in the basic model (1). We therefore have to drop all other country-level variables in the subsequent analysis and can compare the results with those displayed in Table 3.11, Panel A-2, columns (1), (3), and (5), where we also drop country-fixed effects . We analyze the total, mandatory, and voluntary disclosure indices separately. Table 3.13 presents the results.

Table 3. 13 Disclosure and Cultural Effects

Panel A: Disclosure and the impact of cultural clusters

	total		*mand*		*volun*	
size	0.0234	**2.63**	0.0241	**2.10**	0.0245	**2.47**
leverage	0.0154	**3.21**	0.0138	**2.15**	0.0172	**3.16**
internationality	0.0151	**2.43**	0.0197	**2.47**	0.0125	1.85
profitability	0.0089	**4.70**	0.0004	0.16	0.0154	**6.64**
growth opportunities	0.0011	0.37	0.0063	**2.23**	-0.0026	-0.74
future debt increases	0.0328	**2.84**	0.0378	**2.54**	0.0284	**2.23**
future equity increases	-0.0231	-1.92	-0.0301	-1.93	-0.0168	-1.26
speculation	0.0123	0.64	0.0716	**2.66**	-0.0378	-1.67
future abnormal returns	-0.0364	**-3.12**	-0.0537	**-3.58**	-0.0238	-1.87
analyst following	-0.0005	-0.92	0.0001	0.13	-0.0012	-1.84
BIG4	0.0145	0.76	0.0105	0.45	0.0188	0.82
German cluster	0.0709	**3.93**	0.1242	**4.96**	0.0252	1.24
Scandinavian cluster	0.0561	**2.65**	0.0644	**2.39**	0.0510	**2.21**
UK cluster	0.0730	**3.86**	0.0648	**2.56**	0.0823	**3.97**
French cluster	0.0759	**3.88**	0.0633	**2.59**	0.0873	**4.03**
constant	0.4628	**16.43**	0.5848	**15.38**	0.3689	**11.09**
industry fixed effects	yes		yes		yes	
N	385		385		385	
F	8.31		7.08		12.36	
R^2	0.2357		0.2681		0.1918	
Vuong Z-statistic	-2.34		-2.50		-2.58	
Vuong p-value (1-sided)	0.0097		0.0062		0.0050	

Panel A presents results of OLS estimation and t-statistics based on robust standard errors. The dependent variable is *total* in model (1) and (2), *mand* in model (3) and (4), and *volun* in model (5) and (6). Industry fixed effects are included in the models as indicated. For the regression analysis, statistical significance is based on two-sided t-tests. The cut-off-values for significance levels are: 2.58 for significance at the 1%-level, 1.96 for the 5%-level, and 1.65 for the 10%-level; t-values in bold indicate significances at the 5%-level. We also present Z-statistics and corresponding p-values of Vuong-tests to compare R^2s of the above regressions with R^2s of regressions as presented in models (1), (3), and (5) of Panel A-2 in Table 3.11. Cultural clusters are from a k-means cluster analysis of eleven cultural variables; for details, see Table 3.7.

Panel B: Country regressions

	total				*mand*				*volun*			
	(1)		(2)		(3)		(4)		(5)		(6)	
German cluster	0.0700	**2.40**			0.1311	**3.44**			0.0205	0.76		
Scandinavian cluster	0.0662	2.01			0.0957	**2.47**			0.0452	1.39		
UK cluster	0.0919	**3.27**			0.0779	**4.16**			0.1078	**2.87**		
French cluster	0.0702	**3.37**			0.0679	**4.14**			0.0720	**2.69**		
common law			0.0263	0.63			-0.0130	-0.29			0.0589	1.29
german law			0.0010	0.03			0.0047	0.09			-0.0072	-0.18
french law			-0.0328	-0.86			-0.0499	-1.07			-0.0220	-0.6
constant	0.4542	**28.68**	0.5199	**14.92**	0.5829	**41.29**	0.6739	**15.55**	0.3505	**19.82**	0.3995	**12.22**
N	20		20		20		20		20		20	
F-statistics	4.08		1.68		6.52		1.34		3.19		1.70	
R^2	0.4086		0.1661		0.5040		0.1630		0.4113		0.1910	
Vuong Z-statistic		1.85				1.92				1.48		
Vuong p-value (1-sided)		0.0322				0.0271				0.0699		

Panel B reports results of OLS estimation and t-statistics based on robust standard errors. We aggregate the disclosure indices at the country-level and regress indicator variables for each cultural cluster on the average indices.The cut-off-values for significance levels are: 2.86 for significance at the 1%-level, 2.09 for the 5%-level, and 1.72 for the 10%-level. Figures in bold indicate significances at the 5%-level. We also present Z-statistics and corresponding p-values of Vuong-tests to compare R^2s of model (1) vs. (2), (3) vs. (4), and (5) vs. (6).

Panel C: Country-level regressions with extracted country-fixed effects

	total		*mand*		*volun*	
German cluster	0.0846	**4.04**	0.0725	**3.51**	0.0863	**2.98**
Scandinavian cluster	0.0865	**2.61**	0.0855	**2.16**	0.0811	**2.67**
UK cluster	0.0998	**5.89**	0.0708	**3.43**	0.1173	**8.05**
French cluster	0.0541	1.83	0.0283	0.97	0.0712	**2.31**
constant	-0.0978	**-5.80**	-0.0720	**-3.49**	-0.1131	**-7.99**
N	20		20		20	
F	9.88		4.84		17.24	
R^2	0.4488		0.3845		0.4510	

For Panel C, we first estimate firm-level OLS regressions with robust standard errors using the full set of firm-specific and country-specific controls plus country-fixed effects. We subsequently regress these country-fixed effects on cultural-cluster indicator variables using OLS estimation with robust standard errors. The cut-off-values for significance levels are: 2.86 for significance at the 1%-level, 2.09 for the 5%-level, and 1.72 for the 10%-level. Figures in bold indicate significances at the 5%-level. All continuous independent variables are standardized and calculated as defined in the Appendix to Chapter 3.

Panel A shows firm-level regressions on all three disclosure indices. In short, the statistical and economical significances of all coefficients are comparable to our findings without cultural indicators. In addition, the coefficients on all cultural indicators are statistically and economically highly significant (with the only exeption of the German cluster (c1) in the voluntary model). Since the Greek cluster (c5) is the benchmark cluster, all coefficients load positive. We test for the differences in explanatory power between the models presented here (with cluster indicators) and the models presented in Panel A-2 of Table 3.11 (models (1), (3), and (5) without cluster indicators) via a Vuong-test. All differences in R^2s are highly significant (p-values<0.01). Cultural clusters are able to explain more than 22% more of the variation in the total and mandatory disclosure index, and 43% more of the variation in the voluntary disclosure index.

Next, we aggregate – as in section 3.4.3 – the disclosure indices at the country level and regress indicator variables for each cultural cluster on the average indices. The benchmark cluster is again the Greek cluster (c5). Models (1), (3), and (5) in panel B of Table 3.13 present the results. To compare the explanatory power of this approach with an approach using a classification based on legal origins, we also present regression results when we include indicator variables for a country's legal origin (models (2), (4), and (6)). First, the coefficients on cultural clusters are statistically and economically highly significant and load positive in eight out of ten cases.[54] This is not surprising given that we had chosen the Greek cluster (c5) as our benchmark cluster. The opposite is true for regressions of legal origins on disclosure indices. All their coefficients are insignificant; the explanatory power of the models (2), (4), and (6) are very modest compared to the explanatory power of the models (1), (3), and (5). The differences in R^2s, again tested via a Vuong-test, are highly significant. Our findings highlight that there is something beyond legal origins. Cultural clusters – and hence, discrepancies in cultural values across countries – seem to explain corporate disclosure behavior far better than legal origins.[55] Finally, we also extract country-fixed effects from firm level regressions using the full model including all firm and country level variables. We then regress country-fixed effects on indicator variables for each cultural cluster. Panel C of Table 3.13 presents the results. In summary, cultural clusters explain on average up to 45% of the extracted country-fixed effects. Given that we have already controlled for twelve firm-level and five country-level variables, a R^2 of more than 40% indicates that cultural clusters truly add something to explain risk management disclosure behavior.

In total, Hypothesis 3a is supported: cultural clusters do have a significant impact on mandatory and voluntary risk management disclosures.

Impact of cultural values on disclosure

We now analyze which cultural value explains managers' disclosure practices best and test for Hypothesis 3b. We therefore regress three distinct sets of cultural values on each disclosure index after controlling for corporate characteristics, managers' disclosure incentives, and industry membership. Table 3.14 presents the empirical evidence. Models (1) and (4) focus on the four Hofstede (1991, 2001) cultural values, models (2) and (5) on the Schwartz (1994, 1999, 2004) values, and models (3) and (6) on the GLOBE Project (House et al. 2004) cultural values.

---

[54] There are only two exemptions: the German and Scandinavian clusters do not have a significant impact on voluntary disclosures; this is in line with the descriptive statistics presented in Panel B, Table 3.7.

[55] Note that it was legitimate to use legal origins as instrumental variables in the models presented in section 4. They fulfill the exclusion restriction while at the same time being relevant for the strength of enforcement.

Table 3. 14 Disclosure and Cultural Values

	mand						volun					
	(1)		(2)		(3)		(4)		(5)		(6)	
Hofstede UA	0.054	**2.48**					0.036	**2.31**				
Hofstede PD	-0.047	**-3.25**					0.016	1.15				
Hofstede IND	-0.027	-1.83					0.014	1.17				
Hofstede MAS	0.004	0.48					0.001	0.05				
Schw. AUT-EMB			0.022	**2.14**					-0.029	**-3.69**		
Schw. HAR-MAS			0.025	**2.49**					-0.012	**-1.45**		
Schw, EGL-HIE			-0.024	**-2.15**					-0.009	-0.80		
Globe UA					0.055	**3.81**					0.031	**2.45**
Globe GE					0.013	1.04					0.031	**3.16**
Globe FO					-0.038	**-2.51**					-0.037	**-2.82**
Globe AS					0.042	**2.61**					0.024	1.85
Globe HO					0.022	1.72					0.032	**3.05**
firm controls	yes		yes		yes		yes		yes		yes	
industry FE	yes		yes		yes		yes		yes		yes	
N	385		385		385		385		385		385	
F-statistics	6.18		5.97		6.31		10.48		14.89		9.61	
R^2	0.2487		0.2354		0.2585		0.1501		0.1829		0.1840	
p-value (Wald-test)	0.0059		0.0353		0.0001		0.0617		0.0001		0.0006	

This table presents results of OLS estimation and t-statistics based on robust standard errors. The dependent variable is *mand* in model (1), (2), and (3), and *volun* in model (4), (5), and (6). Industry fixed effects and firm-öevel controls are included in all models. Hofstede UA/PD/IND/MAS denote the *uncertainty avoidance/power distance/individualism/masculinity* cultural values introduced by Hofstede (1991, 2001). HAR, EMB, HIE, MAS, AFF AUT, INT AUT, and EGL denote the *harmony, embeddedness, hierarchy, mastery, affective autonomy, intellectual autonomy,* and *egalitarianism* cultural values introduced by Schwartz (1994, 1999, 2004). Globe UA/FO/PD/IC/HO/PO/IGC/GE/AS denote the *uncertainty avoidance, future orientation, power distance, institutional collectivism, human orientation, performance orientation, in-group collectivism, gender egalitarianism,* and *assertiveness* cultural values introduced by the GLOBE Project (2004). Firm controls include the following variables: *size, leverage, internationality, profitability, growth opportunities, future debt (equity) increase, speculation, future positive abnormal return,* and *number of analyst.* For the regression analysis, statistical significance is based on two-sided t-tests. The cut-off-values for significance levels are: 2.58 for significance at the 1%-level, 1.96 for the 5%-level, and 1.65 for the 10%-level. Figures in bold indicate significances at the 5%-level. All continuous independent variables are standardized and calculated as defined in the Appendix to Chapter 3.

Hofstede cultural values

We find that *uncertainty avoidance* is positively related to the mandatory disclosure index (model (1), coeff. = 0.0540), as expected. Its coefficient is statistically significant at the 5%-level (t-value = 2.48). The more uncertainty avoidant a culture is said to be, the more managers disclose and reveal to the public to mitigate uncertainty. This is consistent with the notion that costs associated with non-disclosure are expected to be greater in high uncertainty avoidant societies. The general public in those societies, including share- and stakeholders, has a greater demand to reduce uncertainty regarding a firm's risk management activities. Managers not complying with this demand are expected to suffer from hiding information, either in form of a loss in reputation, or a drop in their compensation level.

Managers in societies with a stronger emphasis on *power distance* comply less with mandatory disclosure rules (coeff. = -0.0473; t-value = -3.25). This finding is also consistent with our expectations. In high power distant societies, less powerful members accept that power is distributed unequally. Hence, managers are less penalized when they do not comply with mandatory disclosure rules since they exercise power in deciding what and how much to disclose.

Individualism has a negative impact on mandatory disclosure (coeff. = -0.0266, t-value = -1.83). The more individualistic a society is said to be, the less are individuals integrated into groups. Ties between insiders and outsiders of a firm are loose. Hence, managers try to withhold information by disclosing less.

Finally, the coefficient on *masculinity* is statistically and economically insignificant (coeff. = 0.0040, t-value = 0.48). This is consistent with prior research.

In total, the joint impact of all Hofstede cultural values on the amount of mandatory disclosure is statistically significant. The p-value of a Wald-test of all four Hofstede variables indicates a 1%-significance level (p-value = 0.0030). The impact of *uncertainty avoidance,* as measured by Hofstede, on mandatory disclosure is by far the largest, which is in line with our expectations.The degree of uncertainty avoidance is expected to have the largest influence on risk management and financial instruments disclosures.

Focusing on the voluntary disclosure model (model (4)), all Hofstede variables do not exhibit a significant impact on the voluntary disclosure index. The only exemption is *uncertainty avoidance* (coeff. = 0.0359, t-value = 2.41). Managers disclose more voluntarily in high uncertainty avoidant societies. Joint tests of significances corroborate that Hofstede cultural values have a slight impact on voluntary disclosures (Walt-test p-value = 0.0682).

Schwartz cultural values

The Schwartz cultural value set consists of six cultural values: autonomy, embeddedness, egalitarianism, hierarchy, harmony, and mastery. Autonomy itself is split into affective and intellectual autonomy. We will not distinguish between the two variants of autonomy and calculate a country's autonomy orientation as the average of the affective and intellectual scores. Since an emphasis on one cultural value typically accompanies a de-emphasis on the polar type, we collaps each bipolar cultural dimension to a single one by calculating its difference (as suggested in Schwartz, 2004). This approach is justified by the notion that a higher value for a certain cultural dimension (e.g. *autonomy*) typically coincides with a lower value for its bipolar counterpart (here, e.g., *embeddedness*). We therefore end up with three bipolar cultural values: *autonomy vs. embeddedness*, *harmony vs. mastery*, and *egalitarianism vs. hierarchy*.

We find that *autonomy vs. embeddedness* has a negative and significant impact on mandatory disclosure (coeff. = -0.0219, t-value = -2.14), and a negative impact on voluntary disclosure (coeff. = -0.0285, t-value = -3.69). The dimension of autonomy vs. embeddedness characterizes the relation between the person and the group, which is the most critical cultural dimension in general (Schwartz, 1999). It deals with the desirable degree of independence of the person from groups. *Autonomy* stresses the degree of self-direction and flexibility of thoughts, whereas *embeddedness* emphasizes the maintenance of the status quo and relies on social order, moderation and wisdom. With regard to risk management and financial instruments disclosure, the higher the degree of *autonomy* in a society, the less managers comply with mandatory disclosure rules. On the other hand, the higher the degree of *embeddedness*, the more they provide voluntary disclosures. Our findings are consistent with intuition, since *embeddedness* focuses more on the social welfare of the group, whereas *autonomy* focuses more on the person.

Harmony vs. mastery is positively correlated with mandatory risk disclosures (coeff. = 0.0219, t-value = 2.14), and negatively correlated with voluntary risk disclosures (coeff. = -0.0124, t-value = -1.95). The bipolar dimension addresses the desirability of harmony with the social and natural environment. Whereas *harmony* points to accepting the world as it is and relates to living in a world in peace, *mastery* supports the idea of getting ahead through active self-assertion and refers to values such as influence, competence, and ambition. In consequence, a stronger emphasis on *harmony* causes more compliance with mandatory disclosure rules, whereas a stronger emphasis on *mastery* causes more voluntary disclosures.

Egalitarianism vs. hierarchy has a positive and significant impact on mandatory disclosure (coeff. = 0.0239, t-value = 2.15), and a negative, but insignificant, impact on voluntary disclosures (coeff. = -0.0086, t-value = -0.80). The bipolar cultural value deals with the desirability of equal allocation of roles. Whereas *egalitarianism* relates to showing concern for the welfare of others and bears on the values social justice, loyalty and honesty, *hierarchy* corresponds to the legitimacy of an unequal distribution of power. (*Hierarchy* as measured by Schwartz corresponds to *power distance* as measured by Hofstede.) Consequently, we expect and find a positive impact of *egalitarianism* and a negative impact of *hierarchy* on mandatory disclosure compliance.

In total, the joint impact of all Schwartz cultural values on the mandatory and voluntary disclosure indices is statistically significant. The p-value of a Wald-test of all three Schwartz variables indicates a 5%-significance level (p-value = 0.0327) for the mandatory model, and a 1%-significance level (p-value = 0.0000) for the voluntary disclosure model.

Globe cultural values

The Globe cultural value set consist of nine different dimensions. Due to multicollinearity problems, we focus only on those dimensions which we expect to be related to risk management disclosures: *uncertainty avoidance* is the extent to which a society, organization, or group relies on social norms, rules and procedures to alleviate unpredictability of future events. We expect a positive impact of *uncertainty avoidance* on disclosure. *Assertiveness* represents the degree to which individuals are assertive, dominant and demanding in their relationships with others. We do not have any prediction on the impact of *assertiveness* on disclosure. *Gender egalitarianism* is the degree to which a collective minimizes gender inequality. We expect a positive correlation with disclosure. *Future orientation* measures the extent to which a collective encourages and rewards future-oriented behaviors such as delaying gratification, planning and investing in the future. Again, we expect a positive correlation with disclosure. Finally, *humane orientation* is the degree to which a collective encourages and rewards individuals for being fair, altruistic, generous, caring and kind to others. The impact of *humane orientation* on disclosure is expected to be positive.

Models (3) and (6) in Table 3.14 confirm (most of) our expectations. The impact of *uncertainty avoidance* is positive and significant in both the mandatory (coeff. = 0.0545, t-value = 3.81) and voluntary (coeff. = 0.0307, t-value = 2.45) disclosure model. This is consistent with our findings in models (1) and (4) when analyzing the Hofstede measure of *uncertainty avoidance.* The coefficient on *assertiveness* is positive and significant in the mandatory model (coeff. = 0.0420, t-value = 2.61) and the voluntary model (coeff. = 0.0244, t-value = 1.85). *Gender egalitarianism* exhibits no significant impact on mandatory disclosure compliance (coeff. = 0.0128, t-value = 1.04), but a highly significant impact on voluntary disclosure (coeff. = 0.0305, t-value = 3.16). *Future orientation* has a negative and significant impact on both mandatory (coeff. = -0.0381, t-value = -2.51) and voluntary (coeff. = -0.0365, t-value = -2.82) disclosure. This is in contrast to our expectations. Managers seem to disclose less today to defer disclosures into the future. Finally, the impact of *human orientation* on mandatory disclosures is positive but barely significant (coeff. = 0.0220, t-value = 1.72), whereas it is positive and highly significant on voluntary disclosure (coeff. = 0.0321, t-value = 3.05).

In total, the joint impact of all five Globe cultural values on the mandatory and voluntary disclosure indices is statistically significant. The p-value of a Wald-test of all five Globe variables indicates a 1%-significance level for both the mandatory (p-value = 0.0002) and the voluntary (p-value = 0.0003) disclosure model.

In total, Hypothesis 3b is supported by our data: cultural values do exhibit a significant impact on the amount of mandatory and voluntary risk management disclosures. The largest impact comes from the cultural value *uncertainty avoidance*. A one standard deviation increase in *uncertainty avoidance* translates into a more than 5% increase in the mandatory disclosure index and more than a 3% increase in the voluntary disclosure index.

3.5.3 Enforcement and Cultural Values

In this section, we explore the interplay of enforcement and culture and test for hypothesis 4a and 4b.[56] We hypothesize that the impact of enforcement on firms' mandatory disclosure practices is conditional on a country's cultural values (H4a). The reasoning is as follows: countries have to design institutional structures to enforce disclosures in order to assure the required amount of disclosures. A country's strength of enforcement as well as its cultural values are, however, highly interdependent. Societies with a strong emphasis on *uncertainty avoidance*, for example, do not need to rely on strong enforcement mechanisms since members of the society have internalized uncertainty avoidant behavior. We therefore expect that the impact of *enforcement* on mandatory disclosures is less pronounced in high uncertainty avoidant cultures.

---

[56] Since the strength of *enforcement* only plays a role for the mandatory disclosure index, we only analyze the mandatory disclosure index in this section.

Interaction of enforcement and culture

We analyze how the impact of enforcement on mandatory disclosures varies for countries with a low and high emphasis on different cultural attributes based on Hofstede's cultural values.[57] We estimate the full basic model (1) with industry fixed effects. We introduce interaction terms of *enforcement* and dummy variables for each cultural variable. Each dummy variable is assigned a value of 1 if the country's cultural value is above the sample median value of the respective cultural variable, and 0 otherwise. Table 3.15 presents our results.

Table 3. 15 Enforcement and Cultural Values

Panel A: Differences in disclosures and enforcement across cultures

	uncertainty avoidance		*power distance*		*individualism*		*masculinity*	
	low	high	low	high	low	high	low	high
mand	0.6369	0.6820	0.6843	0.6361	0.6825	0.6449	0.6495	0.6752
enforcement	-0.9120	0.6696	0.6573	-0.8226	-0.1450	0.1327	-0.0879	0.0805
p-value (t-test mand)	**0.0027**		**0.0014**		**0.0097**		0.0554	
p-value (t-test enforcement)	**0.0000**		**0.0000**		**0.0032**		**0.0495**	

Panel A presents mean mandatory disclosure scores and mean strengths of enforcement values for sub-samples of countries. The sub-samples are constructed based on the sample median values of Hofstede's *uncertainty avoidance, power distance, individualism,* and *masculinity* indices. We also report one-sided p-values for t-tests of differences in means across sub-samples.

[57] We only focus on the Hofstede cultural values. If we substitute *uncertainty avoidance* as measured by Hofstede with *uncertainty avoidance* as measured by Globe, and *individualism* (Hofstede) by *autonomy* (Schwartz), our results still hold.

Panel B: The interplay of enforcement and cultural values

	uncertainty avoidance		*power distance*		*individualism*		*masculinity*	
enforcement	0.0568	**2.97**	-0.0009	-0.02	0.0450	**3.04**	0.0583	**3.73**
conditional variable	0.0409	1.90	-0.0392	-0.87	-0.0360	-1.82	0.0250	1.17
*enforcement * cond. var.*	-0.0201	-1.63	0.0476	0.87	-0.0142	-1.63	-0.0152	-0.82
size	0.0243	**2.14**	0.0218	1.91	0.0228	**2.02**	0.0258	**2.20**
leverage	0.0111	1.69	0.0104	1.62	0.0104	1.59	0.0124	1.91
internationality	0.0240	**2.87**	0.0232	**2.74**	0.0228	**2.73**	0.0232	**2.78**
profitability	0.0007	0.27	0.0003	0.11	0.0006	0.26	0.0007	0.27
growth opportunities	0.0100	**3.00**	0.0096	**3.02**	0.0096	**3.15**	0.0108	**3.42**
future debt increases	0.0349	**2.35**	0.0335	**2.24**	0.0327	**2.19**	0.0340	**2.28**
future equity increases	-0.0338	**-2.16**	-0.0333	**-2.11**	-0.0321	**-2.04**	-0.0324	**-2.05**
speculation	0.0748	**2.95**	0.0769	**2.94**	0.0759	**2.92**	0.0722	**2.76**
future abnormal returns	-0.0466	**-3.02**	-0.0490	**-3.17**	-0.0470	**-3.02**	-0.0455	**-2.90**
analyst following	-0.0003	-0.42	-0.0001	-0.18	-0.0002	-0.30	-0.0001	-0.13
BIG4	0.0070	0.57	0.0019	0.17	-0.0120	-0.93	0.0006	0.05
absence	0.0378	**4.80**	0.0312	**2.74**	0.0317	**3.37**	0.0314	**2.70**
divergence	0.0300	1.26	0.0323	1.38	0.0284	1.18	0.0283	1.19
business sophistication	-0.0367	**-2.87**	-0.0367	**-2.80**	-0.0261	-1.75	-0.0390	**-3.08**
equity market development	-0.0153	-1.45	-0.0093	-0.81	-0.0126	-1.18	-0.0137	-1.24
constant	0.6230	**16.33**	0.6719	**13.18**	0.6590	**17.27**	0.6286	**16.13**
industry fixed effects	yes		yes		yes		yes	
N	385		385		385		385	
F-statistics	7.81		6.88		7.14		7.34	
R^2	0.2859		0.2830		0.2881		0.2875	

Panel B presents results of OLS estimation and t-statistics based on robust standard errors. In all models, *mand* is the dependent variable. We proxy for various cultural attributes with the Hofstede cultural values *uncertainty avoidance, power distance, individualism,* and *masculinity.* We assign the *conditional variable* a value of 1 if the country has above sample median values of *uncertainty avoidance, power distance, individualism,* and *masculinity,* and 0 otherwise. Industry fixed effects are included in the models as indicated. For the regression analysis, statistical significance is based on two-sided t-tests. The cut-off-values for significance levels are: 2.58 for significance at the 1%-level, 1.96 for the 5%-level, and 1.65 for the 10%-level; t-values in bold indicate significances at the 5%-level. All continuous independent variables are standardized and calculated as defined in the Appendix to Chapter 3.

Panel A highlights that the mandatory disclosure index as well as the strength of enforcement differ significantly across the subsamples of countries with low vs. high values for each cultural variable. The mandatory disclosure index (strength of enforcement) for firms in high uncertainty avoidant societies is on average 0.6820 (0.6696), whereas it is in low uncertainty avoidant societies only 0.6369 (-0.9120). The differences are highly significant at the 1%-significance level (p-values=0.0027 (0.0000)). Concerning the means of *mand* and *enforcement* in high vs. low power distant societies we find that differences in *mand* (0.6361 vs. 0.6843) are significant at the 1% level (p-value = 0.0014), and differences in *enforcement* (-0.8226 vs. 0.6573) are also significant at the 1% level (p-value = 0.0000). The mandatory disclosure index (strength of enforcement) for firms in societies with a strong emphasis on *individualism* is on average 0.6449 (0.1327), whereas it is in societies with a low emphasis on *individualism* 0.6825 (-0.1450). The differences are highly significant at the 1%-significance level (p-values=0.0097 (0.0032)). Concerning the means of *mand* and *enforcement* in high vs. low masculine societies we find that differences in *mand* (0.6752 vs. 0.6495) are significant at the 10% level (p-value = 0.0554), and differences in *enforcement* (0.0805 vs. -0.0879) are significant at the 5% level (p-value = 0.0495).

Panel B presents our findings in a multilevel setting. The first model focuses on *uncertainty avoidance*, the second analyzes the effect of *power distance*, the third model examines *individualism*, and the fourth model focuses on *masculinity*. Note again that the magnitudes and significances of all coefficients are consistent with our previous findings.

Focusing on the first model, we find – as expected – a statistically significant positive coefficient on *uncertainty avoidance* (coeff. = 0.0409, t-value = 1.90). Societies with a strong emphasis on *uncertainty avoidance* disclose significantly more than "uncertainty-neutral" or "uncertainty-loving" societies. The main effect of *enforcement* is positive and significant (coeff. = 0.0568, t-value = 2.97), indicating that *enforcement* has a positive impact on mandatory disclosures in low uncertainty avoidant cultures (countries from the France cluster (c4) and the Greece cluster (c5), see Table 3.12). Further, we find that the interaction effect of *enforcement* and *uncertainty avoidance* is, as expected, negative (coeff. = -0.0201). Its impact is, however, only barely significant at conventional levels (t-value = -1.63). Nevertheless, our findings reveal that *uncertainty avoidance* and *enforcement* act as substitutes, or – to interpret it differently – that the strength of *enforcement* incorporates a society's uncertainty avoidance.

In the second model, we analyze the impact of *power distance* and *enforcement* on disclosure. *Power distance* represents the extent of inequality within a society. More specifically, it measures the extent to which the less powerful members accept and expect that power is distributed unequally. We therefore expect that managers in societies with a high emphasis on *power distance* disclose less, and that enforcement is of particular importance in these countries. Our hypotheses are not really supported by the data. Whereas the directions of impacts are confirmed, all effects are statistically insignificant. The econometric model suffers from a large multicollinearity problem, indicated by variance inflation factors far above 100 (mean VIF = 12.77).

The third model focuses on *individualism*. In societies with a high emphasis on *individualism* everyone is expected to look after him-/herself. We therefore expect managers in high individualistic societies to comply less with mandatory disclosure rules. In addition, we expect *enforcement* to have a larger impact on mandatory disclosures in individualistic societies compared to its impact in societies that stress collectivism. The data confirm our main hypotheses. *Individualism* has a significant negative influence on mandatory disclosures (coeff. = -0.0360, t-value = -1.83). The coefficient on *enforcement* is positive and significant (coeff. = 0.0450, t-value = 3.46). The interaction term, however, is negative, contrary to what we had expected (coeff. = -0.0142). However, the coefficient is only barely significant (t-value = -1.63). Summing the main effect and the interaction effect still results in an economically positive and significant impact of *enforcement* on mandatory disclosures.

Finally, the last model presents results on the *masculinity* cultural value. In line with prior studies, we find no significant impact of *masculinity* on disclosure (coeff. = 0.0250, t-value = 1.17). The impact of *enforcement* in feminine societies is positive and significant (coeff. = 0.0583, t-value = 3.73), the impact in masculine societies is smaller (coeff. on interaction term = -0.0152, t-value = -0.82).

In sum, hypothesis 4a is supported by the data. We conclude that societies with a weak emphasis on uncertainty avoidance, a strong emphasis on power distance, and a weak emphasis on masculinity should enhance their enforcement mechanisms to assure the required level of corporate mandatory disclosures.

Predicted strength of enforcement based on cultural values

In our final set of analyses we directly address the concern that enforcement mechanisms are embedded in a country's cultural system. We therefore regress *enforcement* on Hofstede's four cultural variables. The R^2 lies at 0.7094. We then take the predicted values based on this regression (*enfo_p*) and compute the differences between the observed levels of enforcement and the predicted level of enforcement (*enfo_r*). *Enfo_p* measures the indirect impact of culture on disclosure via the mediator variable *enforcement*. *Enfo_r* measures the isolated impact of enforcement on disclosure that goes beyond what cultural values predict. Table 3.16, Panel A presents the predicted and residual enforcement figures per country.

Table 3. 16 Direct and Indirect Effect of Culture on Enforcement and Disclosure

Panel A: Predicted and residual enforcement based on cultural values

	observed	Hofstede	
	enforcement	enfo_p	enfor_r
Austria	0.5890	0.6858	-0.0969
Belgium	-0.0043	-0.9617	0.9574
Czech Republic	-1.5301	-0.8466	-0.6834
Denmark	1.2245	1.7288	-0.5043
Finland	0.9332	0.6669	0.2664
France	-0.5352	-0.9626	0.4274
Germany	0.3310	0.0959	0.2351
Greece	-1.9316	-1.4859	-0.4457
Hungary	-1.4905	-0.5142	-0.9763
Ireland	0.5353	0.5313	0.0040
Italy	-2.0735	-0.4681	-1.6054
Luxemburg	0.8598	-0.0237	0.8835
Netherlands	0.7613	0.9072	-0.1459
Norway	0.7412	1.1143	-0.3731
Poland	-2.3189	-1.4355	-0.8833
Portugal	-1.0880	-1.3507	0.2628
Spain	-0.8555	-0.8099	-0.0455
Sweden	0.9134	1.2783	-0.3649
Switzerland	0.9784	0.1303	0.8481
United Kingdom	0.6426	0.5636	0.0790
Total	-0.2084	-0.0578	-0.1081
F-statistic		352.80	
R^2		0.7094	

Panel A presents results of a regression of *enforcement* on Hofstede's cultural. *Enfo_p* is the predicted value of enforcement based on the regressions of *enforcement* on cultural values. *Enfo_r* is the difference of *observed enforcement* and *enfo_p*.

Panel B: Predicted and residual enforcement and their effect on disclosure

	mand	
enforcement_predicted	0.0697	**3.22**
enforcement_residual	0.0263	**2.58**
uncertainty avoidance	0.0354	**1.92**
individualism	0.0081	0.63
masculinity	0.0197	1.45
size	0.0238	**2.05**
leverage	0.0126	1.93
internationality	0.0229	**2.74**
profitability	0.0002	0.08
growth opportunities	0.0105	**3.46**
future debt increases	0.0324	**2.15**
future equity increases	-0.0318	**-1.99**
speculation	0.0732	**2.75**
future abnormal returns	-0.0468	**-2.94**
analyst following	0.0000	0.00
BIG4	0.0308	1.28
absence of acc. standards	-0.0141	-0.93
divergence of acc. standards	0.0207	1.43
business sophistication	-0.0385	**-2.67**
equity market development	-0.0141	-1.26
constant	0.6358	**17.42**
industry fixed effects	yes	
N	385	
F	6.70	
R^2	0.2886	

Panel B presents results of a regression of *mand* on *enfo_p, enfo_r,* and three cultural values plus control variables.The cut-off-values for significance levels are: 2.58 for significance at the 1%-level, 1.96 for the 5%-level, and 1.65 for the 10%-level. Figures in bold indicate significances at the 5%-level. All continuous independent variables are standardized and calculated as defined in the Appendix to Chapter 3.

We hypothesize *enforcement_predicted* and *enforcement_residual* to be positive and significant in a regression on the mandatory disclosure index. We also include the Hofstede cultural values in our regressions to measure the direct impact of culture. Panel B of Table 3.16 presents our findings. In general, the coefficients on *enforcement_predicted* and *enforcement_residual* are positive and highly significant. Note, however, that one cannot interpret these coefficients as the impact of *enforcement* on mandatory disclosures. The significant and positive coefficients solely confirm that the decomposition of *enforcement* into a predicted and a residual component can reasonably well explain disclosure behavior. It is noteworthy to point out that the impact of *enforcement_predicted* (coeff. = 0.0697, t-value = 3.22) is more than twice as large as the impact of *enforcement_residual* (coeff. = 0.0263, t-value = 2.58). Besides, *uncertainty avoidance* is positively related to mandatory disclosures (coeff. = 0.0354, t-value = 1.92). *Individualism* and *masculinity* are also positively related to mandatory risk disclosures, their impact is, however, insignificant. In total, this confirms that cultural values have both an indirect impact on disclosure (via the mediator variable *enforcement*), as well as a direct impact on managers' disclosure decisions. Hypothesis 4b is therefore supported.

3.6 Conclusion

In this study, we examine firms' compliance with mandatory disclosure rules. We focus on European firms that adopted IFRS and analyze their 2007 annual reports with regard to mandatory (and voluntary) risk management and financial instruments disclosures.

We find a huge variation in corporate risk management disclosures among our sample firms. Firms comply with mandatory disclosure rules with an average of 66% only. This might cause some concern, given that all firms are subject to the same accounting rules. To explore the huge variation in mandatory and voluntary disclosures, we classify determinants of disclosure into four main groups: *managers disclosure incentives'*, *accounting standards, business structure*, and *institutions*. All groups taken together form a comprehensive picture of a firm's disclosure incentives. We find that each group taken alone and all groups together have a significant impact on disclosure behavior.

A further analysis of the mandatory disclosure index reveals that the strength of a country's legal enforcement is more pronounced for firms that face a higher demand for accounting information by outsiders. We also find that country characteristics explain more than 60% (40%) of the variation in cross-country mandatory (voluntary) disclosure.

We further document that cultural values account for a huge part of variation in disclosure indices. A cluster analysis of various cultural values reveals that mandatory and voluntary disclosures vary significantly across five cultural clusters. The explanatory power of cultural clusters in a regression on the mandatory disclosure index is twice as large as a regression of legal origins on the same index. We also find that cultural values have a direct impact on firms' disclosure practices. For instance, firms in societies with a strong emphasis on uncertainty avoidance disclose more, both mandatorily and voluntarily. Finally, we find that cultural values affect managers' disclosure practices through enforcement both directly and indirectly.

We contribute to the literature in various ways. First, we show that mandatory and voluntary disclosures are not determined by accounting standards alone. Our study supports the view that accounting harmonization is unlikely to be achieved without harmonizing enforcement and alignment of disclosure incentives across countries and firms. Second, we analyze the impact of differences between previously relevant local GAAP and current IFRS standards on firms' disclosure behavior. Third, we contribute to the literature on the impact of enforcement and institutions on disclosure practices. Our study directly examines the influence of enforcement on (1) firms' compliance with mandatory accounting rules, and (2) firms' voluntary disclosure choices. Fourth, we also contribute to the literature on the importance of culture for accounting. Finally, we also contribute to the literature on risk management and financial instruments disclosure by analyzing risk management disclosures.

Our results have implications for standard setters and policy makers. Our findings indicate that cultural values and habits can explain huge parts in variations of disclosure indices across European countries. This suggests that identical monitoring of each member country by EU institutions is not appropriate. Instead, a tailored monitoring of each country dependent on cultural values and habits would be more efficient than imposing the same monitoring efforts on all countries. The ongoing crisis in the European Union which mainly affected Southern European countries corroborates our conclusion. Cultural habits do not only manifest in governmental budget discipline. They also affect companies' disclosure and disclosure behavior. Hence, when concluding that certain member states should be under greater scrutiny of supervisory councils, companies in these countries should also be on a more pronounced watch of regulators. This certainly helps to ensure consistent financial disclosure across all member states.

Appendix to Chapter 3

Variable Definitions

Dependent variables:

total	total unweighted disclosure score based on a maximum of 99 disclosure items; non-disclosure of irrelevant items is not penalized (*annual reports*)
mand	mandatory unweighted disclosure score based on a maximum of 25 disclosure items; non-disclosure of irrelevant items is not penalized (*annual reports*)
volun	voluntary unweighted disclosure score based on a maximum of 74 disclosure items; non-disclosure of irrelevant items is not penalized (*annual reports*)

Independent variables:

size	the natural log of total assets in millions USD (*Worldscope)*
leverage	total debt/total assets ratio (*Worldscope)*
internationality	foreign assets/total assets ratio; firms with missing data are assumed not to have foreign assets (*Worldscope)*
profitability	net income/net sales ratio (*Worldscope)*
growth opportunities	market value of common equity divided by book value of common equity (*Datastream, Worldscope)*
future debt increase	dummy variable coded 1 if the firm has a debt increase superior to the median debt increase of the sample in the next two years, and 0 otherwise (*Worldscope)*
future equity increase	dummy variable coded 1 if the firm has a equity increase superior to the median equity increase of the sample in the next two years, and 0 otherwise (*Worldscope)*
future positive abnormal return	dummy variable coded 1 if the firm shows a positive market-adjusted stock return over the next year, and 0 otherwise; we use the DJ STOXX 600 as the market index (*Datastream*)

speculation	dummy variable coded 1 if the firm states in its annual report that it engages in speculative activities with derivatives, and 0 otherwise (*annual reports*)
competition	Herfindahl index calculated over net sales and two-digit SIC industry classification; it ranges from 0 to 1 whereas a higher value indicates smaller competition (*Worldscope)*
number of analysts	the number of unique analysts making a forecast of the firm's annual earnings (*I/B/E/S*)
BIG4 auditor	dummy variable coded one if the firm is audited by a BIG4 audit firm, and 0 otherwise (*Worldscope)*
absence	the number of accounting topics not covered under national GAAP but regulated by IFRS (*Ding, Jeanjean and Stolowy (2005)*)
divergence	number of accounting topics covered under both IFRS and national GAAP but which prescribe different accounting methods (*Ding, Jeanjean and Stolowy (2005)*)
enforcement	factor score of a principal component factor analysis with rotated factor matrix of the following four variables: (1) rule of law, (2) regulatory quality, (3) government effectiveness, (4) corruption index (variables are taken from *Kaufmann et al. (2009)*)
business sophistication	average value of the following three variables: (1) investment freedom, (2) financial freedom, (3) business freedom (variables taken from *Heritage Foundation (2009)*)
equity market development	market capitalization of traded stocks/GDP (*World Bank*)
legal systems	dummy variables indicating whether a country has an English, German, French, or Scandinavian legal origin (*LaPorta et al. (1998)*)
industry	dichotomous variable used to represent different industries at the two-digit SIC-code level (*Worldscope)*

Hofstede (1991, 2001) cultural values:

uncertainty avoidance	deals with a society's intolerance for uncertainty and ambiguity. It indicates to what extent a culture affects its members' preferences towards unstructured situations. Uncertainty avoiding cultures try to minimize the possibility of such situations by strict laws and rules, safety and security measures.
power distance	is the extent to which the less powerful members of organizations and institutions accept and expect that power is distributed unequally.
individualism	measures the degree to which individuals are integrated into groups. On the individualist side we find societies in which the ties between individuals are loose except within the nuclear family. On the collectivist side are societies in which people are integrated into strong, cohesive in-groups.
masculinity	versus its opposite, femininity, refers to the distribution of roles between the genders. Masculine societies stress achievement, heroism, assertiveness and material success. Feminine societies stress relationships, modesty, caring for the weak and quality of life.

Schwartz (1994, 1999, 2004) cultural values:

intellectual autonomy	emphasizes self-direction and flexibility of thoughts
affective autonomy	stresses stimulation and hedonism
embeddedness	emphasizes the maintenance of the status quo and relies on social order, respect for tradition, moderation and wisdom
egalitarianism	relates to sharing basic interests and showing concern for the welfare of others and bears on the values equality, social justice, loyalty and honesty
hierarchy	corresponds to the legitimacy of an unequal distribution of power and resources and applies to values such as authority, wealth and humbleness
harmony	points to accepting the world as it is and relates to unity with nature, protecting the environment, and world in peace

mastery	supports the idea of getting ahead through active self-assertion and refers to values such as influence, competence, daring and ambition

Globe (2004) cultural values:

power distance	is the degree to which members of a collective expect power to be distributed equally
uncertainty avoidance	is the extent to which a society, organization, or group relies on social norms, rules and procedures to alleviate unpredictability of future events
humane orientation	is the degree to which a collective encourages and rewards individuals for being fair, altruistic, generous, caring and kind to others
institutional collectivism	reflects the degree to which individuals are integrated into groups within the society
in-group collectivism	focuses on the degree to which individuals have strong ties to their small immediate group
assertiveness	represents the degree to which individuals are assertive, dominant & demanding in their relationships with others
gender egalitarianism	is the degree to which a collective minimizes gender inequality
future orientation	measures the extent to which a collective encourages and rewards future-oriented behaviors such as delaying gratification, planning and investing in the future
performance orientation	proxies for the degree to which a collective encourages and rewards group members for performance improvement and excellence

Chapter 4

Conclusions

Disclosure studies have been a significant part of the accounting and finance literature over the past decades. However, important questions regarding the observed levels of disclosure, the determinants of disclosure, as well as the consequences of disclosure remain still unanswered. This thesis addresses each of these questions in a specific research setting and tries to shed light on European firms' disclosure practices around the adoption of IFRS.

The first study is motivated by the empirical evidence that some firms from non-English speaking countries publish an annual report in English in addition to their local language annual report, while other firms do not. Prior research has already analyzed the determinants of publishing an English annual report. However, the more interesting question is whether those firms experience economic benefits after the disclosure of narrative and financial information in a widely spoken language. We hypothesize that firms issuing an annual report in English will (1) experience a decrease in information asymmetry, (2) an increase in their analyst following, and (3) attract new and more foreign investors.

To test these hypotheses, we sample 113 firms from 15 European countries. Each firm decided to publish an annual report in English for the first time between 2004 and 2007. We analyze proxies for information asymmetry (bid-ask spreads, zero return trading days), analyst following (number of analysts issuing at least one EPS forecast during the year), and foreign ownership (number of foreign owners to total owners for each firm-year observation) before and after the release of the English annual report. We control for the adoption of IFRS, for the information content of annual reports, for cross-listing, and for many other factors as well.

Our research design addresses two major problems: (1) disentangling the "news" from the "information asymmetry" effect of publishing an English annual report by employing a difference-in-differences setting, and (2) controlling for a self-selection bias by benchmarking our results to a control group of firms selected via a propensity score matching procedure. The combination of both techniques encounters most problems associated with a potential self-selection bias and allows controlling for any other confounding factors.

We find that all our hypotheses are confirmed by the underlying data. Firms publishing an annual report in English experience reductions in information asymmetry, and increases in analyst following and foreign ownership. All these findings are in relation to a group of control firms, which are as similar as possible to the treatment firms, but which do not release an English annual report. Furthermore, all results are corroborated when using an econometric approach suggested by Heckman (1979).

Our study thus contributes to the literature on market participants' responses to firms' communication policy and disclosure patterns. While prior literature has identified the use of the English language as a possible explanation for various phenomena observed in capital markets (home bias, institutional ownership, trading behavior etc.), our study is the first to directly address the question of the possible economic consequences of issuing an annual report in English.

The study could be extended in a number of different directions. One possibility would be to analyze how financial analysts' forecast properties may be influenced by the language of the annual report. Another possibility would be to extend the examination of the "language barrier issue" beyond the annual report.

The second study is motivated by the important debate regarding the effects of accounting standards as prescribed by International Financial Reporting Standards (IFRS) on firms' disclosure behavior. We investigate mandatory disclosure compliance and voluntary disclosure patterns using a sample of 385 firms from 20 European countries in the year 2007. We construct three different disclosure indices – a total disclosure index, as well as a mandatory and voluntary disclosure index. We document that firms comply on average to only 66% with mandatory disclosure rules. We also find that the mean of the voluntary disclosure index is only at 40%. Especially our first finding causes for serious concern, given that all firms are subject to the same set of accounting standards.

In a series of tests we analyze the determinants of firms' disclosure practices. Firstly, we find that four different groups of determinants – *managers' incentives, firms' business structure, accounting standards,* and *countries' institutions* – equally affect the mandatory as well as the voluntary disclosure index. Sensitivity analyses show that our results hold when we (i) extract country-fixed effects, (ii) collapse our data set at the country level, and (iii) control for a possible endogeneity problem of enforcement via a two stage least squares (2SLS) regression.

Secondly, we find that enforcement is generally positively and significantly related to mandatory disclosure compliance. We also find that the (perceived) strength of enforcement at the firm level is conditional on outsiders' demand for accounting information. The higher outsiders' demand for information, the stronger the positive impact of enforcement on the mandatory disclosure index.

Thirdly, firms' disclosure patterns vary significantly across five cultural clusters – which we obtain via a cluster analysis of 20 different cultural values. We also find that cultural values *per se* are highly correlated with the disclosure indices. The highest impact thereby comes from *uncertainty avoidance*.

The study contributes to prior research on the determinants of disclosure. While previous studies typically have analyzed disclosure patterns of U.S. firms by using relatively old data from the 1992/1993 CIFAR index, our study analyzes a large dataset of nearly 400 European firms form the financial year 2007. We also contribute to the growing literature on the role of enforcement, institutions, and culture. The results of this study are of particular interest to accounting standard bodies when assessing the effects of financial reporting standards.

Our results should be, however, interpreted with caution. Firstly, the construction of the mandatory as well as the voluntary disclosure index involves some degree of subjectivity. Secondly, our results rely on *risk management and financial instruments* disclosure and cannot be easily generalized to a broader disclosure behavior. Thirdly, we only observe a cross-section of firms' disclosure such that we cannot identify how disclosure evolves over time. Each of these drawbacks, however, provides ample opportunities to extend the research area in the near future.

References

Adelopo, I. A., and R. C. Moure. 2010. Time and Country Specific Institutional Effects on Corporate Social Disclosure by Financial Institutions: Evidence from Fourteen European Countries. *SSRN eLibrary*.

Adrem, A. H. 1999. Essays on disclosure practices in Sweden – Causes and effects. In *Ph.D. dissertation*: Lund University, Sweden.

Ahmed, A. S., and C. Takeda. 1995. Stock Market Valuation of Gains and Losses on Commercial Banks' Investment Securities: An Empirical Analysis. *Journal of Accounting and Economics* 20 (2):207-225.

Ahmed, K., and J. K. Courtis. 1999. Associations between corporate characteristics and disclosure levels in annual reports: A meta-analysis. *The British Accounting Review* 31 (1):35-61.

Ali, A., T.-Y. Chen, and S. Radhakrishnan. 2007. Corporate disclosures by family firms. *Journal of Accounting & Economics* 44 (1/2):238-286.

Ali, A., and L.-S. Hwang. 2000. Country-Specific Factors Related to Financial Reporting and the Value Relevance of Accounting Data. *Journal of Accounting Research* 38 (1):1-21.

Allayannis, G., and E. Ofek. 2001. Exchange Rate Exposure, Hedging, and the Use of Foreign Currency Derivatives. *Journal of International Money and Finance* 20 (2):273-296.

Altamuro, J., and A. Beatty. 2010. How does internal control regulation affect financial reporting? *Journal of Accounting & Economics* 49 (1/2):58-74.

Antia, M., J. B. Lin, and C. Pantzalis. 2007. Cultural Distance and Valuation of Multinational Corporations. *Journal of Multinational Financial Management* 17 (5):365-383.

Archambault, J. J., and M. E. Archambault. 2003. A multinational test of determinants of corporate disclosure. *The International Journal of Accounting* 38 (2):173-194.

Armstrong, C. S., M. E. Barth, A. D. Jagolinzer, and E. J. Riedl. 2010a. Market Reaction to the Adoption of IFRS in Europe. *Accounting Review* 85 (1):31-61.

———. 2010b. Market Reaction to the Adoption of IFRS in Europe. *The Accounting Review* 85 (1):31-61.

Armstrong, C. S., J. E. Core, D. J. Taylor, and R. E. Verrecchia. 2011. When Does Information Asymmetry Affect the Cost of Capital? *Journal of Accounting Research* 49 (1):1-40.

Armstrong, C. S., A. D. Jagolinzer, and D. F. Larcker. 2010c. Chief Executive Officer Equity Incentives and Accounting Irregularities. *Journal of Accounting Research* 48 (2):225-271.

Arya, A., and B. Mittendorf. 2007. The interaction among disclosure, competition between firms, and analyst following. *Journal of Accounting & Economics* 43 (2/3):321-339.

Ashbaugh-Skaife, H. A., J. Gassen, and R. LaFond. 2006. Does Stock Price Synchronicity Represent Firm-Specific Information? The International Evidence: Available at SSRN: http://ssrn.com/abstract=768024.

Bae, K.-H., R. M. Stulz, and H. Tan. 2008a. Do local analysts know more? A cross-country study of the performance of local analysts and foreign analysts. *Journal of Financial Economics* 88 (3):581-606.

Bae, K.-H., H. Tan, and M. Welker. 2008b. International GAAP Differences: The Impact on Foreign Analysts. *The Accounting Review* 83 (3):593-628.

Baginski, S. P., J. M. Hassell, and M. D. Kimbrough. 2004. Why Do Managers Explain Their Earnings Forecasts? *Journal of Accounting Research* 42 (1):1-29.

Baker, H. K., J. R. Nofsinger, and D. G. Weaver. 2002. International Cross Listing and Visibility. *Journal of Financial and Quantitative Analysis* 37:595-521.

Ball, R. 1995. Making accounting more international: Why, how, and how far will it go? *Journal of Applied Corporate Finance* 8:19-29.

———. 2006. International Financial Reporting Standards (IFRS): pros and cons for investors. *Accounting & Business Research* 36:5-27.

Ball, R., S. P. Kothari, and A. Robin. 2000. The Effect of International Institutional Factors on Properties of Accounting Earnings. *Journal of Accounting and Economics* 29 (1):1-51.

Ball, R., A. Robin, and J. S. Wu. 2003. Incentives versus standards: properties of accounting income in four East Asian countries. *Journal of Accounting & Economics* 36 (1-3):235.

Ball, R., and L. Shivakumar. 2005. Earnings quality in UK private firms: comparative loss recognition timeliness. *Journal of Accounting & Economics* 39 (1):83-128.

Barker, R. G. 1998. The market for information -- evidence from finance directors, analysts and fund managers. *Accounting & Business Research* 29 (1):3-20.

Barth, M. E., W. R. Landsman, and M. H. Lang. 2008. International Accounting Standards and Accounting Quality. *Journal of Accounting Research* 46 (3):467-498.

Beaver, W. H. 1981. Market Efficiency. *The Accounting Review* 56 (1):23-37.

Bekaert, G., C. R. Harvey, and C. Lundblad. 2007. Liquidity and Expected Returns: Lessons from Emerging Markets. *Review of Financial Studies* 20 (6):1783-1831.

Bekaert, G., C. R. Harvey, C. T. Lundblad, and S. Siegel. 2010. The European Union, the Euro, and Equity Market Integration. In *Working Paper*: Available at SSRN: http://ssrn.com/abstract=1573308.

Berger, A. N., and G. F. Udell. 1998. The Economics of Small Business Finance: The Roles of Private Equity and Debt Markets in the Financial Growth Cycle. *Journal of Banking and Finance* 22:613-673.

Bertrand, M., E. Duflo, and S. Mullainathan. 2004. How much Should we Trust Difference-in-Differences Estimates. *Quarterly Journal of Economics* 119 (1):249-275.

Beyer, A., and I. Guttman. 2011. Voluntary Disclosure, Manipulation and Real Effects. *Rock Center for Corporate Governance at Stanford University Working Paper No. 85.*

Board, O. 2009. Competition and Disclosure. *The Journal of Industrial Economics* 57 (1):197-213.

Bodnar, G. M., J. R. Graham, C. R. Harvey, and R. C. Marston. 2012. Managing Risk Management. *SSRN eLibrary*.

Bodnar, G. M., G. S. Hayt, and R. C. Marston. 1996. 1995 Wharton Survey of Derivatives Usage by US Non-Financial Firms. *FM: The Journal of the Financial Management Association* 25 (4):113-133.

———. 1998. 1998 Wharton survey of financial risk management by US non-financial firms. *FM: The Journal of the Financial Management Association* 27 (4):70.

Bodnar, G. M., G. S. Hayt, R. C. Marston, and C. W. Smithson. 1995. Wharton Survey of Derivatives Usage by U.S. Non-Financial Firms. *FM: The Journal of the Financial Management Association* 24 (2):104-114.

Bonaccorsi, A. 1992. On the Relationship Between Firm Size and Export Intensity. *Journal of International Business Studies* 23 (4):605-635.

Botosan, C. A. 1997. Disclosure Level and the Cost of Equity Capital. *The Accounting Review* 72 (3):323-349.

Botosan, C. A., and M. A. Plumlee. 2002. A Re-examination of Disclosure Level and the Expected Cost of Equity Capital. *Journal of Accounting Research* 40 (1):21-40.

Bradshaw, M. T., B. J. Bushee, and G. S. Miller. 2004. Accounting Choice, Home Bias, and U.S. Investment in Non-U.S. Firms. *Journal of Accounting Research* 42 (5):795-841.

Bradshaw, M. T., and G. S. Miller. 2008. Will Harmonizing Accounting Standards Really Harmonize Accounting? Evidence from Non-U.S. Firms Adopting U.S. GAAP. *Journal of Accounting, Auditing & Finance* 23 (2):233-263.

Breuer, W., B. Quinten, and A. J. Salzmann. 2009. Bank vs. Bond Finance: A Cultural View of Corporate Debt Financing. *SSRN eLibrary*.

Burgstahler, D. C., L. Hail, and C. Leuz. 2006. The Importance of Reporting Incentives: Earnings Management in European Private and Public Firms. *Accounting Review* 81 (5):983-1016.

Burns, N., and S. Kedia. 2006. The impact of performance-based compensation on misreporting. *Journal of Financial Economics* 79 (1):35-67.

Bushee, B. J. 2001. Do Institutional Investors Prefer Near-Term Earnings over Long-Run Value? *Contemporary Accounting Research* 18 (2):207-246.

Bushee, B. J., and G. S. Miller. 2012. Investor relations, firm visibility, and investor following. *The Accounting Review* 87 (3):867-897.

Bushman, R. M., J. D. Piotroski, and A. J. Smith. 2004. What Determines Corporate Transparency? *CFA Digest* 34 (4):27-28.

Byard, D., Y. Li, and Y. Yu. 2010. The effect of mandatory IFRS adoption on analysts' forecast error. *Journal of Accounting Research* 49 (1):69-96.

Campbell, D., A. Cornelia Beck, and P. Shrives. 2005. A note on comparative language interrogation for content analysis: The example of English vs. German. *British Accounting Review* 37 (3):339-350.

Campbell, J. L. 2006. Institutional Analysis and the Paradox of Corporate Social Responsibility. *American Behavioral Scientist* 49 (7):925-938.

———. 2007. Why would corporations behave in socially responsible ways? An institutional theory of corporate social responsibility. *Academy of Management Review* 32 (3):946-967.

CESR. 2010. Activity Report on IFRS Enforcement 2009. Paris: Committee of European Securities Regulators.

Chalmers, K., and J. M. Godfrey. 2004. Reputation costs: the impetus for voluntary derivative financial instrument reporting. *Accounting, Organizations & Society* 29 (2):95.

Chan, K., V. Covrig, and L. Ng. 2005. What Determines the Domestic Bias and Foreign Bias? Evidence from Mutual Fund Equity Allocations Worldwide. *Journal of Finance* 60 (3):1495-1534.

Chan, K., A. J. Menkveld, and Z. Yang. 2008. Information Asymmetry and Asset Prices: Evidence from the China Foreign Share Discount. *Journal of Finance* 63 (1):159-196.

Chan, K. H., K. Z. Lin, and P. Lai Lan Mo. 2003. An Empirical Study on the Impact of Culture on Audit-Detected Accounting Errors. *Auditing* 22 (2):281-295.

Chang, L. S., and K. S. Most. 1985. *The Perceived Usefulness of Financial Statements for Investors Decisions*. Miami, FL.: Florida International University Press.

Chang, L. S., K. S. Most, and C. W. Brain. 1983. The utility of annual reports: an international study. *Journal of International Business Studies* 14 (1):63-84.

Charles, M. 2007. Language Matters in Global Communication: Article Based on ORA Lecture, October 2006. *Journal of Business Communication* 44 (3):260-282.

Chavent, M., Y. Ding, L. Fu, H. Stolowy, and H. Wang. 2006. Disclosure and determinants studies: An extension using the Divisive Clustering Method (DIV). *European Accounting Review* 15 (2):181-218.

Cheng, S., and X. Xu. 2006. The role of peer performance in managerial compensation surrounding the 1996 Telecommunications Act. *Journal of Accounting & Public Policy* 25 (5):596-608.

Chordia, T., R. Roll, and A. Subrahmanyam. 2000. Co-Movements in Bid-Ask Spreads and Market Depth. *Financial Analysts Journal* 56:23-27.

Christensen, H. B., L. Hail, and C. Leuz. 2011. Capital-Market Effects of Securities Regulation: The Role of Prior Regulation, Implementation and Enforcement. *SSRN eLibrary*.

Christensen, H. B., E. Lee, and M. Walker. 2008. Incentives or Standards: What Determines Accounting Quality Changes Around IFRS Adoption? In *SSRN eLibrary*: Available at SSRN: http://ssrn.com/abstract=1013054.

Chui, A. C. W., S. Titman, and K. C. J. Wei. 2010. Individualism and Momentum around the World. *Journal of Finance* 65 (1):361-392.

Cooke, T. E. 1989. Disclosure in the Corporate Annual Reports of Swedish Companies. *Accounting & Business Research* 19 (74):113-124.

Core, J. E. 2001. A review of the empirical disclosure literature: discussion. *Journal of Accounting and Economics* 31 (1-3):441-456.

Covrig, V. M., M. L. DeFond, and M. Hung. 2007. Home Bias, Foreign Mutual Fund Holdings, and the Voluntary Adoption of International Accounting Standards. *Journal of Accounting Research* 45 (1):41-70.

Dahlquist, M., and G. Robertsson. 2001. Direct Foreign Ownership, Institutional Investors, and Firm Characteristics. *Journal of Financial Economics* 59 (1):413-440.

Daske, H., L. Hail, C. Leuz, and R. Verdi. 2008. Mandatory IFRS Reporting around the World: Early Evidence on the Economic Consequences. *Journal of Accounting Research* 46 (5):1085-1142.

———. 2013. Adopting a Label: Heterogeneity in the Economic Consequences Around IAS/IFRS Adoptions. *Journal of Accounting Research* 51 (3):495-547.

DeAngelo, L. E. 1981. Auditor size and audit quality. *Journal of Accounting & Economics* 3 (3):183-199.

DeHaan, E., F. Hodge, and T. Shevlin. 2012. Does Voluntary Adoption of a Clawback Provision Improve Financial Reporting Quality? *Contemporary Accounting Research* Forthcoming.

DeMarzo, P., and D. Duffie. 1995. Corporate incentives for hedging and hedge accounting. *Review of Financial Studies* 8 (3):743-771.

Demirgüç-Kunt, A., T. Beck, and V. Maksimovic. 2002. *Financing Patterns Around the World: The Role of Institutions*: The World Bank Group.

Diamond, D. W., and R. E. Verrecchia. 1991. Disclosure, Liquidity and the Cost of Capital. *Journal of Finance* 46 (2):1325-1359.

Ding, Y., O.-K. Hope, T. Jeanjean, and H. Stolowy. 2007. Differences between domestic accounting standards and IAS: Measurement, determinants and implications. *Journal of Accounting and Public Policy* 26 (1):1-38.

Ding, Y., T. Jeanjean, and H. Stolowy. 2005. Why do national GAAP differ from IAS? The role of culture. *The International Journal of Accounting* 40 (4):325-350.

Djankov, S., E. Glaeser, R. La Porta, F. Lopez-de-Silanes, and A. Shleifer. 2003. The new comparative economics. *Journal of Comparative Economics* 31 (4):595.

Dobler, M. 2008. Incentives for risk reporting—A discretionary disclosure and cheap talk approach. . *The International Journal of Accounting* 42 (3):184-206.

Dobler, M., K. Lajili, and D. Zéghal. 2011. Attributes of Corporate Risk Disclosure: An International Investigation in the Manufacturing Sector. *Journal of International Accounting Research* 10 (2):1-22.

Dvorak, T. 2005. Do Domestic Investors Have an Information Advantage? Evidence from Indonesia. *Journal of Finance* 60 (2):817-839.

Dye, R. A. 1998. Investor Sophistication and Voluntary Disclosures. *Review of Accounting Studies* 3 (3):261-287.

Ellis, J. A., C. E. Fee, and S. E. Thomas. 2012. Proprietary Costs and the Disclosure of Information About Customers. *Journal of Accounting Research* forthcoming.

ESMA. 2011. Activity Report on IFRS Enforcement in 2010. Paris: European Securities and Markets Authority ESMA.

EU, E. P. a. C. 2002. Regulation (EC) No 1606/2002 of the European Parliament and of the Council of 19 July 2002 on the application of international accounting standards. In *1606/2002*, edited by E. P. a. Council. Bruxelles.

Fama, E. F., and M. C. Jensen. 1983. Separation of ownership and control. *Journal of Law & Economics* 26 (2):301-326.

Fiss, P. C., and E. J. Zajac. 2004. The Diffusion of Ideas over Contested Terrain: The (Non)adoption of a Shareholder Value Orientation among German Firms. *Administrative Science Quarterly* 49 (4):501-534.

Florou, A., and P. F. Pope. 2009. Mandatory IFRS Adoption and Investor Asset Allocation Decisions. *SSRN eLibrary*.

Gonedes, N. J. 1976. The Capital Market, The Market for Information, and External Accounting. *Journal of Finance* 31 (2):611-630.

Graham, J. R., C. R. Harvey, and H. Huang. 2009. Investor Competence, Trading Frequency, and Home Bias. *Management Science* 55 (7):1094-1106.

Gray, S. J. 1988. Towards a Theory of Cultural on the Development of Accounting Influence Systems Internationally. *Abacus* 24 (1):1-15.

Greif, A. 1994. Cultural beliefs and the organization of society: A historical and theoretical reflection on. *Journal of Political Economy* 102 (5):912.

Grinblatt, M., and M. Keloharju. 2000. The investment behaviour and performance of various investor types: A study of Finland's unique data set. *Journal of Financial Economics* 55 (1):43-67.

———. 2001. How Distance, Language, and Culture Influence Stockholdings and Trades. *Journal of Finance* 56 (3):1053-1073.

Guay, W., and R. Verrecchia. 2006. Discussion of an economic framework for conservative accounting and Bushman and Piotroski (2006). *Journal of Accounting & Economics*, 149-165.

Hail, L. 2002. The impact of voluntary corporate disclosures on the ex-ante cost of capital for Swiss firms. *European Accounting Review* 11 (4):741-773.

———. 2011. Discussion of Consequences and Institutional Determinants of Unregulated Corporate Financial Statements: Evidence from Embedded Value Reporting. *SSRN eLibrary*.

Hail, L., and C. Leuz. 2006. International Differences in the Cost of Equity Capital: Do Legal Institutions and Securities Regulation Matter? *Journal of Accounting Research* 44 (3):485-531.

Hales, J., X. I. Kuang, and S. Venkataraman. 2011. Who Believes the Hype? An Experimental Examination of How Language Affects Investor Judgments. *Journal of Accounting Research* 49 (1):223-255.

Hassan, M. S. S., Norman Mohd; Rahman, Mara Ridhuan Che Abd 2007. Determinants of Financial Instruments Disclosure Quality among Listed Firms in Malaysia. In *Working Paper Series*: Universiti Kebangsaan Malaysia.

Hau, H. 2001a. Geographic patterns of trading profitability in Xetra. *European Economic Review* 45 (4-6):757-769.

———. 2001b. Location Matters: An Examination of Trading Profits. *Journal of Finance* 56 (5):1959-1983.

Healy, P. M., A. P. Hutton, and K. G. Palepu. 1999. Stock Performance and Intermediation Changes Surrounding Sustained Increases in Disclosure. *Contemporary Accounting Research* 16 (3):485-520.

Healy, P. M., and K. G. Palepu. 2001. Information asymmetry, corporate disclosure, and the capital markets: A review of the empirical disclosure literature. *Journal of Accounting and Economics* 31 (1-3):405-440.

Heckman, J. J. 1979. Sample Selection Bias As A Specification Error. *Econometrica* 47 (1):153-161.

HeritageFoundation. *Index of Economic Freedom*. The Heritage Foundation 2007 [cited. Available from http://www.heritage.org/Index/Explore.aspx?view=by-region-country-year.

Hill, P., and H. Short. 2009. Risk disclosures on the second tier markets of the London Stock Exchange. *Accounting & Finance* 49 (4):753-780.

Hofstede, G. 1991. *Cultures and organizations: Software of the mind: Intercultural cooperation and its importance for survival*. New York: McGraw-Hill.

———. 2001. *Culture's consequences: Comparing values, behaviors, institutions and organizations across nations*. 2nd ed. London: Sage Publications.

Holthausen, R. W. 2003. Testing the relative power of accounting standards versus incentives and other institutional features to influence the outcome of financial reporting in an international setting. *Journal of Accounting and Economics* 36 (1-3):271-283.

———. 2009. Accounting Standards, Financial Reporting Outcomes, and Enforcement. *Journal of Accounting Research* 47 (2):447-458.

Hope, O.-K. 2003a. Disclosure Practices, Enforcement of Accounting Standards, and Analysts' Forecast Accuracy: An International Study. *Journal of Accounting Research* 41 (2):235-272.

———. 2003b. Firm-level Disclosures and the Relative Roles of Culture and Legal Origin. *Journal of International Financial Management & Accounting* 14 (3):218-248.

House, R. J., P. J. Hanges, M. Javidan, P. W. Dorfman, and G. V., eds. 2004. *Culture, Leadership, and Organizations: The GLOBE Study of 62 Societies*. Thousand Oaks: Sage.

Iatridis, G. 2008. Accounting Disclosure and Firms' Financial Attributes: Evidence from the UK Stock Market. *International Review of Financial Analysis* 17 (2):219-241.

Iskandar-Datta, M., and Y. Jia. 2013. Valuation Consequences of Clawback Provisions. *The Accounting Review* 88 (1):171-198.

Jaggi, B., and P. Y. Low. 2000. Impact of Culture, Market Forces, and Legal System on Financial Disclosures. *The International Journal of Accounting* 35 (4):495-519.

Jeanjean, T., C. Lesage, and H. Stolowy. 2010. Why do you speak English (in your annual report)? *The International Journal of Accounting* 45 (2):200-223.

Jensen, M. C. 1986. Agency Costs of Free Cash Flow, Corporate Finance, and Takeovers. *American Economic Review* 76 (2):323.

Jin, G. 2005. Competition and Disclosure Incentives: An Empirical Study of HMOs. *RAND Journal of Economics* 36 (1):93-112.

Jin, Y., and P. Jorion. 2006. Firm value and hedging: Evidence from US oil and gas producers. *Journal of Finance* 61 (2):893-919.

Joos, P., and M. Lang. 1994. The Effects of Accounting Diversity: Evidence from the European Union. *Journal of Accounting Research* 32 (3):141-168.

Joos, P. W., P. 2004. (Non)convergence in international accrual accounting: The role of institutional and real operating effects. In *Working Paper*: Sloan School of Management, MIT.

Judge, A. 2006. Why and How UK Firms Hedge. *European Financial Management* 12 (3):407-441.

Jung, W., and Y. Kwon. 1988. Disclosure When the Market is Unsure of Information Endowment of Managers. *Journal of Accounting Research* 2:146-153.

Kai, L., D. Griffin, Y. Heng, and Z. Longkai. 2011. National culture and capital structure decisions: Evidence from foreign joint ventures in China. *Journal of International Business Studies* 42 (4):477-503.

Kalev, P. S., A. H. Nguyen, and N. Y. Oh. 2008. Foreign versus local investors: Who knows more? Who makes more? *Journal of Banking & Finance* 32 (11):2376-2389.

Kaufmann, D., A. Kraay, and M. Mastruzzi. 2009. Governance Matters VIII: Aggregate and Individual Governance Indicators, 1996-2008. *SSRN eLibrary*.

Kim, O., and R. E. Verrecchia. 1994. Market liquidity and volume around earnings announcements. *Journal of Accounting & Economics* 17 (1/2):41-67.

Klein, A. 2002. Economic Determinants of Audit Committee Independence. *The Accounting Review* 77 (2):435-452.

Kwok, C. C. Y., and T. Solomon. 2006. National Culture and Financial Systems. *Journal of International Business Studies* 37 (2):227-247.

La Porta, R., F. Lopez-De-Silanes, and A. Shleifer. 2006. What Works in Securities Laws? *Journal of Finance* 61 (1):1-32.

La Porta, R., F. Lopez-de-Silanes, A. Shleifer, and R. Vishny. 1997. Legal Determinants of External Finance. *Journal of Finance* 52 (3):1131-1150.

———. 2000. Investor protection and corporate governance. *Journal of Financial Economics* 58 (1/2):3-27.

———. 2002. Investor Protection and Corporate Valuation. *Journal of Finance* 57 (3):1147-1170.

La Porta, R., F. Lopez-de-Silanes, A. Shleifer, and R. W. Vishny. 1998. Law and finance. *Journal of Political Economy* 106 (6):1113.

Laksmana, I. 2008. Corporate Board Governance and Voluntary Disclosure of Executive Compensation Practices. *Contemporary Accounting Research* 25 (4):1147-1182.

Lambert, R., C. Leuz, and R. Verrecchia. 2011. Information Asymmetry, Information Precision, and the Cost of Capital. *Review of Finance* forthcoming.

Lambert, R., C. Leuz, and R. E. Verrecchia. 2007. Accounting Information, Disclosure, and the Cost of Capital. *Journal of Accounting Research* 45 (2):385-420.

Landes, D., ed. 2000. *Culture makes almost all the difference.* edited by S. P. H. L. E. Harrison. New York: Basic Books.

Lang, M. H., K. V. Lins, and D. P. Miller. 2003. ADRs, Analysts, and Accuracy: Does Cross Listing in the United States Improve a Firm's Information Environment and Increase Market Value? *Journal of Accounting Research* 41 (2):317-345.

Lang, M. H., and R. J. Lundholm. 1996. Corporate Disclosure Policy and Analyst Behavior. *The Accounting Review* 71 (4):467-492.

Larcker, D. F., S. A. Richardson, and I. Tuna. 2007. Corporate Governance, Accounting Outcomes, and Organizational Performance. *The Accounting Review* 82 (4):963-1008.

Lawrence, A., M. Minutti-Meza, and P. Zhang. 2011. Can Big 4 versus Non-Big 4 Differences in Audit-Quality Proxies Be Attributed to Client Characteristics? *The Accounting Review* 86 (1):259-286.

Lehavy, R., L. Feng, and K. Merkley. 2011. The Effect of Annual Report Readability on Analyst Following and the Properties of Their Earnings Forecasts. *The Accounting Review* 86 (3):1087-1115.

Lesmond, D. A., J. P. Ogden, and C. A. Trzcinka. 1999. A new estimate of transaction costs. *Review of Financial Studies* 12 (5):1113-1141.

Leuz, C. 2010. Different approaches to corporate reporting regulation: how jurisdictions differ and why. *Accounting & Business Research* 40 (3):229-256.

Leuz, C., D. Nanda, and P. D. Wysocki. 2003. Earnings management and investor protection: an international comparison. *Journal of Financial Economics* 69 (3):505-527.

Leuz, C., and R. Verrecchia. 2000. The Economic Consequences of Increased Disclosure. *Journal of Accounting Research* 38:91-124.

Lev, B. 1988. Toward a Theory of Equitable and Efficient Accounting Policy. *The Accounting Review* 63 (1):1-22.

Levine, R. 1999. Law, finance and economic growth. *Journal of Financial Intermediation* 8:8-35.

Levitt, A. 1998. The Importance of High Quality Accounting Standards. *Accounting Horizons* 12 (1):79-82.

Lewis, M. P. 2009. *Ethnologue: Languages of the World.* edited by M. P. Lewis. Vol. 16. Dallas, Texas: SIL International.

Li, F. 2010a. The Information Content of Forward-Looking Statements in Corporate Filings-A NaÃ¯ve Bayesian Machine Learning Approach. *Journal of Accounting Research* 48 (5):1049-1102.

Li, K., and N. R. Prabhala. 2006. Self-Selection Models in Corporate Finance. In *Handbook of Corporate Finance: Empirical Corporate Finance, Volume A, Chapter 2, Handbooks in Finance Series*, edited by B. E. Eckbo. North-Holland: Elsevier, 39-83.

Li, S. 2010b. Does Mandatory Adoption of International Financial Reporting Standards in the European Union Reduce the Cost of Equity Capital? *Accounting Review* 85 (2):607-636.

Linsley, P. M., and P. J. Shrives. 2000. Risk management and reporting risk in the UK. . *Journal of Risk* 3 (1):115-129.

Linsley, P. M., and P. J. Shrives. 2006. Risk reporting: A study of risk disclosures in the annual reports of UK companies. *British Accounting Review* 38 (4):387-404.

Linsmeier, T. J., D. B. Thornton, M. Venkatachalam, and M. T. Welker. 2002. he effect of mandated market risk disclosures on trading volume sensitivity to interest rate, exchange rate, and commodity price movements. *The Accounting Review* 77 (2):343-377.

Lopes, P. T., and L. L. Rodrigues. 2007. Accounting for financial instruments: An analysis of the determinants of disclosure in the Portuguese stock exchange. *International Journal of Accounting* 42 (1):25-56.

Lundholm, R. J. 1988. Price-Signal Relations in the Presence of Correlated Public and Private Information. *Journal of Accounting Research* 26 (1):107-118.

Magee, S. 2009. Foreign Currency Hedging and Firm Value: A Dynamic Panel Approach. *SSRN eLibrary*.

Merton, R. C. 1987. A Simple Model of Capital Market Equilibrium with Incomplete Information. *Journal of Finance* 42 (3):483-510.

Meyer, J. W., and B. Rowan. 1977. Institutionalized Organizations: Formal Structure as Myth and Ceremony. *The American Journal of Sociology* 83 (2):340-363.

Myers, S. C. 1977. Determinants of Corporate Borrowing. *Journal of Financial Economics* 5 (2):147-175.

Myers, S. C., and N. S. Majluf. 1984. Corporate financing and investment decisions when firms have information that investors do not have. *Journal of Financial Economics* 13 (2):187-221.

Nabar, S., and K. K. Boonlert-U-Thai. 2007. Earnings Management, Investor Protection, and National Culture. *Journal of International Accounting Research* 6 (2):35-54.

Nickerson, C., and E. B. de Groot. 2005. Dear Shareholder, Dear Stockholder, Dear Stakeholder: The Business Letter Genre in the Annual General Report. In *Genre Variation in Business Letters*, edited by P. Gillaerts and M. Gotti. Bern: Peter Lang., 325-346.

Nobes, C. W. 1998. Observations on measuring the differences between domestic accounting standards and IAS. *Journal of Accounting and Public Policy* 28 (2):148-153.

O'Brien, P. C., and R. Bhushan. 1990. Analyst Following and Institutional Ownership. *Journal of Accounting Research* 28 (3):55-82.

Pagano, M., A. A. Roell, and J. Zechner. 2002. The Geography of Equity Listing: Why Do Companies List Abroad? *Journal of Finance* 57 (6):2651-2694.

Petersen, M. A. 2009. Estimating Standard Errors in Finance Panel Data Sets: Comparing Approaches. *Review of Financial Studies* 22 (1):435-480.

Petersen, M. A., and R. G. Rajan. 1994. The Benefits of Lending Relationships: Evidence from Small Business Data. *The Journal of Finance* IL (1):3-37.

Portes, R., and H. Rey. 2005. The determinants of cross-border equity flows. *Journal of International Economics* 65 (2):269-296.

Raffournier, B. 1995. The determinants of voluntary financial disclosure by Swiss listed companies. *European Accounting Review* 4 (2):261-280.

Ramnath, S., S. Rock, and P. Shane. 2008. The financial analyst forecasting literature: A taxonomy with suggestions for further research. *International Journal of Forecasting* 24 (1):34-75.

Rauch, J. E. 1999. Networks versus markets in international trade. *Journal of International Economics* 48 (1):7-35.

Rosenbaum, P. R., and D. B. Rubin. 1983. The Central Role of the Propensity Score in Observational Studies for Causal Effects. *Biometrika* 70:41–55.

Salter, S. B., and D. J. Sharp. 2001. Agency effects and escalation of commitment: do small national culture differences matter? *The International Journal of Accounting* 36 (1):33-45.

Sarkissian, S., and M. J. Schill. 2004. The Overseas Listing Decision: New Evidence of Proximity Preference. *Review of Financial Studies* 17 (3):769-809.

Schwartz, S. 1999. A Theory of Cultural Values and Some Implications for Work. *Applied Psychology: An International Review* 48:23-47.

———, ed. 1994. *Beyond individualism/collectivism: New cultural dimensions of values.* edited by H. C. U. Kim and C. K. Triandis, S. C. Choi, & G. Yoon: Sage.

———, ed. 2004. *Mapping and Interpreting Cultural Differences around the World.* edited by H. Vinken, Soeters, J., Ester, P. Leiden: Brill.

Seyhun, H. N. 1998. *Investment Intelligence from Insider Trading*. Cambridge, MA: MIT Press.

Shackleton, M. B., A. Panaretou, and P. A. Taylor. 2012. Corporate risk management and hedge accounting. *Contemporary Accounting Research* forthcoming.

Shleifer, A. 2005. Understanding Regulation. *European Financial Management* 11 (4):439-451.

Singhvi, S., and H. Desai. 1971. An empirical analysis of the quality of corporate financial disclosure. *The Accounting Review* 46 (1):129-138.

Sonney, F. 2009. Financial Analysts' Performance: Sector Versus Country Specialization. *Review of Financial Studies* 22 (5):2087-2131.

Stulz, R. M., and R. Williamson. 2003. Culture, openness, and finance. *Journal of Financial Economics* 70 (3):313.

Sufi, A. 2007. Information Asymmetry and Financing Arrangements: Evidence from Syndicated Loans. *Journal of Finance* 62 (2):629-668.

Tesar, L. L., and I. M. Werner. 1995. Home bias and high turnover. *Journal of International Money and Finance* 14 (4):467-492.

Tetlock, P. C., M. Saar-Tsechansky, and S. Macskassy. 2008. More Than Words: Quantifying Language to Measure Firms' Fundamentals. *Journal of Finance* 63 (3):1437-1467.

Thakor, A. V. 2012. Information Disclosure and Opinion Divergence.

Tucker, J. W. 2010. Selection bias and econometric remedies in accounting and finance research. *Journal of Accounting Literature* 29:31-57.

Vashishtha, R. 2012. Evidence on the role of banks in borrowers' disclosure. In *2012*: The Wharton School.

Vergoossen, R. G. A. 1993. The use and perceived importance of annual reports by investment analysts in the Netherlands. *European Accounting Review* 2 (2):219-244.

Verrecchia, R. E. 2001. Essays on disclosure. *Journal of Accounting and Economics* 32 (1-3):97-180.

Vielmeyer, U. 2004. *Risikoorientierte Unternehmenspublizität: Theorie Und Empirie.* . Frankfurt/M., Germany: Lang.

Wallace, R. S. O., and K. Naser. 1995. Firm-Specific Determinants of the Comprehensiveness of Mandatory Disclosure in the Corporate Annual Reports of Firms Listed on the Stock Exchange of Hong Kong. *Journal of Accounting & Public Policy* 14 (4):311-368.

Wang, S., W. Li, and L. Cheng. 2009. The impact of H-share derivatives on the underlying equity market. *Review of Quantitative Finance & Accounting* 32 (3):235-267.

WEF. 2008. The Financial Development Report 2008: World Economic Forum.

Welker, M. 1995. Disclosure Policy, Information Asymmetry, and Liquidity in Equity Markets. *Contemporary Accounting Research* 11 (2):801-827.

Westphal, J. D., and E. J. Zajac. 1994. Substance and Symbolism in CEOs' Long-term Incentive Plans. *Administrative Science Quarterly* 39 (3):367-390.

White, H. 1980. A heteroskedasticity-consistent covariance matrix estimator and a direct test for heteroskedasticity. . *Econometrica* 48 (4):817-838.

Zarzeski, M. T. 1996. Spontaneous harmonization effects of culture and market forces on accounting disclosure practices. *Accounting Horizons* 10 (1):18.

Springer Gabler
springer-gabler.de

Qualität entscheidet

Publizieren Sie Ihre Dissertation bei uns – ohne Druckkosten-Zuschuss!

- Print- und eBook
- Zitierfähigkeit und hohe Sichtbarkeit durch SpringerLink
- Qualitative Titelauswahl
- Namhafte Herausgeber
- Renommierte Schriftenreihen
- Hochwertige Bücher

Neu: ohne Zuschuss!

Ein Buch ist nachhaltig wirksam für Ihre Karriere.
Zeigen Sie, was Sie geleistet haben.

Marta Schmidt | Lektorin Forschungspublikation
Tel +49(0)611 / 7878 - 237 | marta.schmidt@springer.com

Unter springer.com/research sind wir jederzeit für Sie erreichbar

A08562

Made in the USA
Monee, IL
13 September 2026

62973771R00105